D0876365

The See-Through Years

The See-Through Years

Creation and Destruction in Texas Architecture and Real Estate 1981-1991

by Joel Warren Barna

photography by BlackmonWintersKuhner

Rice University Press, Houston

Printed in the United States of America
First Edition 1992

Requests for permission to reprint material from this work should be addressed to
Rice University Press
Post Office Box 1892
Houston, Texas 77251

Barna, Joel Warren, 1951-
The see-through years: creation and destruction in Texas architecture, 1981-1991 / by Joel Warren Barna; photography by BlackmonWintersKuhner
p. cm.
Includes bibliographical references and index.
ISBN 0-89263-316-6: $39.95
1. Commercial buildings—Texas. 2. Architecture, Modern—20th century—Texas. 3. Texas—Economic conditions. I. BlackmonWintersKuhner II. Title
NA6212.B37 1992
720'.964'09048—dc20 92-50336
CIP

To

Laura and Solomon,

who are always above the line,

and to

Theodore and Dorothy Barna

CONTENTS

List of Illustrations

Foreword

About ten years ago, I happened on *The Last American City, An Intrepid Walker's Guide to Houston,* a now out-of-print book by Douglas Milburn and Thomas Stanley Richmond.[1] Except for noting that certain buildings were associated with civic pride, I can't remember having paid much attention to architecture before that. Growing up in Houston, I had seen it as more or less fixed—houses, roads, museums, churches strewn about here, and hospitals, schools, and workplaces plopped down there. Milburn and Richmond's book revealed what I had never noticed before. It was Houston as process, a constructed record of decisions made by people.

I have learned since that *The Last American City* is part of a long American tradition of minority reports dealing with architecture in social, psychological, political, and economic terms, standing beside the books in which architecture is examined under the more common rubrics of stylistic lineage and relative aesthetic merit. In Texas, this minority tradition has included recent distinguished work by David Dillon, Bruce Webb, Richard Ingersoll, and Peter Papademetriou, all of whom I have learned from, and Stephen Fox, whose affectionate but tough-minded

Houston: An Architectural Guide I have studied carefully and often.[2] I offer *The See-Through Years* as an extension of that tradition. The title comes from speculative office towers without tenants—"see-through" buildings, in developer jargon—that would become symbols for the vast sums poured into unproductive real estate gambles during the 1980s and for the middle-class lemon socialism that followed.

I discuss here about two hundred architectural projects—only a small part of the architectural output of the 1980s. But, as I hope will be plain, what follows is not a guidebook but a series of connected meditations on relationships and ideas, with certain buildings providing the focus.

With the exception of those from some unbuilt projects, there are no plans on the pages that follow. This is a serious omission in a book about architecture, and I feel that I owe readers an explanation. I wanted this book to represent an independent view. Being myself unable to draw the required plans, I would have had to request them from the architects whose works were to be included, a confidence that might have implied an obligation or a deception. To avoid such compromises, I cite published sources for plans in the footnotes. This also explains why I commissioned Craig Blackmon, Willis Winters, and Craig Kuhner to shoot the wonderful photographs for the book, instead of following the usual practice in architectural journalism of relying on photographs supplied free by the architects. Their photographs—and their counsel—make for a better book than would have been produced otherwise.

Many people made suggestions that helped me develop the primitive idea I jotted down outside Ninfa's on Kirby Drive in Houston on a Sunday afternoon in June 1989. They include Mark Branch, Laura Furman, Sandy Heck, Lila Knight, Jack Kyle, Willard Spiegelman, Ray Don Tilley, and Susan Williamson. Douglas Pegues Harvey provided encouragement and key insights. Joan Marik gave important material support. Susan Fernandez and Susan Bielstein of Rice University Press worked with both speed and patience. Stephen Fox, in particular, gave generously, again and again, of his time and his inexhaustible expertise.

The Anchorage Foundation of Texas awarded me a grant that allowed me to take a month off from my job in 1991 to work fulltime on this book. For this assistance, and for the help of those I haven't named here, I am very grateful. *J.W.B.*

A businessman in a gray suit and ostrich-skin cowboy boots stops at a pay phone near Sugar Land and calls his partner at their office in the Galleria.

"Bill," he says, "this is Jimmy. I've got some good news and some bad news."

"What's the good news?" Bill asks.

"A farmer down here in Fort Bend County will let us have a thousand acres of rice fields for twenty dollars per acre."

"Good God," says Bill. "We're saved! We can put in fifty thousand condos, sell them for $200,000 apiece, and make a billion dollars. So what's the bad news?"

"The son of a bitch wants $500 down."

Houston real estate joke, ca. 1983

Energy is a very fast-moving business on pay-out. I have to drill a well every seven years because the well's gone by then, produced out. But if I build a building, it has a forty-year life. The long-term economics are what make it look interesting.

George Mitchell
in an interview in Houston North *Magazine, November 1980*

We have come to a time when a sense of order is no longer inherent in the process of living. We are freed from many of the incessant tasks which gave form to living in previous generations. The electric light turns night into day. Central air conditioning creates one long temperate season. The car takes away nearness as a condition for relationships so that our friends can be scattered all over and our neighbors remain unknown. We inhabit an expanded world of abstract realities which we try to interpret through a contracted world of familiar symbols.

Bruce C. Webb and Peter Jay Zweig
"Gone to Texas: The Search for a Symbolic Landscape"
Texas Architect, *November/December 1982*

The way to wealth is debt.

Trammell Crow, quoted in
Risk, Ruin and Riches: Inside the World of Big Time Real Estate
by Jim Powell, 1986

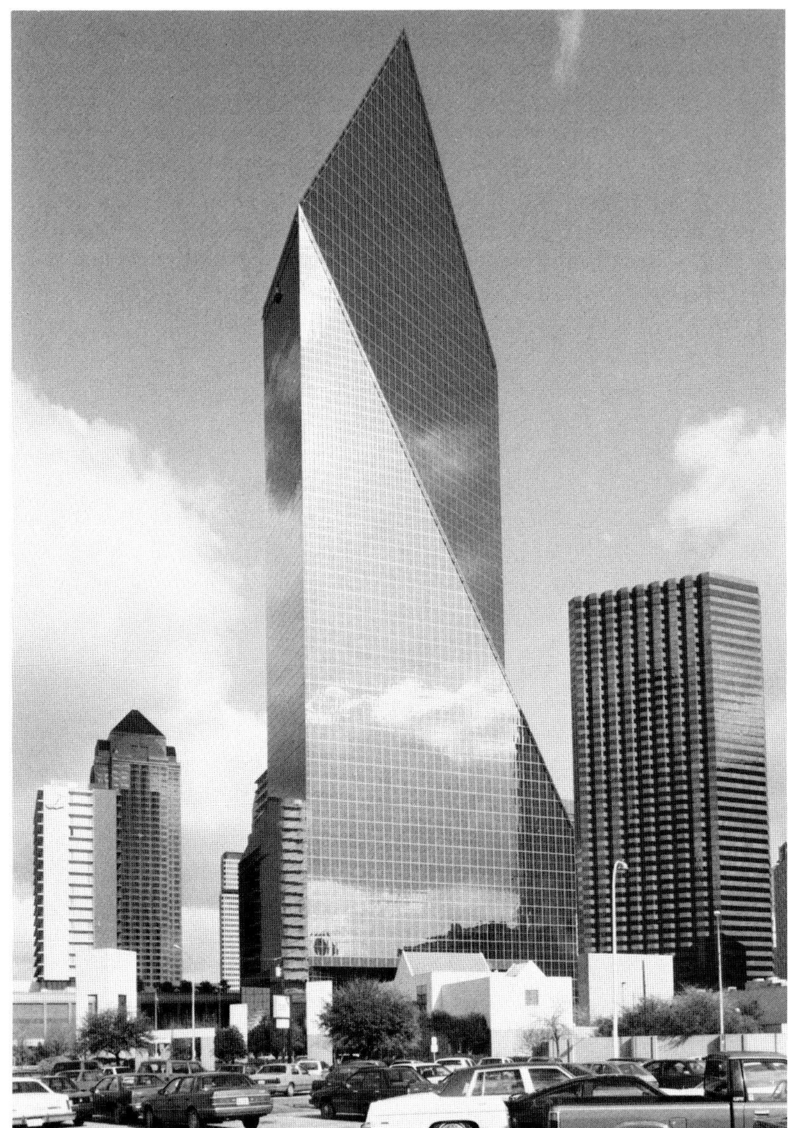

Allied Bank Tower at Fountain Place, Dallas (1986), by I.M. Pei & Partners

1
J.R. McConnell Died for Our Sins

The green glass wedge that was originally called the Allied Bank Tower at Fountain Place when completed in Dallas in 1985, and the red-granite-faced, step-gabled skyscraper in Houston called RepublicBank Center when it was completed in 1983—these are very diverse-looking buildings. Each gives mute testimony to different paths taken over several years of planning, risk-taking, and labor by architects, developers, bankers, engineers, interior designers, contractors, builders, materials suppliers, and construction workers.

Both buildings are also reticent about the role each played in the cataclysmic unfolding of the great ritual of creation and destruction that was enacted all over Texas in the 1980s: the ritual of real estate, which dominated the spiritual life of the state for a decade. These soaring towers express an insistent language of hope and confidence, language that drowns out any confession of cupidity, frailty, and delusion that in retrospect seems more appropriate.

The Allied Bank Tower was developed by Criswell Development Company, a relatively new player in a city where the real estate game was dominated by mega-builder Trammell Crow, offshoots of his companies, and such Canadian giants as Olympia & York, Campeau, and Cadillac Fairview.[1]

Allied Bank, the company that rented enough of the space to have the building named in its honor, was based in Houston and was then controlled by Houston's one-time political kingmaker, Walter Mischer. Following changes in state laws that had previously limited competition by prohibiting "branch banking," Allied was expanding its operations into the Dallas area in the mid-1980s; the North Texas real estate market was still hot, even though Houston's was floundering as energy prices fell. Being lead tenant in the tower gave these newcomers immediate visibility among a crowd of lenders eager to put money into the continuing economic miracle of the Dallas-Fort Worth area.

Allied Dallas was designed by Harry Cobb, one of the principals of the New York architects I.M. Pei and Partners, which had several other major Dallas buildings to its credit, including the Dallas City Hall. Later commissions would include the city's new symphony hall.

Pei and his partners have always liked abstract, platonic forms, particularly triangles and trapezoids, which, the architects say, spring from analysis of the dynamics of movement inside and outside their buildings and which present the viewer with razor-sharp perspectives along cleanly detailed walls. The miraculously precise corner of the East Wing of the National Gallery in Washington, D.C., one of the most photographed spots in a city of monuments, is perhaps the best-known example of this proclivity. In keeping with this bent, the design of Allied Bank Tower at Fountain Place has more than a little in common with Pei's trapezoid-shaped, granite-and-steel-skinned Arco Tower (1983) to the southeast.

With its pitched top, Allied Dallas seems to paraphrase the tops of Philip Johnson and John Burgee's Pennzoil Place,[2] completed in 1976 in Houston, although it could just as well be said that the triangles-sliced-from-a-square planning of Pennzoil was a citation of Pei's geometries.

At Pennzoil, developer Gerald D. Hines had shown that people in his profession, previously known for market-driven conservatism and penuriousness that squeezed the architectural vitality out of the budgets of speculative office buildings, could make money by hiring well-known architects

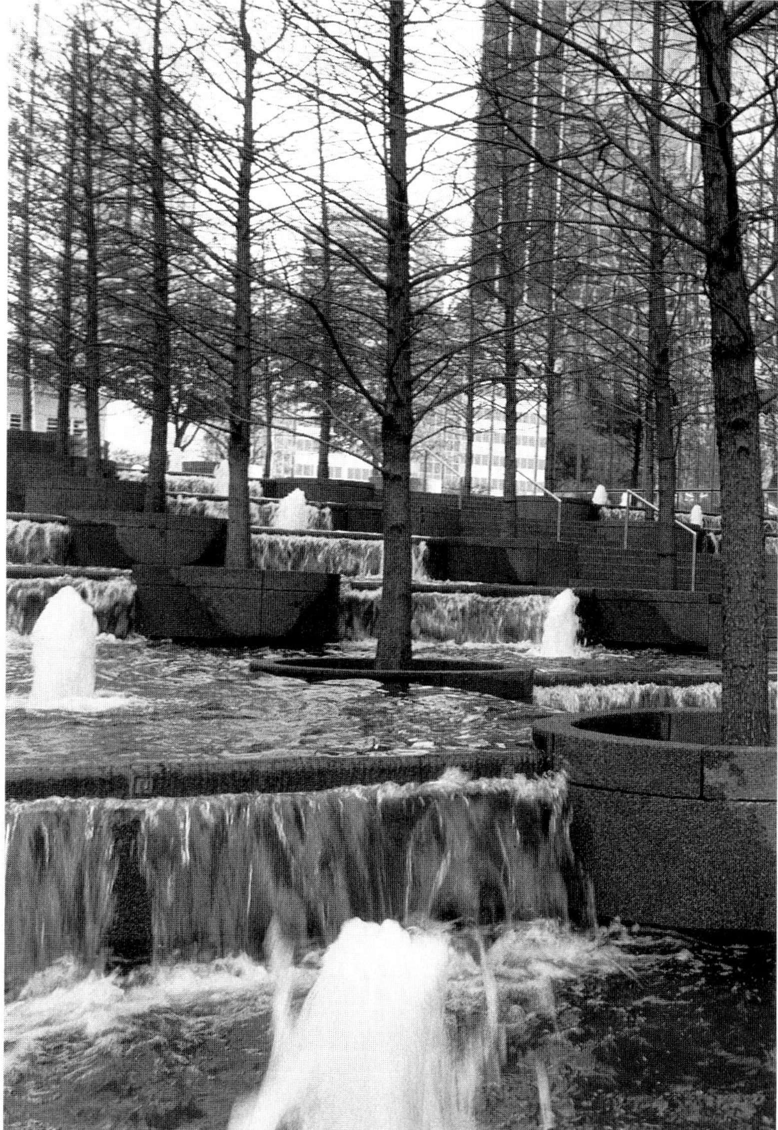

Fountain Place fountains, Dallas, designed by landscape architect Dan Kiley

Dallas City Hall (1978), by I.M. Pei and Partners

and by paying a few percent more to include the distinctive details such architects designed. Pennzoil was one of the few office buildings in Texas to be famous for something other than being tall. Splitting the project into two thirty-five-story towers, Hines said, made it possible to have two lead tenants, which made both financing and leasing easier. It also freed up leasable space that would have been taken by a larger structural core and more elevators in a single seventy-story building. Pennzoil was also the first serious office building in decades not to have a flat top, and it sent a shock of delight through architectural and development circles. Writing in the American Institute of Architects' national magazine, *Architecture*, one critic, Carleton Knight III, said that Pennzoil changed architectural history, while another, John Pastier, suggested that the role of "city of the future" passed from Los Angeles to Houston "with the completion of a single building, Pennzoil Place."

Developers all over the country took notice; in Texas, in terms of hiring for the most prestigious jobs, Pennzoil's success meant that major in-state firms, some among the biggest in the country, became spear carriers in the

Pei-and-Johnson opera. But development was a growth industry, and there was plenty of other business to go around. The Pennzoil strategies of splitting sites into two or more phased buildings (this was later applied at Fountain Place in Dallas, of which the second phase has yet to be built) and of "breaking out of the box" to give every building a "distinctive" shape were applied so often that by the mid-1980s they had lost their effectiveness. In addition, building managers found that volumes with odd geometries were hard to use efficiently and thus hard to rent, and the underlying conservatism of the market reasserted itself. By the mid-1980s, most new buildings were again being designed with floors shaped like thick rectangles, which could be more easily adapted for potential renters. At the same time, the design approach called postmodernism (a muddled and in some ways inverted version of its namesake in literary theory) was leaving the East Coast academies and becoming the mainstream American architectural style for office buildings.[3] Postmodernists condemned almost all modernist design—particularly the boxy skyscrapers of the 1960s and early 1970s—for its abstract lack of reference to historical form and decoration and its lack of connection to human scale and urban texture. Instead, sometimes playfully,

Arco Tower, Dallas (1983), by I.M. Pei and Partners, at center

sometimes in dead earnest, postmodernists proposed designs with historical precedents from antiquity to Art Deco.

So, when the Allied Tower was built, its modernist abstractness and its hard-to-market shape made it something of a relic, a tardy reminder of Pennzoil Place when everyone else was trying new and different strategies for creating distinctive skyscraper images, to fulfill the needs of developers for marketing position. Nevertheless, Allied's design was a critical success, even with postmodernists; in 1989 it won an award in a national competition organized by the AIA. The developers, architects, and landscape architects involved (Dan Kiley of Vermont chief among them) had created one of the most generous urban spaces in Texas at the base of the trapezoidal tower and had done well a number of things that had been done rather poorly at Pennzoil Place. Pennzoil's bronze-glass curtain wall, for example, slams into a low granite parapet at the very edge of its property line, offering pedestrians nothing to look at but the dusty venetian blinds of the street-level offices; it's as if the architects, with all their attention to the dynamics of the building's top, had forgotten that people would be entering it from the street. Fountain Place, by comparison, delivers what the name implies: It has a small forest of cypress trees and acres of cascading fountains set within the tower's zigzag footprint. In the courtyard on the north side of the building (forming what would have been the central space of the complex if the planned second tower had been built) is a fountain shooting from holes in the granite pavement. Fountain Place is one of the most successful fragments of public space in Dallas.

Part of the building's allure comes from its skin. Instead of the dull bronze glass and projecting bronze mullions of Pennzoil or the gray granite and steel clips of the Arco Tower, Allied Bank Tower has a curtain of green glass held together by an internal structure with the thinnest possible mullions; it is as close to seamless as was practicable at the time. Both up close and from a distance, it reads as a single prismatic object rather than a collection of parts. It is a commonplace among postmodernist and neotraditionalist critics that tall glass-skinned buildings are scaleless and fail to give meaning to cities that badly need it. Allied Bank Tower at Fountain Place may be tricky in scale, but it fairly sings with imagery.

As a statement on banking in the 1980s, Allied Tower says: Banks are not the rigid structures they once were, wrapped in stone columns that prop some people up and act as bars to keep others out; in the world of modern finance, money is water. It is available, like salvation, to all, dissolving social distinctions and forming a crystalline structure with its own internal logic. Money is self-regulating and thus uninhabited by the functionaries usually found framed by the windows of office buildings. And it reflects back at you whatever you bring to it.

RepublicBank Center in Houston was created to portray money and banking with similarly reassuring cheerfulness, but the architects used a vocabulary of masonry and historical references.[4] Developed by Gerald D. Hines Interests, the building was to be the new headquarters of the Dallas-based RepublicBank, which was itself expanding into the territory of its Houston-based rivals and wanted a signature image to establish its presence. Designed by Philip Johnson and John Burgee, RepublicBank Center was greeted on its completion in 1984 as the thoroughly postmodern tower that Johnson and Burgee had set out to create when they announced their much more celebrated AT&T Building in New York.[5]

Pennzoil Place, Houston (1976), by Philip Johnson & John Burgee, which rewrote the rules for speculative office buildings

RepublicBank Center, with 1.2 million square feet of space, has the rectangular floor plates of the mid-'80s tower, but it also has a separate twelve-story banking hall, with a ribbed and gabled roof and obelisk-like finials, grand entrances with Romanesque arches, and a series of finial-capped gabled setbacks, echoing the form of the banking lobby's roof. The designers took advantage of a technological change that affected the economics of curtainwall design worldwide: the computerization of stone-cutting machinery in Italy, which allowed stone to be cut into inch-thick panels that could be attached to buildings as if they were glass (the panels, hung from the building frame, bear no external weight, and they are joined at the edges by a caulk-like sealant), and in many cases for less than the cost of glass. RepublicBank's granite skin was quarried in Vermont, cut in Italy, and shipped to Houston for millions of dollars less than processing the stone in the United States would have cost. Despite its thinness, the stone skin is not flush or highly polished (the way it is on I.M. Pei's nearby 1982 Texas Commerce Tower, the tallest building in Houston); instead the slightly roughened panels are set in a frame that steps in and out, simulating the effect of rusticated and ashlar masonry blocks. From the freeways that loop around and into downtown, the rusty-colored stepped-up massing of the building is striking, particularly in the light of the setting sun.

The imagery deployed by the building's designers, seen under such circumstances, is almost delirious. The great architectural delineator Hugh Ferriss, in his celebrated studies of New York's setback regulations, portrayed buildings as mountains; RepublicBank Center is the most mountain-like American building of the 1980s. Complete with what seem to be tree-topped ridges, it rises from the foothills of Jones Hall and the Alley Theatre and the low commercial structures at the freeway's edge to mediate between them and the heights of the other office buildings farther south on Louisiana Street; it actually gains strength from thus deferring to the scale of the buildings around it, while the Texas Commerce Tower sticks out nearby like a naked stump.

The historical references are the tower's most astounding attributes, however. Philip Johnson, who must be unacquainted with Texas secondary education, is famous for having remarked that one "cannot not know history,"[6] and for hijacking raw chunks of history for use in new contexts. RepublicBank is a case in point: Its skylit jewel box of a banking hall was

RepublicBank Center (1983), Houston, by Johnson/ Burgee Architects

made to look, on its exterior, like a sixteenth-century Dutch guild hall, albeit one scaled to be seen from the freeway at sixty miles per hour. Why this image? For one thing, it linked the bank to one of the few architectural sources that could convey a sense of historical continuity without the troubling links to monarchical or dictatorial power that other styles carry. The image was not money as water, but money as republican virtue, conferring on the bank, and on banking in general, a defining role in a city where economic freedom was valued almost as much as financial muscle. But the image is much stronger. No doubt few driving by RepublicBank Center will recall consciously that, while the royal houses of post-Reformation England and Europe were battling for empires, the free cities of the Netherlands, led with probity and wisdom by representatives of the business community, were making their country into a major economic and military power. But can it be a coincidence that Johnson and Burgee gave Houston a Dutch-style building when the burghers of Texas saw themselves increasingly as rivals to the bankers of New York, a city that owed its early ascendancy to the merchant-warriors of New Amsterdam? RepublicBank Center is not a history lesson but an act of appropriation, a

Jeff Debevec

RepublicBank Center, banking-hall exterior

RepublicBank Center, lobby interior

The Alley Theatre (1969), centerpiece of the 1960s-era Houston cultural district

claim that Houston, not the decaying empire of New York, was home to the legitimate children of the American business spirit. This theme of appropriation had been missing from most high-style American architecture for over a generation; in Texas in the 1980s it would be rediscovered, elaborated on aesthetically, and travestied morally.

In the case of both RepublicBank Center and Allied Bank Tower in Dallas, the imagery speaking for the bank, and for the world of banking, was true only in unintended ways. Money *was* as free-flowing as water and as democratic as the market could make it in the 1980s, but it wasn't flowing to support Texas banks. The economic miracle of North Texas in the early 1980s, it turned out, was a bubble inflated by money plundered from the deregulated savings-and-loan industry.[7] Not long after Allied Bank Tower in Dallas was built, Allied Bank, on the brink of failure, was purchased by First Interstate Bank of Los Angeles. RepublicBank, after absorbing a number of other troubled Texas institutions, was itself engulfed by North Carolina National Bank

(NCNB, which later became NationsBank), in a sale hurried through by federal regulators eager to prop up consumer confidence in the banking system. The takeover was subsidized, like that of MCorp and First City Texas, by almost obscene amounts of tax money. A 1991 congressional report puts the public cost of the NCNB/RepublicBank deal at $6.6 billion.[8] Each building now bears the name of the out-of-state institution that kept its previous owners out of bankruptcy court (at least for the time being); the proud architectural language of First Interstate Bank Tower in Dallas and NationsBank Center in Houston mocks the aspirations to symbolic dominance that drove the conception and funded the construction of each.

Gains and Losses in the 1980s

Real estate is an engine, powered by money, that generates and consumes vast wealth. Sometimes this process unfolds slowly and conservatively, as when land values rise gradually over the course of generations so that the accidental foresight of ancestors rewards heirs with prosperity. Sometimes the engine runs faster. At such times, as happened during the 1980s in Texas, money can seem particularly fluid; in social terms, it seems

Texas Commerce Tower, Houston (1981), by I.M. Pei and Partners

that money can act as a truly democratizing force, both leveling and ennobling whatever it touches. Thus the iconography of money used at Allied/First Interstate and Republic/NCNB made sense for their times, no matter how these buildings read today. As particularly coherent statements of late-modernist and postmodernist design, they form stylistic bookends for the architectural development of tall buildings in the 1980s, and thus they are also useful for illustrating some of the decade's design trends. In the great movement that was born with rising oil prices in the 1970s and died in a thousand bankruptcy courts before the 1980s was half over, these buildings are only two among thousands of more or less equivalent episodes, each pointing beyond itself to the deeper layer of signs that underlies the overt symbolism used by architects. This is the meta-level at which every exchange of money for land and buildings delineates the structure not only of the particular real estate transaction involved—who buys, who sells; who gains, who loses—but social relationships throughout the whole of the encompassing society. It is the layer of real estate, which, in our society, embodies a complex system of signs and a ritual within which those signs are coordinated.

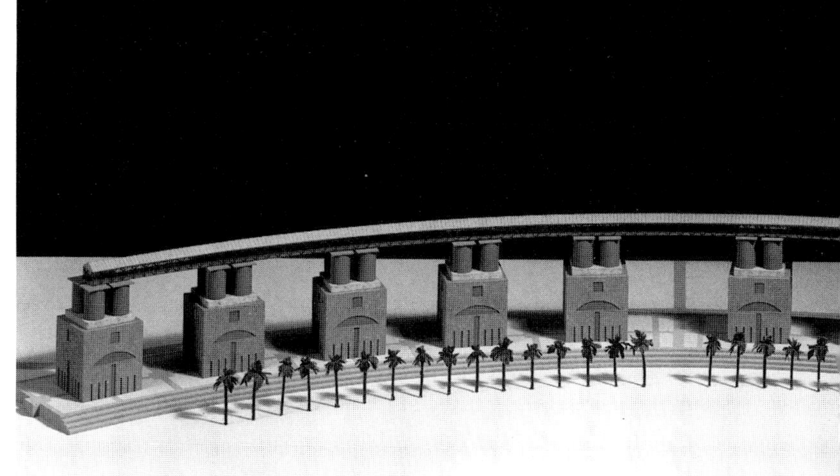

Model showing residential towers in the Grand Reef's central crescent

If there is a central, representative figure who defined this meta-level of signs as it operated in Texas in the 1980s, perhaps the best candidate would be J.R. McConnell, a failed developer who, in the infirmary of the county jail in Houston on July 4, 1988, stripped the insulation from the cord of an electric wheelchair recharger, wrapped the bare wires around his leg, and convinced a fellow inmate to plug the device into a wall outlet. By killing himself, McConnell accomplished the single most exemplary act of the 1980s, an act that, for all its intimacy of scale, illuminates the ritual nature of real estate, which must be understood for the architecture of the 1980s to make any kind of overall sense. Nobody's life and death had a more mythic quality than McConnell's.[9]

McConnell arrived in Houston in 1979 with twenty-three cents in his pocket and a beat-up Camaro. He scraped by at first only by selling a camera and other personal belongings in a K mart parking lot and by doing house repairs in Houston's inner-city Heights and Montrose neighborhoods. Soon after, however, he founded the ironically named Guaranty Investments, Inc., one of a hundred and twenty companies he would control. By 1985, he had amassed holdings valued at $500 million, with properties in California and Tennessee as well as Houston, Galveston, San Antonio, and Corpus Christi. His biggest impact was felt in Galveston, where (emulating Hines's profitable lead) he acted out a predilection for both historic preservation and high-profile contemporary architecture. He funded restoration and adaptation projects along the historic Strand. And he gained headlines and *eclat* by hiring the East Coast architect Michael Graves (whom Hines, although he later chose him to design an unbuilt residence in Houston, has yet to embrace for a major building) to design Grand Reef, a $900-million, 440-acre mixed-use retail-golf

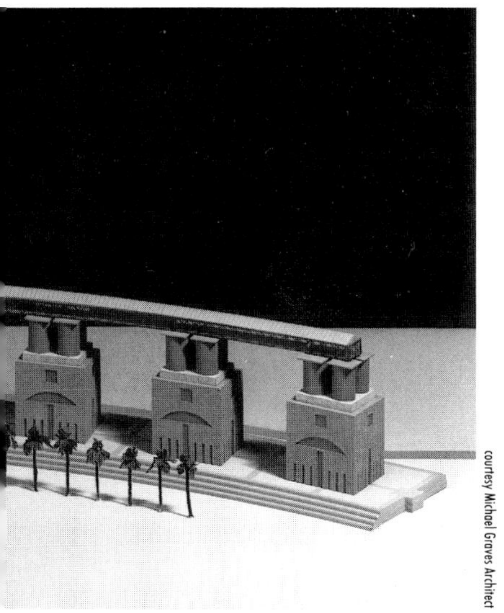
courtesy Michael Graves Architect

course-condominium project that, had it been built, would have changed the focus of development from the west to the east end of the island.[10]

But in 1986 McConnell filed for personal bankruptcy, promising to eventually repay the estimated $200 million owed to financial institutions and limited partners that his assets would not cover. As the court-appointed bankruptcy trustees began selling off McConnell's properties to pay his debts, they reportedly discovered that many of the properties had competing liens. They had been pledged as collateral to one institution, and, fraudulently, it was alleged, to others. Creditors began checking into his background and found that, before he came to Houston, McConnell had been convicted and given a five-year probated sentence for land fraud in Florida. A savings-and-loan sued. Then the Ticor title-insurance company filed suit against McConnell and eighteen of his associates, alleging that they had faked the titles of properties to bilk Ticor out of $100 million. In 1987, following an FBI investigation, McConnell and five associates were charged in federal court with defrauding a bank and a savings and loan of some $5.7 million, although federal officials said the total figure reaped by the group was closer to $162 million, making it the largest case of its kind to date.

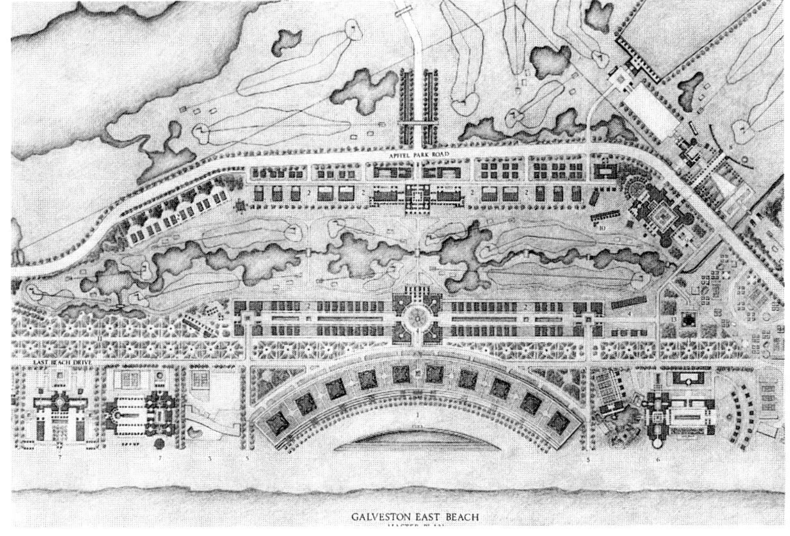

Site plan, Grand Reef development, Galveston, by Michael Graves

courtesy Michael Graves Architect

Reflecting on McConnell's death, I was reminded of a passage in Spiro Kostof's history of world architecture in which Kostof recounts the roles of the emperor of Byzantium and the bishop of Constantinople in the liturgy of the early Christian mass as it was celebrated in the great cathedral of Hagia Sophia. Kostof shows how the building's shape and decoration contributed to a reenactment of the symbolic marriage of divine and earthly power that formed the heart of the ceremony; the architecture of the building, with its vast dome giving physical expression to an entire cosmic order, cannot be understood except in the context of its use, Kostof says.[11]

The world of Texas real estate during the 1980s was no less byzantine and no less mystical than the one described by Kostof. Indeed, the symbolism of a divinely ordained order of emperor and church, with social roles neatly mapped for everyone below, has a simple, appealing clarity, compared with the swirling chaos of economic, political, social, and psychological forces that played themselves out in the Texas landscape of the last decade.

As social scientists have shown in their studies of ancient civilizations and of other cultures that we take to be less perfect than our own, myths are more than just stories about events that didn't really happen—a titan sacrificing his life to bring fire to humankind, and so on. Myths are narratives that echo the needs and aspirations of the people who tell them, and they play a powerful role in holding cultures together. Similarly, rituals are actions that, by common agreement, change meaning or status for those involved. By saying certain words in certain framing situations, for example, people change the definitions of their lives, becoming soldiers or priests or spouses.

The most important rituals are organized around an embedded myth, and they take the form of ceremonies in which value is conferred on something or taken away from something else. Kostof's example of the mass in Hagia Sophia provides a perfect example—in it the Byzantine emperor comes to church wearing a crown won through military conquest and participates in a ritual that declares his power to be divine and eternal, not merely human and contingent. At the same time, the ritual described by Kostof expresses a radical reframing of the role of Christianity, changing it from a religion of outsiders who had been anticipating the end of the world into a pillar of imperial power, which not only gives Christianity's blessing to the emperor but elevates the church's communicants to participation in the emperor's temporal authority.

Myths and rituals work best when everyone involved forgets or otherwise suspends awareness of the fact that they are projections that serve social ends, just as a play succeeds only when the members of the cast and audience agree to treat the "unreal" as provisionally "real." In fact, the willingness to accept without question the system of rituals and myths constructed by a given group is sometimes what constitutes membership in the group, and groups often go to great lengths to enforce belief.

Many rituals—politics, law, sports, fashion—give structure to social relations, and the power of each stems from multilayered meanings. Real estate in our society constitutes a ritual of vast influence, touching everything from family relationships to political structures. It exists as a ritual because of the simple fact that, for believers, it creates and destroys value.[12]

There is an indisputably rational basis for real estate. Land is useful. Crops can be grown on it and buildings can be built on it, and that usefulness can be expressed in monetary terms. But real estate as a business enterprise depends on the expectation that real property is or will be worth more than this use value. That makes sense. After all, as Mark Twain said of land, "They've stopped making it," while the number of possible users is constantly increasing. This sensible basis has almost nothing to do, however, with Texas in the early 1980s, when people expected land values to rise forever. Speculative value, that which matters most in real estate, is purely a social construct, which exists only as long as people treat it as "real." In addition, almost nothing is sold purely for mere use or even unalloyed speculation in our society. Instead most sales depend on accompanying fictions of personal transformation: Buy this toothpaste and you will be more lovable; rent this space and you will be more deserving of success. Real estate is the most transformative of commodities, with the possible exception of automobiles. These factors make real estate's ritualized nature nearly invisible, particularly when its fictions triumph. If one stands to profit from selling a piece of property, one won't be likely to remind a potential buyer that both are acting out a kind of socially sanctioned delusion.

As the story of J.R. McConnell demonstrates, Texas real estate in the 1980s included failure as well as success. The really amazing thing about real estate—a quality that elevates it to a plane with the world's great religions—is that not only its successes but its failures are taken as proof of the ritual's power. Like what used to be called the wheel of Fortuna, real estate creates a loser for every winner—Texas up one decade, New York up the next, while Texas languishes—and it operates in cycles. The psychological power of real estate lies in the fact that both losers and winners in our society tend to see their fortunes as reflections of personal character, not impersonal forces. Instead of seeing flaws in the system when large numbers of people lose their savings in real estate, we blame the losers for their lack of intelligence or industriousness. The socially constructed nature of the real estate market disappears behind a fog of details and numbers that help cloak the market's winners in an aura of metaphysical wisdom, the trappings of a princely caste.

The myth embedded in the Texas real estate ritual in the 1980s was this: "The prince brings prosperity." Although it was almost never articulated, this myth was acted out in the structure within which the princes of the market closed their financing deals, marked their territories with billboards, and climbed into the society columns. It embodied the belief that riches would flow to the whole of society if these few, who apparently possessed the fructifying blessings of a beneficent heaven, were allowed to create the physical and cultural arrangements required for the orderly operation of society—arrangements best expressed through architecture.

The chief method employed by architects for demonstrating the validity of the myth was appropriation, like that used by Johnson and Burgee for RepublicBank Center in Houston. Working for a given prince, the architect's job was to come up with images that would give his projects value while taking value from everything else, convincing onlookers that they stood in the presence of the anointed, and that all other claims to legitimacy were false. This process was played out hundreds of times during the 1980s, at the scale of the region, the city, the street, the office building, the neighborhood, the house. The importance of this process, as would be shown throughout the decade, was that it was a zero-sum game, *requiring* that losers be generated to balance out winners.

Of course, the myth of the prince bringing prosperity is not unique to Texas, nor to the 1980s. If anything, it is the commonest myth of American democracy, at least in this century. Nor is the appropriation of historic imagery anything new—it forms a constant in Western architecture at least since the Renaissance. But in Texas during the 1980s, the myth was held so fervently and the consequences of the strategies of appropriation used to advance it were so calamitous as to present a kind of distillation of what is otherwise a diffuse universal process.

What made this process so important in Texas in the 1980s was an ongoing struggle between two economic principles that have vied to rule the consciousness of the American public at least since the 1920s. The first of these principles is based in classical economics, with its emphasis on savings and productivity, on living within one's means, on deferring gratification, and, most of all, on avoiding debt. The second principle was formulated by British economist John Maynard Keynes, who treated demand as the ultimate economic force. Keynes said that a country could do what an individual consumer could not: It could, in aggregate, "spend itself rich" by stimulating overall growth in the economy through deficit spending, and "save itself poor" by choking off capital needed to stimulate demand.

Something like a vernacular Keynesianism fueled the public participation in the stock market speculation of the 1920s, while the U.S. government's actions were dictated by a classical economic stance. Governmental and public positions switched in response to the market crash of 1929; the new Roosevelt administration began using deficit spending to create jobs and stimulate economic growth, while the public, scared by the crash, bank panics, and widespread unemployment, reembraced classical principles. This attitude was continued by the wartime austerity required of the public during the 1940s.

After the war, however, the government greatly expanded its stimulative policies (embraced by the Republican Party when Eisenhower succeeded Truman), creating tax breaks and government insurance programs aimed at increasing home ownership, and directly funding new highways, college scholarships, and other programs. In the 1950s, for the first time, both the business climate and public psychology came into alignment with these government policies; lenders, prodded by federal insurance and new regulations into lending up to 90 percent of a house's purchase price, were matched by a growing population willing to take on debt at unprecedented rates, not just for new suburban houses but for cars, appliances, clothes, and education. The 1950 census was the first in which more than 50 percent of U.S. households were owner-occupied. (The ratio climbed to 61 percent in 1960 and 62 percent in 1970 and leveled off at 65.6 percent in 1980, falling back to 63.9 percent later in the decade.)

And the vast experiment worked: The new suburban America spent itself rich, becoming an economic force that led the global economy into recovery.

This represented a momentous psychological change. For the head of the typical American family in the 1930s, debt had looked like a noose; to the middle-class or even working-class paterfamilias of the 1950s, debt had lost its terror; it had become, as Constance Perin points out in *Everything in Its Place*, the road to home ownership, which is to say first-class citizenship.[13] Beyond that, debt opened up myriad paths to the pursuit of happiness held as a right since the country's inception and given new meaning in a culture that more and more equated personhood with consumption of goods.

The change went even deeper, into the expectations about life cycles and relationships between generations that undergirded family life throughout the country. Parents, whose authority was tied up with helping their children learn to defer gratification and to educate themselves to take places in adult society, adopted spending patterns that must have seemed to parents, before the novelty turned into necessity, both liberating and threateningly infantile.

By the beginning of the 1960s, as Barbara Ehrenreich wrote in *Fear of Falling, The Inner Life of the Middle Class*, classical economics had become the province of a few reactionaries; like polio and poverty, it seemed on the verge of being eradicated. All that remained, prominent social theorists wrote, was to remove the noneconomic barriers that kept certain groups out of the mainstream, and society could be engineered into economic, social, and cultural parity. Ehrenreich says that the pundits stopped calling for federal Great Society programs before they were enacted, and turned instead to worrying that America would soon lack incentives for excellence.[14]

The combination of expensive social programs with the ongoing war in Vietnam, however, not only splintered the consensus for governmental activism aimed at benefiting the "lower" classes, says Ehrenreich; it also stimulated inflation that wove itself into the country's economic structure, particularly after the first Arab oil embargo, when energy prices jumped a thousand percent and higher costs fanned out through practically all goods and services.

The steep climb in U.S. real estate prices arose from and fed off this inflationary climate; real estate prices continued to climb faster than general inflation through the 1970s. A psychological corner was turned sometime during the Nixon administration, when real estate prices shot through a critical barrier: It was no longer possible to pay for a typical middle-class house on a single middle-class income. American women had been entering the job market in large numbers since the 1960s. Now, for most families, the participation of a working wife was not an option but a necessity; a family that didn't have two breadwinners was in danger of slipping out of the middle class, of having its first-class citizenship revoked. It was at this point that the liberal consensus of the country, already strained during the 1960s, snapped irrevocably. Middle-class families, struggling to keep their heads above water, Ehrenreich says, lost interest in other people's problems, and the mood of the country became increasingly conservative during the Ford and Carter administrations as inflation continued unchecked.

The middle class did not, however, want to give up its Keynesianism; debt, like governmental economic intervention and inflation, had become inextricable parts of every family's budget. President Ronald Reagan, who swept into office on a tide of change that promised to reverse the excesses of the 1970s, talked like a classical economist, denouncing the trillion-dollar national debt and extolling the virtues of a bygone era, when families lived within their means. Then, with the blessing of voters who elected Republican administrations and Democratic congresses, the federal government tripled that unimaginable number in a little over eight years, in large part to support transfer payments to middle-class recipients. At the same time, corporate and private borrowing kept pace: Analysts estimated that $8 trillion in debt was created by government, business, and consumers in the 1980s. Lots of the money that was borrowed went overseas for oil and manufactured goods, while some of it went into American manufacturing and research. Hundreds of billions of dollars went into speculation in real estate.

The psychological effect of the 1980s debt binge was a mixture of euphoria and desperation. As the 1980s unfolded, people found that, even with two earners, some families were having trouble qualifying for loans in the fastest-growing and most prosperous areas of the country. But people hung onto the idea that real estate was the solution, not the problem—even after inflation in most other sectors of the economy cooled. The only hope was that a family could get on the escalator and start trading up, perhaps by taking out a mortgage that stretched the family's paychecks paper thin. In an economy in which millions of families were living with this risk, the princes of the real estate market, getting rich by taking risks with borrowed money, were more than just distant businesspeople: They were the guarantors that the ritual would work for everyone.

Nowhere was this truer than in Texas, where, in the early 1980s, events matched the predictions of the myth that the prince brings prosperity to all. Energy price inflation that started in the 1970s helped Texas, even though it hurt the rest of the country; rising oil prices meant rising profits for Texas-based companies, siphoned off from the economies of the unlucky oil-consuming states of the Northeast and Midwest, providing capital and jobs that drew immigrants and further investment. Real estate became an attractive place to store the rising tide of oil money,[15] providing an inflation-derived return that matched or even surpassed speculative return from the oil business. Not only did banks and individuals who invested directly in the real estate developments of princes such as Trammell Crow, Gerald D. Hines, or Austin's John Watson make money on their investments; a much broader social benefit flowed from the growth of values in high-profile real estate transactions downward into the market, lifting single-family houses and raw land at the same time. Families who had done nothing more canny than buy and occupy an in-town bungalow or a '50s-suburb ranch house found, once the boom started, that they could sell out and buy a bigger house or a place in the country, or that they could pay for a child's education or their own retirement. Like the Christians of Byzantium, pipe fitters and nurses and college professors throughout Texas found themselves partaking in some of the princes' glory and wealth.

On top of this, a new aristocracy arose in the real estate market who also found a way to ride the real estate boom to stratospheric heights. Besides J.R. McConnell, these were the crooked developers and skim-off artists such as Don Dixon of Vernon Savings, Edwin McBirney of Sunbelt Savings, Stanley Adams of Lamar Savings, and a host of others who gained control of savings-and-loan institutions and discovered new ways to create wealth from debt—using federally insured deposits. These characters could not have succeeded without the mechanisms of deregulation created by Congress, which tried in the late 1970s to save the S&L industry from impending failure by lifting the limits on the interest that depositors could be paid and by taking the lid off the kinds of investments S&Ls could make, or without the Reagan administration's ideological conviction that the only problem with the American economy was government interference with the creativity of entrepreneurs.

The fountain of creativity unleashed by deregulation in Texas spewed forth a new way of converting long-term debt into risk-free short-term wealth. This was done by paying everyone for everything with the '80s drug of choice, "OPM"—other people's money—backed by federal deposit insurance. In a typical transaction, a developer would go to an S&L (perhaps owned by the developer himself or controlled by friends) and borrow 100 percent of the value of a proposed project (as shown on his self-generated pro forma statement and backed by a report from a compliant appraisal company), and perhaps additionally secure the loan with the deed to another property whose value had been inflated through a series of secret land-flip transactions. So far so good, except that the pyramid of inflated values couldn't last. The real creativity came in opportunities to make the loan supply not only spending cash for the developer but profits for the S&L itself. This was done simply by using loan funds to pay whatever points and fees the S&L wanted to charge, converting deposits immediately into profits before a cent has been invested in the project or paid back to the S&L, and enabling the S&L's board to pay itself and its officers big salaries and bonuses. And just in case there might be fluctuations in the market that would squeeze the developer's ability to keep up the interest payments, the S&L set up an exquisite creation, an interest escrow account—using borrowed funds—that would make payments on the loan for a given period, so that the project would be protected from going into default (thereby exposing the crookedness underlying the original pro forma, appraisals, and land flips) even if it were a flop, and even if some or all the funds loaned for it had been skimmed off and used for some other purpose. Finally, there was "walking money" loaned to the developer; it might be used for a new Mercedes, a trip to Las Vegas with S&L regulators, or some other little celebration of untrammeled entrepreneurialism. Billions of dollars were looted using variations of these devices.

Such insanity is increasingly costly, but by the early 1980s oil prices had started to fall. The cities most tied to oil production—Houston, Beaumont, Midland, and Odessa—felt the blow first. The bust spread to Dallas and

Austin later, as a hoped-for boom in electronics died under the assault of growing Japanese production. Still, because of a confluence of financial commitments and the S&L deregulation that allowed a hemorrhage of capital into real estate just when it made the least sense, building continued. It was during this period that Allied Bank Dallas and RepublicBank Center were built.

Then, late in the decade, winners became losers statewide. Time ran out on the speculative bubble; the real estate market inexorably began paring property values down by 10 to 15 percent per year until they approached use value, dragging real estate prices downwards, closer into line with wage levels and other fundamentals of the economy. But the old prices didn't quite evaporate: in the late '80s, a seller who bought for $100,000 and hoped to sell for twice as much was suddenly required to bring $10,000 or $20,000 to the closing to pay for the difference between his mortgage and the buyer's offer. By the last third of the decade, any real estate investment was not just risky but crazy. People began to discover that some of the princes were, in fact, pretenders—J.R. McConnell, for example.

It is fair to say that the 1980s represent a loss of innocence for Texas, if not a fall from grace; it was the decade when the availability of easy money from just being lucky enough to live on top of extractable natural resources was superseded by the necessity to be more like the rest of the country, depending on manufacturing, services, and other, more intellectually strenuous ways of making a living. In the '80s, the cumulative sins of decades came to a peak: The Texas middle class tried to climb too high, converting debt to capital the way that only the rich had been able to in previous generations, and were punished for their pride. Texans thought they were in control of the mystery of real estate, but the essential volatility underlying the ritual reasserted itself. Real estate's forgotten duality was again revealed: the ritual creates but it also, simultaneously, destroys.

Indeed, although hidden from the white middle class during the early 1980s by the effects of the boom, the destructive side of the real estate equation is, in the long run, more important.

Perhaps the first effect of the '80s boom came in relation to the future: The advent of the two-wage-earner house represented a fundamental shift in social expectations whose effects, it can be predicted, will reach far into the next century. Future buyers became losers relative to contemporary sellers.

But the value-consuming power of the real estate market is even more fundamental: it creates losers even in a stable market, without excessive speculation. It is through this operation that real estate helps regulate social relations, keeping the rich and the poor in their respective positions. Real estate takes away value, for example, based on the criterion of race; almost by definition, the houses and lots and commercial buildings where black people live are worth less than those in predominantly white neighborhoods. Studies show, in addition, that even in a rising market, property in a black neighborhood will appreciate by a smaller percentage than land in a white neighborhood. Economists and social geographers find little exceptional in this: members of any given group tend to want to live in proximity to each other, and since white people as a group tend to have higher incomes, they can spend more buying property, creating higher values in the locales they favor.[16]

Real estate also creates losers by its propensity to treat land as a bank in which capital can be profitably invested even though nothing is built. The most deleterious effects of this propensity can be seen in downtowns, such as Dallas's, where land is most valuable for banking if it is stripped of the historic buildings that make up the city's built connection with the past. In central Dallas, despite a nationally recognized preservation ordinance that gives property owners tax breaks, almost half of the pre-Second World War buildings standing in 1980 had been torn down by the end of the decade, and some 38 percent of the downtown lots were occupied not by buildings but by surface parking.[17] A similar percentage of downtown Houston is vacant, and for the same reasons: Tax laws led the owners to tear the buildings down while they waited for a big deal to come along. For people who live in a neighborhood that will be cleared so that the land can be banked, the time frame of their experience includes a past; by comparison, the calculation of value in real estate time starts today and looks to the future—the past has no value, except as a tax liability. The loser in such a situation is the community at large, which has its physical connection with history truncated, if not obliterated.

In fact, perhaps the most important function of both sides of the real estate equation lies in its demonstration that we live in a two-tiered economic system in which a small number of people with their hands on the levers of capital can win big, while the rest can win but never on the same scale. The market in real estate is free in one sense. Just as the late-night TV hucksters promise, it is possible, with luck and ambition, to parlay a small initial investment into control over a lot of property. Trammell Crow started small, as did Gerald Hines, and, of course, J.R. McConnell. The boundary between the top tier and the bottom is, in that sense, fluid enough to admit those with the initiative to climb up. But admission is controlled by access to capital and by expertise reserved for a few princes, which tends to keep the number of successful climbers rather small.

For everyone else, the structure of the typical real estate transaction is a simulacrum of the free market touted by ideologues; consumers in the second tier are free to buy where they like, but only from within the range of products and sites offered by the princes at the top. The names chosen for the marketing of suburban housing tracts or condominium projects often attempt to compensate for any possible alienation caused by this stair-stepping in the market by conveying a sense that the lucky home buyer is purchasing a share in old-world aristocracy, if not royalty (Kingwood, Nottingham Village), or a hint that buyers will reside in a nature preserve (The Oaks of Glenwood, The Woodlands), or that they are holders of an original land grant (Travis Country, First Colony). Of course, the life of the suburban homeowner, with its lawnmowings and cracked slabs and traffic jams, may be pleasant enough, but it seldom lives up to the expectations promoted by the princes of the market.

If Texans sinned in the 1980s, it was by sending out too many climbers and by trying to capture too much of the increase in value spun off by the princely doings of those with access to capital and information. The downfall started when unemployment began rising and homeowners began having trouble meeting their mortgages. Then they rediscovered a forgotten fact: Capital in the modern world is mobile, and labor has to be mobile to benefit from its shifts. But when a large percentage of a family's two incomes is going into the mortgage of a house for which there are suddenly no buyers, mobility is hard to come by, mostly because the owners can't leave without losing their investment. For typical second-tier purchasers in the real estate market of the mid-1980s, real estate changed. It was as if an unseen hand had flipped a switch on the escalator they were riding and they were suddenly going down instead of up. Many took the way out used by J.R. McConnell and dozens of other princes when times got tough. They walked away, "gave the house back to the bank," took off for Boston, or California, or Florida, where there was hope for work. Enough people fled their homes in Houston's newest suburbs to create what a writer in *Cite* magazine called "suburbia deserta."[18] Others sat it out and watched their equity erode, learning the lesson that real estate has, as one Houston stockbroker puts it, "no value, only a price," and that it ties working people down—at least scrupulous people—when most other influences in the economy push them to move like gray-suited nomads.

Besides this didactic effect, the real estate bust in Texas had other functions, the chief of which was to reestablish the social order that real estate helps constitute and that the earlier boom had threatened. Princes, with access to enough capital to stay mobile, on top; the rest, pinned down by debt. J.R. McConnell was an expiatory offering for the whole state, one man sacrificed so that the boom cycle could start again, as it did, modestly, in late 1988. J.R. McConnell died for our sins.

Of course, he did not see himself that way. McConnell killed himself fifteen days before he was to come to trial and thus was never convicted of any wrongdoing; in his suicide note he accepted no guilt, blaming the judicial system for keeping him from making good on his debts. All but two of his associates were acquitted in 1989, although they got off by blaming it all on McConnell, who wasn't there to defend himself.

The allegations of fraud against McConnell make him seem like an anomaly. But in key respects he was not. McConnell had a vision of possibilities, and the ability to convey it to other people. A Galveston realtor who had worked with McConnell said of him after he died: "Had he been able to be conventional in the way he financed things, he would have been second to none. The guy had real vision, but he had a little larceny in his heart."

People bought things from McConnell; more important, they bought into what he had to offer, investing in his vision. Early on, they were rewarded. Later, they lost. Families were unable to sell their homes because of the fraudulent use of titles to their properties. Bankruptcies rippled out through the list of McConnell's creditors; among them were two banks and seven savings and loans, all of which later went under.

This is what makes McConnell an exemplar, not an anomaly. McConnell's alleged fraud helped bring down several financial institutions. That is no inconsiderable feat, but the collapse of the Texas real estate market in the late 1980s caused the closure of no fewer than one hundred and sixty-eight S&Ls and three hundred and thirty-four banks (as of July 1990), and dozens more were left teetering on the brink. Not coincidentally, the amount of vacant commercial real estate created in Texas at the time became a national scandal: At the bottom of the bust, there was more unrented office space in the tenantless towers of Houston than there was total office space in Atlanta and Denver combined. Not long afterward, not coincidentally, the number of real estate properties foreclosed on in Texas rose to astronomical levels: In Dallas, Harris, Bexar, and Travis counties alone between 1985 and 1989, there were 213,964 property foreclosures, and over 90 percent of them involved single-family dwellings, real estate analysts say. Harris County by itself accounted for 121,072 foreclosures during this five-year period. (The number of foreclosures in Harris County peaked at 31,015 in 1987, compared with 1,386 in 1980.) Behind these figures is the fact that nearly 400,000 people in a single county lost their homes, along with their down payments and the thirty percent or more of their family incomes that had been paid toward housing costs. Extrapolating from available figures, real estate analysts say, it is possible to estimate that a million men, women, and children lost their homes in Texas in half a decade, a displacement of historic dimensions.[19]

Compared with the ruin visited on the people who lost their homes, the banks and savings and loans lost mere paper profits. But these losses have been translated again into real problems. The federal government's 1989 bailout plan for the savings-and-loan industry promises to convert as much as $500 billion in tax revenues to a fund to absorb industry losses, most of which, although certainly not all, derive from real estate speculation, and a large part of which can be traced to Texas. The children and grandchildren of all U.S. citizens will be paying on this debt with taxes that might have been used for education, roads, medical research, and the space program. Higher bank-insurance fees and the borrowing by the federal government required to support the savings-and-loan bailout, analysts say, will keep interest rates higher than they might otherwise have been for years to come, raising the cost of capital needed for productive industries at a time when the U.S. is already struggling to deal with increased global competition. The Texas real estate bust could help turn the U.S. into a second-rate economic power.

Main Street, downtown Dallas, 1991

Seen in this context, the skyline monuments for Momentum Bank, Allied Bank, RepublicBank, Interfirst Bank, and others, intended by their builders and architects to represent the economic vitality of whole regions, have ended up as monuments to a colossal social tragedy, their glass or stone facades and soaring profiles seeming to deride not just the hopes of their creators but the aspirations of those who inherit the resulting mess. The social and economic changes of the 1980s, centering on the real estate debacle, left Texas city centers punctuated by tall buildings, but these were set among empty lots in all-but-deserted streets and surrounded by an urban fabric in which pockets of affluence struggled to avoid the fate of other neighborhoods dragged down into the decaying infrastructure. So much money had been gambled and lost in real estate that the decade left significant parts of the private realm and most of the public realm in Texas hollowed out; dozens of the state's colleges and school systems, its social services, its courts and hospitals and sewer systems, like all but the upper layer of its neighborhoods, were left as see-through shells that the merest puff of additional economic tribulation could bring down. It is a common-

Main Street, downtown Houston, 1991

place of architectural criticism that societies create buildings to symbolize their underlying order and aspirations. In the 1980s in Texas, however, the process seemed to work in reverse; all those see-through office buildings helped create a society in their own image.

Perhaps tragicomedy describes the situation better, however, since there is surely comedy in the fact that the managements of all these leading institutions, presumably representing the best financial minds in the region, commissioned office towers whose architecture attracted national attention, only to have their vaults vacuumed by a sagging real estate market. Allied, Republic, Interfirst—where are the banks of yesteryear? The upright burghers who ran these institutions, used to a social structure and a built environment (of their making) that supported the sense that they were leaders of society by right, found themselves victims of the same belief in the mystery of real estate that took J.R. McConnell from a K-Mart parking lot to his act of expiation in the Harris County jail.

Most comic of all is the fact that the delusion that led to creation of these bank towers was not merely local. Indeed, as the 1980s started, the cities of the Sunbelt in general and Texas in particular were looked on as the hope of America, the only logical sites of growth in coming decades. In 1980, a blue-ribbon group called the President's Commission for a National Agenda for the Eighties, set up a year earlier by then-President Jimmy Carter, issued a report, *Urban America in the Eighties: Perspectives and Prospects*, urging that national policy be organized to commit a kind of urban triage, abandoning the moribund cities of the industrial Northeast to market forces that would kill them off in the '80s, and stimulating the same market forces as they attracted immigrants and capital to the growing suburbs of Houston, Dallas, San Antonio, and Atlanta. By the middle of the decade, however, people were walking away from their houses in Houston's suburbs and out-of-state banks were taking over the troubled assets of the Texas banks; meanwhile, New York, Philadelphia, Boston, Cleveland, Washington, D.C., Princeton, and a half dozen other northeastern cities were sprouting new office towers and sprawling at their edges in a pattern that local critics denounced as "Houstonization." And by the early '90s, when the effects of overbuilding drove prices down and threatened the stability of banks in the Northeast, it was being called "the Southwest disease."[20] Proponents of the free market, during the congressional debate over the savings-and-loan bailout, proposed that Texas cities be abandoned to their fate, turning the logic that once favored Texas to its detriment. McConnell's deals, like those of scores of his compatriots, went sour partly because money that Texans thought divine providence had intended for their exclusive use was being drawn instead to the financial and real estate markets of the Northeast, which had been, wrongly, presumed dead.

The Unhealable Split, Farbism, and Old and New Money

Real estate is a ritual connecting buyers and sellers and distributing gains and losses not only to individuals within social groups but to whole regions and societies; the system is confirmed by dozens of mechanisms, from government tax and spending policies to the advertisements in the Sunday newspaper supplements.

Real estate also embodies another, subtler process. It allows for exchanges between the world of economics and the world of culture; it mediates between money and meaning. This is especially true of architecture, the subcategory of real estate that converts financial and political resources, land, materials, and the expertise and labor of designers, contractors, and construction workers into structures and places for use. (The distinction between "building" and "architecture" can be set aside here; every building can be seen as conveying meaning to someone, which is enough to qualify it as architecture.)

In our society we have many means for achieving this mediation—indeed, almost all institutions from academia to the zoo must play such a role at one time or another—and both television and popular songs, to cite just two obvious examples, touch more people more intimately than does architecture.

But songs and television shows are transitory things, made boring or forgettable in hours or minutes, while works of architecture tend to last because they represent such huge investments of time, energy, materials, and money. Hanging around from year to year, a building channels visions and expectations from the moment of its creation into its future, wrapping a section of the past around the ephemeral concerns of the present. All meaning comes from relationships, and buildings are accorded the role of relationship-bearers par excellence, acting not only as foreground objects but as backgrounds that frame contemporary activities and concerns in terms of the built human past.

Buildings are commodities—units of exchange stripped down to a state of commensurability with other such units, molecules in the sea of the monetary system. On the other hand, they are unique constituents of the cultural memory, reefs lifted above the waves of economic calculation by our inescapable need to quell what architect and writer Michael Benedikt calls "the fear that we will be overcome by the dread muteness of objects and the heedlessness of nature," an anxiety that pecks at us with every entropic second.[21]

Both economic and cultural realms exert equal claims on architecture, and, as a result, the pursuit of architecture oscillates uncomfortably between them. This oscillation is part of the constitution of every work of architecture; each building reflects the social relationships through which it was created, and the simplest diagram of those relationships, in our society, is a triangle, with economic forces in one corner, cultural forces in another, and the public, as an audience, in the third. For simplicity's sake, I will start by taking developers as the most self-interested epitomes of the different owners, managers, and clients who make up our society's economic forces (and will treat those forces as separable from the rest of the society); similarly, I will treat architects as separable from and representative of the whole panoply of cultural forces at work. The simplification of complex roles and forces into such a triangle does some violence to the intricate meshing of our social fabric, but it also helps reveal some of the underlying problems of architecture over the last decade. For a start, it is obvious that, like all triangles, the one formed by developers, architects, and the public is fraught with desire, anger, and shifting loyalties.

In *The Social Life of Things*, the anthropologist Arjun Appurdai examines the rules governing the roles of producers and consumers in the creation and use of commodities and cultural objects. One of the chief means of differentiating such roles, Appurdai suggests, lies in considering the knowledge about the process of production and exchange possessed by each of the participants. Paraphrasing the French sociologist Pierre Bourdieu, Appurdai suggests that the type of knowledge a person has about a commodity or cultural object, and the way in which it was acquired, determines the way that person will relate to the exchange process (indeed, that it delineates that person's role in society). Appurdai cites examples from New Guinea, Zimbabwe, and colonial Bolivia.[22] But the production of architecture in Texas during the 1980s would do just as well. The framework, again greatly simplified, goes as follows.

Developers, in their corner of the triangle, control knowledge about such matters as financial packaging, land purchases, and hiring of designers and contractors; they create commodities for sale to the public. They are custodians of capital, whose goal is profit and whose skill lies in managing access to money and reading the demands of the market. As they become more successful, prestige and social standing become as important to them as profit. At this point, a new triangulation of new money, old money, and the professional custodians of cultural power comes into play.

Relative to the public for whom they are providing architecture, developers are clearly members of an elite class, controlling both money and land. Likewise, developers hold elite status relative to architects, who are far from the most important part of the team assembled by developers to produce architectural projects.

Architects, in their corner, to the extent that they can be separated from the commodification process and seen as possessing a separate, specialized knowledge, are the custodians of expertise about production techniques (e.g., the weight-bearing capacity of concrete, ways to use flashing around metal doors), history, and formal considerations (e.g., the psychological implications of a given roof angle, the gender of column capitals, the relative visual weight of brick and stone); what they know is largely self-referential, of concern to other specialists, and what they know of the public is based on observations that ignore or deny the importance of the economic marketplace. Architects specialize in creating and controlling access to cultural objects.

The "cultural capital" (Bourdieu's phrase) that architects represent places them, also, in an elite class relative to the public, and even, in a sense, relative to developers. This elite status, however, rests uneasily, since it is based on education and performance, both of which have to be maintained over lifetimes and over generations through unremitting effort. It is this education-based status that links the profession of architecture to the middle class, while control of capital links developers, even lower-end ones, to the real upper class. In fact, architects are among the most uneasy members of the professional middle class. Doctors and lawyers and accountants have established monopolies that govern the market for their services. Architects have no such control; indeed, industry analysts estimate that at present more than half the commercial buildings in the U.S. and almost all the houses are designed and built without benefit of services by a professional architect. For all but a few architects, fees have fallen over the last generation, and control over various aspects of the design and construction-administration process has been parceled out to other people, from acousticians to interior designers to leasing agents.[23] As architects come under threat of economic marginalization, they tend to protect their cultural prerogatives all the more jealously. At the same time, the public seems to resent the elitism of architects much more than that of developers; the world of economics is seen as an open system, to which the members of the public can aspire, while the world of culture is not.

The two types of knowledge possessed by developers and architects are always in competition. Architects work to restrain the tendency, naturally shown by developers who are trying to maximize profits, to cut back on the aesthetic qualities that stimulate the public's desire to choose one building over another in a competitive marketplace, to build structures with no meaning beyond their roles as commodities. Conversely, they sometimes work to restrain developers from throwing money at projects—misusing materials or historically validated visual codes in a way that will make the project an expensive exercise in bad taste. Developers try to restrain architects from creating works that are so expensive or so idiosyncratic that the public, or those parts of it identifiable as potential consumers, won't want them—works, that is, that can't be made into commodities. (Arguments over just such issues fill the biographies of developers that have appeared in the last decade,[24] and, indeed, they are familiar to most people who have worked with an architect.)

One example of the incomprehension and suspicion that nonarchitects feel for architects was provided by then-Texas Governor Bill Clements in 1989. Clements's fortune came from oil technology, not real estate, but he fits here because his views on the relations between economics and culture are exemplary (during a tour of the University of Texas' Harry Ransom Center, Clements was shown a Gutenberg Bible, about which an employee launched into a rhapsody that began, "We live by it. Our souls are structured by it." Clements replied by asking simply, "How much did it cost?")[25] and because in 1989 he was the most important member of a group of government officials overseeing restoration and expansion of the Texas State Capitol. Clements took the occasion of the unveiling of a schematic model of the Capitol addition to berate architects in general for their propensity to create "a wonderland of architecture" like the nearby University of Texas campus. It's hard to know what set Clements off; the architects for the project had been assiduously following both the budget and the program of uses set forth by the overseeing politicians, and were guilty, if anything, of excessive modesty in their presentation.

But perhaps the best single example of the developer's view of architects is provided by Dallas businessman Ben Carpenter, son of one of the city's most powerful oligarchs, who created the residential-commercial-office satellite city Las Colinas out of a family ranch northeast of Dallas. Carpenter, easy in both his inherited wealth and his sense of personal achievement, has spoken with unusual candor about Las Colinas's role as a monument to his own taste and sense of vision. He also has spoken publicly

Office buildings in the Las Colinas "urban center"

about the intimate colloquies and man-to-man handshakes among business leaders, highway-department officials, and others, in which he figured prominently and which resulted in the private manipulation of public infrastructure that made possible the creation, first, of the Dallas/Fort Worth Airport, and, second, of Las Colinas.[26]

Carpenter sees nothing to apologize for in this; in his mind, he created something of unique quality in Las Colinas, and that's that. At a symposium at the University of Texas at Austin in 1991, he enumerated the main means of establishing the development's "quality" image. First, he purchased a buffer zone of property in Irving and cleared away the "substandard" houses of its residents. Next, he turned the site's flood-prone swales into decorative features, digging out canals and lakes (the largest, Lake Carolyn, was named for his sister) and forming ridges with the fill dirt. Then he set up a kind of theme-park design code covering everything from building materials to signage to road-shoulder heights, and reinforced it with amenities such as golf courses, equestrian centers, and water taxis. The houses for Las Colinas's twenty thousand or so residents, almost all de-

Canal Walk, Las Colinas, Ben Carpenter's vision of urbanity, designed by HKS

signed in the aggressive North Dallas builders' vernacular, were famed for their sheer expense (described as "exclusivity" and "quality") and for embodying what Gary Cartwright in *Texas Monthly* called Carpenter's obsession with security; armed guards at the entrances, electronic surveillance of practically every room of every house—a mirror of the problems of the city that residents came to Las Colinas to escape. He installed a monorail to connect the buildings of the main office park, and he lined its central canal with fountains, bell towers, bridges, and pastiche false building fronts hiding parking garages, in what he has described as "a continuation of our Spanish and early Texas cattle-raising heritage." He bought bronze sculptures for the plaza of Williams Square, which he touted as a thriving urban space, the next St. Mark's Piazza or Trafalgar Square.

In fact, judged by the standards of traditional architectural discourse, almost none of this works. The sculptures in Williams Square are striking, but, despite the horses and the canals, Las Colinas will never be confused with Venice. The turbid expanse of Lake Carolyn and the canal walk are modest improvements on basic office-park planning, and nothing more.

San Antonio's River Walk

Even the argument that Las Colinas's success in the marketplace is evidence of quality is undercut by the fact that Carpenter's company, driven to the brink of bankruptcy in the mid-'80s, was forced to sell off a sizable chunk of the property and to cede control of the central business park to Lincoln Properties. At best, Las Colinas is a hodge-podge of indifferent buildings, with one distinguishing characteristic: proximity to D/FW Airport, which makes it a good location for globe-hopping executives.

It is just possible, on the other hand, that the ersatz quality of what Carpenter has created could wear away, and it could be anointed with cultural acceptance. San Antonio's Paseo del Rio provides a clear precedent. It is based on a plan called "The Shops of Aragon and Romula," invented out of whole cloth by architect Robert H.H. Hugman in 1929. He devised it as a way of controlling flooding on the San Antonio River downtown while allowing for commercial development and preserving the river's natural vegetation. (Officials had been planning to pave the river over, following a series of killer floods.) Hugman's plan embodies the same appropriation of "Spanish heritage" that Carpenter cites as the ethos of Las Colinas, along with the same implicitly racist message that Anglos, not Mexicans, are the legitimate heirs of the first European conquerors of this region. As if this weren't fake enough, Hugman even recalled in a 1978 speech how the manager of a downtown hotel and compliant city officials rigged a bond election by excluding property owners opposed to the project while including hotel residents "who owned so much as a watch" and who could be counted on to vote properly.[27] All that has been forgotten now; the River Walk is treated as living history and spoken of worshipfully by architects around the state. Of course, the River Walk has a downtown around it, a downtown it has helped preserve beyond the term of other downtowns in Texas.

To Carpenter, none of these factors matters. What he has created is, in his terms, real beauty. He has known from the start that the people most likely to cast aspersions on his achievement would be architects, and that, in doing so, they would be acting out of a self-aggrandizing cultural arrogance. He has been ready to parry architectural criticisms from the start. As David Dillon quotes him in *Dallas Architecture 1936-1986*, Carpenter told the architects at the Dallas firm HKS who designed the canal walk: "I am not interested in authenticities . . . just a change of pace, to warm things up for the people in the office buildings." Architects, he said, only liked "cold modern commercial stuff." Finally, architects "want to win awards" from each other "by doing something new and different."[28]

For now, however, Carpenter and most architects are clearly at odds over who can legitimately interpret the significance of forms in the built landscape. Carpenter's point, like that made by Governor Clements about the Capitol expansion, is that architects simply can't be trusted. If one stands in the developer's vertex, such a charge is self-evidently true.

Architects and developers have different agendas. Each group sees the buildings they cooperate in producing, and the social context in which that process of production takes place, in differing ways. As groups, they constitute what Peter L. Berger and Thomas Luckmann in *The Social Construction of Reality* call social subuniverses, "each seeking to establish itself and to discredit if not liquidate the competing body of knowledge."[29] In justifying their positions in this competition, both developers and architects assert that they speak not just for themselves but for the interests of the public, and they periodically mount direct and indirect appeals for public support; like partners in a bad marriage, each needs the other but tries to escape to carry on a romance with the public. The public's role throughout all this is always to ratify one position or the other, and to do so more or less unconsciously; members of the public are thought to express their sensibilities, if not their actual personalities, through the purchase and use of architectural space and other commodities, which one group or the other identifies as expressing its values.

In seeking to seduce the public this way, architects and developers are attempting not just to win the argument as to whether a given project should best be treated as a commodity or as a cultural object; they are trying to frame the terms in which the argument is expressed so that winning is the only option, trying to establish hegemony over the field in which the struggle takes place. Both sides characterize their opponents as self-interested and coercive. And they construct arguments that are essentially mystifications, projecting their views as natural, inevitable, unchangeable, and unimprovable. Think, for example, of Louis I. Kahn's often-imitated murmurings that features of his projects "wanted to be" positioned where he put them, or the incantatory effect of calling any way of trying to turn a profit on a property its "highest and best use"—perhaps it would make more sense if there were also a commonly used category called "worst and stupidest use."

One of the simplest ways of establishing such hegemony is to recruit to your side members of the opposite camp. Thus, most developers seek out architects who are willing to drop their cultural "pretensions" and get down to the business of creating commodities. Trammell Crow, founder of what was in the late 1980s the world's largest real estate company, got his start as an independent businessman by listening to the needs of some potential clients and by designing and overseeing construction of a warehouse that met those needs. Soon, his business got so big that he could no longer personally attend to every detail, and he began working with architects. But, with few exceptions, he gave them little room to work. Throughout his career he has claimed that he designed the basic concept of his best-known buildings (chiefly relying on atriums, which he reportedly first saw in Milan on vacation and brought back into the vocabulary of American commercial building a decade before John Portman gained acclaim for the supposedly ground-breaking Hyatt Regency hotel in Atlanta) and then engaged architects "to draw up the plans."[30] As the client, Crow was unshakable in his faith that he knew what was best, and, of course, events

Four Leaf Towers, Houston (1982), by Cesar Pelli Associates

supported his view. At the same time, he had the economic power to reinforce his faith. Any architect who didn't agree didn't have to accept his commissions.

By the publicly held mainstream standards of the architectural profession, any designer who works under such conditions at best risks debasing the tradition of architecture and creating projects that diminish the standing of architecture as a public art; at worst, he or she is a traitor to the public trust, abetting in the creation of a counterfeit. Nevertheless, it should be noted that the majority of practicing architects spend most of their careers accepting similar commissions, happily deferring to the power of economic determinism; they are, after all, businessmen and -women themselves, and if such a bargain condemns them to obscurity, it allows them to earn a living in their chosen profession. A few high-profile designers pay similar fealty, at least rhetorically, to the economic realm: Robert A.M. Stern, architect, author, and host of a mid-'80s public-television series on architecture, told an audience at a University of Texas School of Architecture symposium in 1988 that it was time for architects to recognize that they were nothing more than high-priced set designers.[31] (This statement, however, is hardly representative of Stern's career.)

Developers can also make alliances with those in the news media who write on matters relating to architecture. The real estate writers in Texas' newspapers provide many excellent examples of how such alliances work; a typical story about a new building describes costs and financing arrangements and quotes from the principal developers involved, while the architects, being relatively unimportant hirelings, are not even named. Some design critics (as opposed to real estate writers) for the papers in Texas, although they might be expected to have absorbed some of the language

San Antonio "Alamodome" under construction, January 1992

and sensibilities of architects (the way that city-hall reporters ingest the mind-set, if not the policies, of the politicians they cover), routinely misuse or misrepresent both. Instead of explicating the cultural model used in the architectural profession, these critics accept the developer's viewpoint as identical to that of the public. Pam Lewis of the *Houston Post*, for example, used a story covering the 1990 national awards program of the American Institute of Architects to denounce the profession for designing things that the public wouldn't or shouldn't want to buy, implicitly holding up mainstream developer-dominated Texas architecture-without-architects as the ideal that the prize-winning projects failed to achieve.[32] Other newspaper writers show their distance from the concerns of architects by deliberately "misreading" the metaphors projected by different buildings, seeing in them only unintentional humor. Thus, in the early 1980s, *Houston Post* columnist Lynn Ashby compared Cesar Pelli's Four Leaf Towers condominium project, widely praised in the architectural press for the elegance of its glass skin, to "slabs of Spam." Similarly, Pelli's design for St. Luke's Tower, a medical office building in the Texas Medical Center in Houston, has been compared to a pair of up-ended hypodermic syringes. And in 1989, the *San Antonio Light* likened an early scheme by Marmon Barclay Souter Foster Hays of San Antonio for the proposed San Antonio Domed Stadium, with its four corner towers, to a dead armadillo. These misreadings are an important part of the life of every building. The point is that by constructing metaphors at odds with those intended by the architects, these writers show their skepticism of architects' claims to authority even over their own projects.

The most important public spokesman on architectural matters in the 1980s nationally (and a great constructor of humorous metaphorical readings of architecture) was Tom Wolfe, whose *From Bauhaus to Our House*, published in 1981, was a stinging critique of the architectural profession for its adherence to ideas based on what he saw as an outmoded and ill-conceived 1920s European political radicalism. By closing itself off in an effort to protect these ideas, Wolfe charged, the architecture profession had failed in its proper task, which was to provide buildings celebrating the expansive exuberance of American capitalism. Wolfe's ideal city (as he further explained when he addressed the American Institute of Architects's national convention in 1985) was New York before 1940, the city of the Woolworth Building (1913), the first building called "a cathedral of commerce," and the Chrysler Building (1926-30), with its car-part friezes and winged-radiator-cap setback corners paying homage to the country's emerging mania for automobiles. Interestingly, although Wolfe heaped scorn in his AIA speech upon Lever House (1952, Skidmore, Owings & Merrill) and other post-Second World War modernist office buildings in New York, his worst opprobrium was saved for the Sunbelt cities of the 1970s. The cities of America, he said contemptuously, were in danger of becoming "places like Dallas," full of mirror-glass buildings whose abstractness stood as an insult to America. Wolfe started his speech as a critic of architects who have failed their clients, but as he surveyed Dallas and Houston, whose cityscapes are thoroughly dominated by the aesthetic results of developer calculation, his stance shifted. He became the voice of the old wisdom—more than that, the voice of old money—speaking on behalf of the accumulated cultural capital of the Northeast against the claims to legitimacy of the upstart cities of the Sunbelt, and against the real estate developers who lacked the sense to accept the economic and architectural authority of America's historic cultural center (which, by a quirk of timing, was about to experience a building boom even as activity dried up in the Sunbelt). *From Bauhaus to Our House* came out before RepublicBank Center, the closest contemporary Texas skyscraper to Wolfe's eclectic ideal, was completed; it would have been interesting to see how he characterized it.

But the straightforward business of recruiting architects and media representatives from the public into the developer camp inevitably proves insufficient, especially since architects are ceaselessly working to recruit turncoat developers—Harlan Crow or Gerald Hines, for example—who are willing to pay apparent homage to architects as culture lords, in the form of the higher fees and the control over projects demanded by high-profile designers.[33]

Instead, some developers are driven to leave the paths of logical persuasion and to enter a life designed to show that their specialized knowledge of money matters rivals architecture as cultural capital, that it is a competing source of value judgments, of *taste*. They set out to create roles for themselves as tastemakers. As those who spot trends anywhere can attest, the attempt to live such a role involves a dangerous journey into the id, and one is always under threat of losing one's way.

Nevertheless, it is a strategy that seems to come naturally to developers who have just noticed that their money confers elite status on them and who try to take up the responsibility to their new class that their wealth requires.

How else can one explain the actions of Harold Farb, who made millions in the 1970s throwing up apartment complexes for Houston's burgeoning young singles population?[34] Farb was portrayed in silhouette, holding a roll of blueprints, on the parking stickers affixed to the car windows of each of his tenants, making him a ubiquitous, if somewhat anonymous, figure. By the early 1980s, however, that was not enough. He and his young wife, Carolyn, climbed into Houston society through charity balls and other functions that allowed the conspicuous display of their wealth. He developed the San Felipe Plaza office building, a well-detailed structure of pink and gray granite and glass with eroded corners. Designed by Skidmore, Owings & Merrill and finished in 1984, it juts up grotesquely from a low-scale residential neighborhood northwest of the Galleria area, with the sort of antiurban nonchalance that

San Felipe Plaza (1984), Houston, by Skidmore, Owings & Merrill

visitors from other cities find breathtakingly incomprehensible. He released publicity photographs of himself, wearing his characteristic uncomfortable smile and sitting in an aggressively stylish chair in the Michael Graves-designed Sunar office-furniture showroom in Houston, captioned "This is Farb." And he opened a restaurant-night club in which he sang; thousands came to see the gruesome spectacle. Near mid-decade, he and Carolyn divorced. She reportedly got a settlement of $20 million, and he refused to say a word against her to the gossip columnists; they were both guaranteed celebrity status for life, despite the impending eclipse of his fortunes. Farb had not only created himself anew, he had projected a charisma, in the public's eyes, that no architect could compete with and that spilled over to developers throughout Texas. (Interestingly, Carolyn Farb went on to become a patron of high-style architecture, organizing fund-raising events for the Rice Design Alliance as part of her civic activities.)

Developer Donald Trump of New York in the late '80s and early '90s, using his public-relations apparatus to endlessly parade the details of his popular-taste architecture, his self-proclaimed deal-making skills, and his divorce, seems, from this vantage point, to be practicing a warmed-over Farbism. Trump demonstrates, however, that the urge to take on the role of tastemaker is not limited to Texan parvenus. Wherever a developer rises from obscure businessman to hype-crazed public figure, a battle is being waged over the meaning of architecture. Such figures can be seen as aggressive, trying to drive their rivals from the field of discourse by dominating all discussion; they can also be seen as tragic, since the tastemaker role requires large investments of time and money, and it almost always ends in a reversal of fortunes. Farb and Trump, besotted by the fumes of quick money, offered up their very personalities so that the rift between the economic and cultural realms built into architecture's social fabric could be healed, forgetting that such a task is impossible. The attempt brought them low, although Farb has now rebounded, and Trump may do so as well. J.R. McConnell had hardly begun his trajectory in this therapeutic drama, but he ended up paying for the ride with his life.

Farb, Trump, and McConnell were trying to establish the legitimacy of the developer's subuniverse through what Peter Berger and Thomas Luckmann describe as "irrational propaganda" and attempts at "manipulation of prestige symbols." Architects, battling for their own legitimacy both within their group and outside it, generate their own streams of propaganda and prestige symbols. For one thing, they also generate publicity, controlling a number of publications created for just that purpose, including *Architecture*, *Architectural Record*, and *Progressive Architecture*, three of the longest-lived of national magazines, despite the fact that they never have Princess Di or Madonna on their covers. But these magazines, for all their staying power, have tiny audiences. More Americans are interested in monster trucks than in architecture. Some state-level components of the American Institute of Architects have publications, while more-specialized titles, from *Assemblage* to the *Journal of the Society of Architectural Historians*, treat architecture as a pursuit of the mind. Although controversies rage repeatedly in these publications, they are united in one respect. Architecture is treated as a conveyer of meaning while economics is seen as backdrop, secondary to the production of cultural objects.

The same stance, more or less, is taken by design critics at some newspapers around the country. David Dillon, beginning with his 1980 story in *D* magazine, "Why Is Dallas Architecture So Bad?," and continuing as critic of the *Dallas Morning News*, has been one of the most important voices in making the cultural assertions of architects a factor in the city's architectural climate.[35]

But the siren call is strong, and certain individual architects have dropped the tediously linear pursuit of arguing in favor of their expertise in this or that professional or popular journal, and headed, like so many Farbs with T-squares, into the taste-making loop, where their influence has been much more pronounced. Thus, in the mid-1980s, high-style catalogs and department stores around the country began offering jewelry and dinnerware designed by Stanley Tigerman, Richard Meier, and a handful of others, which might have been confined previously to the gift shop of the Museum of Modern Art in New York, and Michael Graves appeared in print ads for some sensible suede shoes.[36] The point is that regular people were presented with a previously unexplored means of buying what Peter Dormer calls "tokens" of architecture,[37] which is to say, tokens of the wealth and taste limited before to those controlling the building process. Purchasing tokens was nothing new, but never before had the public responded so well to the chance to buy things stamped with the name or the look of an identifiable architect, identifiable because he or she was busy helping developers alter the landscapes of just about every contemporary American city. J.R. McConnell had to promise Michael Graves a lot of money to design his proposal for a condominium development in Galveston; by contrast, anybody with $100 or so could call up Williams-Sonoma and order a Graves-designed tea kettle with a little plastic bird on its spout. Walter Benjamin first described how, after the printing press and the camera became widespread, authenticity came to replace exclusivity as the generator of value in paintings and other works of art; in a world in which the images from Van Gogh's paintings can be reproduced millions of times on postcards and cocktail napkins, the museum-authenticated signature of the artist becomes the locus of the irreproducible quality that creates artistic value.

A similar effect applied to the architect-designed tokens of the 1980s. Graves's tea kettle is a work of industrial mass production, just like a Le Corbusier chaise, a Mercedes, or a plastic plate sold at K mart. The association of products with names, beginning with designer blue jeans, was, like the melding of high-style architecture and speculative office development by Gerald Hines, one of the great legacies of the 1970s to the 1980s.

As a merchandising ploy, it gave consumers the illusion that they were buying something "authentic," even when what they were buying was a teeshirt with the word Gucci printed on it. For architects, the opportunity to establish links with a mass market, still wrapped in the museumy trappings of authenticity and provenance, meant the ability to project themselves as cultural arbiters for a previously unreachable audience.

But in the struggle between economics and culture for power to frame the public perception of architecture, even such unprecedented alliances between architects and the public amounted to little. If Bloomingdale's sold a thousand Aldo Rossi espresso pots or Arata Isozaki dinner plates, developers were further rationalizing the building process in ten thousand more ways, leaving less and less space for architects to occupy as free and independent entities. All that architects seemed to accomplish was the cultivation of economic urges among members of the public who otherwise might never have been in the market for whatever the developers had to sell. Architects were creating luxury tokens that ended up as advertisements for other people. In a strange boomerang effect, architects were forming and delivering audiences to developers with their every effort at self-promotion. Indeed, the logic underlying the mass marketing of architect-labeled items tended to reduce design itself—the serviceability and inventiveness imparted by the architect—to a commodity, thus undercutting architects' claims to validity outside the realm of economics. Every architect's assertion of cultural stewardship, it seemed, came to the public wrapped in a frame implying the magisterium of economic forces.

Nothing illustrates this better than the life cycles of recent architectural styles. These typically begin as programs for artistic cleansing and social reform based on a rejection of the values most admired by the leaders of the previous generation, in favor of truer values, which were rediscovered from an even older generation and propounded by a small group of outsiders. Such an impulse is not limited to the twentieth century. Think of John Ruskin's condemnation of what he called the idolatrous meaninglessness of Baldassare Longhena's Santa Maria della Salute in Venice[38] as part of his campaign to replace the previous generation's favored classical architecture with what he saw as the more spiritual Gothic style. These movements almost inevitably themselves mature into mainstream visual codes expressing the power of political and economic elites. Architect Douglas Harvey says that architects want to create the equivalent of the young Bramante's modest but perfectly balanced Tempietto in the cloister of San Pietro in Montorio and end up building the old Bramante's overblown, grandiloquent St. Peter's Basilica. Tom Wolfe was right. The adoption of Bauhaus modernism, and later its glass-prism offshoot, as the architectural style of American business after the Second World War was a travesty of modernism's politically radical roots in early twentieth-century Europe. But then, such an observation was commonplace a long time before Wolfe got around to it (and his ascription to modernist architects of the powers of "a Jacmel Houngan" over businessmen is ludicrous; the triumph of modernist architecture in America makes sense only in the context of social factors that he glides past). And, as I tried to show in my earlier discussion of the Allied Bank Tower at Fountain Place in Dallas, such architecture provides many pleasing metaphors for a truly American attitude toward business practice. (The interesting thing is that the bank inside the building creates the significance of the architectural means employed, not the other way around.)

Just like modernism, postmodernism started as an outsider's critique not just of previous architecture but of the entire cultural order of the Western world, which postmodernists defined as corrupted by colonialism and capitalism, irreparably fragmented, and capable of being reconstructed only through irony, pastiche, and nervous quotations from an inescapable but uncapturable history. The first postmodernist projects, like Charles Jencks's parody of Palladio, the Garagia Rotunda, were both tentative recreations and insiders' jokes. Later, the social critique of modernist urban design led to the adoption within postmodernism of a range of historical building and planning forms, from street-level retail and high-density, low-rise housing, to nonironic use of picturesque building forms and classical ornaments. By the end of the 1980s, postmodernism had become the style of mid-level office parks and shopping malls, and its practitioners were trying without embarrassment to apply planning principles from colonial Virginia to strip shopping centers in North Dallas.

Next came deconstructivism, an offshoot of the fragmented-culture postmodern school of thought that grew out of post-structuralist linguistics and social theory in the 1970s and 1980s in Europe. Again, it started as social critique, and again, it has been absorbed into the dominant economic system, going from purposefully unrealizable drawings by Daniel Libeskind, to hostilely conceived house projects with dorky punning names ("Fin d'ou T Hou S" is one) by Peter Eisenman, to restaurants and stores by Morphosis, to cultural institutions by Frank Gehry, to a sprucing-up campaign intended to raise sales of Kentucky Fried Chicken in Los Angeles.[39] The path, until the last step, seemed to be leading to something increasingly interesting (if increasingly solipsistic), but then it ends up confirming and falling victim to the assertion of deconstructivism's philosophical founders: We live in a culture of gibberish, where economic determinism warps all sources of meaning to its own ends, sucking all cultural innovations into the service of commodification. Architecture? Fried chicken? It's all the same thing.

The paradox of the 1980s in Texas was that, with everything dovetailing to assert that culture is only an unimportant vassal of economics and that architects have no claim on the public consciousness, architecture-as-culture survived, because a handful of Texas developers "distinguished" themselves by using high-style architects, who in turn created what were considered distinctive products.

Why? Because developers needed projects that stood out from the background. Developers were in a market in which, first, both demand and supply were expanding, and later, supply was expanding while demand fell. At the same time, the commodity being offered—office space, for example—was thoroughly standardized. Developers had succeeded too well. In equivalent locations, all buildings were basically alike. They were too plainly commodities, and thus of little differentiable value, since the success of commodification, spilling over into the physical expression of the architecture, drove down the speculative value of the commodity until it matched or fell below its use value. There was no reason to choose one building over another. Developers most needed what they could not provide from within their standard mindset: "a point of difference."[40] And the chief mode of getting that difference, during the 1980s, was through the appropriation of architectural imagery from other places and times. This appropriation was something for which the learning and taste of architects, otherwise merely encumbrances, were indispensable. The 1980s was the decade in which Texas developers were forced to mirror the dilemma experienced by architects. To achieve their economic ends, they had to accept, if briefly and grudgingly, the cultural authority of their rivals over the process.

This situation explains why Philip Johnson and I.M. Pei (followed by Skidmore, Owings & Merrill; Edward Larrabee Barnes; Mitchell/Giurgola; Stanley Tigerman; and others) were so important to Texas architecture in the 1980s; hiring them showed, better than the use of local architects would have done, that the developer was "serious about design," which is to say, willing to accept the role of architectural meaning in creating value.

"Real" Architecture

In doing so, it is worth noting, developers were, in effect, themselves buying "tokens" of architecture. Just as ambitious yuppies bought architect-designed housewares to bask in the glory reflected from a higher social class, developers, being grubby-fingered new-money types, were buying architecture-as-culture in emulation of yet another subuniverse, that of the *really* rich—those with fortunes big enough and old enough to allow them to act as patrons of *real* architecture.

To the rest of the world, architecture may be defined in terms of structures and the meanings they convey. But between the new rich and the old rich exists a line of class division as clear as that between the rich and the nonrich, and architects help define the characteristics of both moneyed classes.

The architects and the two groupings of the rich form a triangle of desire similar to and superimposed on that formed by architects, developers, and the public. In this case, architects cooperate most effectively with old money in manipulating symbols of prestige, providing some of the cultural means by which the two moneyed groups are separated. The best architects of all for this purpose are those, like Philip Johnson, heir to a fortune in Alcoa stock, with old money of their own; they embody the remnants of the nineteenth-century tradition that architects are cultured gentlemen educating the tastes of AT&T executives and other simple tradesmen.

Above the line, with the old money, is architecture. Below the line, with the new money, is building. New money is about replicating itself, about *getting*. Old money is about replicating culture, about *keeping*. The line between the two, at least in Texas, seems to be easily permeable; any fortune can enter a higher cultural realm as soon as its possessor is willing to give it for use on projects that generate no direct profits, and almost anything built with the proceeds of such donations becomes above-the-line architecture. New money builds below-the-line office buildings and malls. Old money builds above-the-line museums and concert halls. One is the world of commerce and production, while the other is the world of culture and authenticity.

In fact, the goal of old money since well before the time of the emperor of Byzantium has been to create buildings so authentically above the line—so far outside the reach of commodification—that they penetrate into an actual state of sacredness; the old rich want a palpable physical world that embodies their elevation above the status of other men, who have to grub away in meeting rooms deciding on the floor-to-area ratios and toilet fixtures of office buildings. They want a plenum of perfect and eternal beauty and order.

Seen this way, the low-slung, semi-industrial, clapboard-sided Menil Collection in Houston is architecture embodying some of Dominique de Menil's lifelong scholarliness and austerely generous spirituality, while the biggest, most expensive granite and steel office building, admired as a symbol of civic pride by common folks and developers alike throughout the world, is irretrievably below the line. The difference between these two states partakes of both Ruskin (who, in *The Seven Lamps of Architecture*, listed unnecessariness and excessive expense, which any given philanthropic activity fairly reeks of in relation to any given income-producing property, among architecture's defining "sacrificial" virtues) and Veblen (who called the display of wealth on music, art, and other luxuries necessary to the barbarian primitivism that wealth breeds in all who possess it).[41]

Above-the-line architects of high-culture buildings, because of their role in helping to create and maintain the physical expression of this class difference between new and old money, are thus allies of the high/old/stable elite against the new/lower/climbing elite.

The critic Diane Ghirardo, writing on the subject of suburban design restrictions in *Architecture California*, has pointed out that old money gets a lot from such transactions. Owners of old fortunes are taking part in a ritual that not only sanctions their tastes "as objectively rather than as socially and culturally conditioned,"[42] but, as much as can happen through the acclaim of mere contemporary mortals, confirms their place above the line of commerce and even above the plane of temporality and mortality.

As one-sided and restricted as such a ritual may seem, there are reasons to think that its operation, in fact, provides a number of benefits for the rest of society. Indeed, the importance of the role of old money and its above-the-line creations can hardly be overstated.

In a world in which economic values have supplanted all others, the old rich have been cast in the role of last bulwark against the world's continual entropic drift into meaninglessness, and as such they are equivalents of saints for this secular age; people look to them to prove that money, however it is amassed, can be used to create a path to spiritual growth. In addition, the old rich embody the myth within the myth that animated Texas real estate in the 1980s; not only do the good princes of the marketplace bring prosperity to all, but the saintly elders of culture make it all worthwhile by creating structures without which the physical world would lack landmarks of significance.

This is what made the flap over the proposed additions to the Kimbell Art Museum in Fort Worth in 1988 so important. A storm of outrage was provoked among architects and connoisseurs around the country when Romaldo Giurgola, at the behest of museum director Edmund Pillsbury, suggested replicating Louis Kahn's original galleries as new wings for the museum. The architects attacking the proposal were establishing their bona fides by helping to defend the sacred realm against the depredations of those below the line, giving the considerable force of their fury to saying that above-the-line buildings are too important to alter.

But the story of the Kimbell was the exception, not the rule. The story of architecture in the 1980s in Texas shows most high-style architects to be untrustworthy allies to the forces of culture—the triangulation of desire is too strong when emissaries from below the line come with the opportunity to design lucrative and interesting projects that represent a change from the dull round of museums and music halls. Pei and Johnson, among others, spent the 1980s alternately selling out and renewing their old-money connections. They created office buildings that were tokens, for example, of what H. Ross Perot got at the Meyerson Symphony Center, partaking of the quality of above-the-line design the same way that suburban breakfast nooks gained cultural snap from the presence of Robert Venturi coffee cups. For a while the alchemy worked, and architecture clasped hands with, and was sold off as, commodity in RepublicBank and Allied Bank and the other hot office towers of the 1980s. But then—about the time that Texas architects were getting in on the action—the commodities thus blessed began their inevitable drift into the relative valuelessness that curses the undifferentiated field of commodity-hood. Sacredness and architecture shook off their links to the sullied world of commerce and retreated once again above the line, which was redrawn to exclude the style of the developer building. Eventually Johnson went to the well once too often, and his work became identified with the world below the line; Gehry and Eisenman and Morphosis and Stephen Holl and others arose to fill the void, while Pei managed a narrow escape.

In the relationship between old money and the world of commodities, the psychological ramifications of cultural creation are sufficient to keep such processes going. But there is another reason why old money has been particularly important in Texas. The life of cities also depends on a combination of *getting*, expressed in population growth, new jobs, and new revenues, and *keeping*, expressed in maintenance of the city's buildings, streets, and institutions. The 1980s marked the crisis point in a gradual erosion of legitimacy for Texas cities, in which keeping was swamped by getting and the urban sphere was nearly consumed by speculation at its periphery. Old money's role in the decade was to provide a way of binding economic growth and development to the central cities of Texas, holding out to the latter a vestige of hope for their survival.

Money is most easily made in the conversion of real estate from low-cost to high-cost uses—from farm to suburban tract housing, for example, or from housing tract to office park. And such conversions are most easily made not in already-built-up cities but at their diffusely utilized peripheries. (The best-known exception is Kenneth Schnitzer's Greenway Plaza development in Houston, built on some three hundred cleared lots of a former residential development.) This fact (along with legal codes, energy costs, and other factors) has molded the style of development that created the Texas landscape, in which tracts and office parks sprawl ever wider, jumping over underutilized land.[43]

As a historical legacy, this style of urban development has made Texas cities increasingly costly and difficult to administer. If Houston, for example, were not spread like patches of lichen throughout pine forests and rice fields, between George Mitchell's Woodlands in the north to Gerald Hines's First Colony in the southwest, its taxpayers could save billions of dollars now devoted to sewer construction, flood control, and road maintenance, and

Towers amid the parking lots in downtown Dallas, 1991

its police and fire services could operate much more effectively. The cost of one infrastructure problem alone—meeting the EPA's standards for rainwater runoff for the Houston area—is expected to be in the billions over the next decade. Dallas and San Antonio, ringed by bedroom suburbs that capture most of the revenues of new growth, are less spread out, but are in even worse long-term financial shape than Houston.[44]

The leapfrog development system loads benefits to the developer at the front end, and it leaves other people to worry about the price of maintaining a hypertrophied infrastructure. Which is to say that it does what Adam Smith said markets should not do: externalize costs.

Any part of a system that can externalize costs so well has an enormous advantage. As a consequence, since the 1950s in Texas, new money has gravitated from the city to the urban edge. The process accelerated into a kind of free-fall in the 1980s; bankers poured money into the suburban projects of dozens of developers, who achieved almost uniformly catastrophic results, while the neighborhoods of the inner cities were redlined.

As a further consequence, the links of economic interest and loyalty between the "developer community" and the city have gradually dissolved, until only a few remain. Among the remaining links, the most important is the envy that developers have for the cultural powers of old money. A city with a museum or a symphony hall funded by above-the-line beneficence represents a vision to which a developer can see himself or his heirs aspiring.

Without the link of envy and aspiration that such cultural centers inspire, developers might simply turn their backs on the city and be drawn further and further away into the outer fringe of wheeling and dealing; the city behind them, with its high costs, its minorities, and its political complexities, would become in their eyes simply the locus of problems. Eventually, developers might decide that the city would be better left to die. Ben Carpenter said during the symposium at the University of Texas in 1991 that he had decided as much about Dallas.[45]

The future survival of the cities of Texas depends on access to the capital controlled by developers and others interested in growth. For now, the cultural power of above-the-line money embodied in architectural projects represents the last best hope of drawing developers back to the city. Meaning and money cannot be divorced if our cities are to live.

Late-1980s builder-vernacular houses in the North Dallas suburb Rockwall

2
Middle-Class Houses of the 1980s

For most families a house is the biggest, most costly commodity that its members will buy or sell. It is also *home*, the most idealized of cultural artifacts, enclosing the most intimate personal space. Balanced between these two poles, houses have always been the average person's peephole on architecture's oscillations. Those oscillations were intensified by the boom and bust of the 1980s in Texas. Houses were called upon to embody conflicting desires for short-term profit and life-long security.

As a result, houses provided the paradigmatic expression of the economic and social forces that shook the state. Many experiments in house design (some inherited from the 1970s) were tried during the 1980s. By decade's end, a characteristic 1980s house style had emerged, found in clusters behind protecting wall, and decorated with architectural features proclaiming that their owners valued tradition and that they were secure in owning property that couldn't be snatched away by time or economic troubles.

Houses have been the most important American building type since the days of Jamestown and the Plymouth Plantation. The early nineteenth-century inventions of dimensioned lumber, machine-made nails, and lightweight "balloon" framing are among the most elegant and significant contributions America has made to world culture.[1] The twentieth-century combination of the small-scale, short-lived construction companies that dominate the house-building market with national, government-backed funding mechanisms for builders and consumers is one of the others.

Although technology, materials, and finance have been central to house design and construction from the start, the underlying focus has always been on the role of the house as a moral force. Religious leaders, feminists, and political reformers in the mid-nineteenth century promoted home ownership and even specific house plans in hopes of achieving such goals as raising the status of women in the family, civilizing the frontier, and dispersing the growing urban working classes to suburban homes where they would stop worrying about collective grievances and turn instead to spiritual growth and approved methods of child rearing.[2]

An ideology of social improvement focusing on health and "natural" living guided the house-building boom of the 1910s and '20s, when most of the bungalows and colonial-style houses in what are now the older neighborhoods of Texas cities were built. This ideology culminated in the ranch houses and "minimal traditional" houses[3] built in the 1950s, which were treated in governmental policy and advertising, television, and other channels for popular culture as shapers of a more truly American America.

Fifties houses had open plans, paralleling a loosening of rules about dress and manners for adults and children. America had won the war, after all. It was okay to relax, and to most people, such relaxation was congruent with less oak wainscoting and more thin-section extruded aluminum around the windows and doors. Kitchens were often separated from the dining room only by a low counter, while the dining room itself was often just a zone within the family room. The idea was that this openness would promote togetherness among the members of the new suburban families. The promise of these '50s house types was of a new path to the pursuit of happiness. As Clifford Clark writes in *The American Family Home 1800-1960*, "At the center . . . was the image of the family as the focus of fun and recreation. Happiness came from raising healthy, independent kids, decorating the home to one's own tastes, and sitting back in the evening with other family members and relaxing in front of the new television set." Children were to be given unique freedom within this new arrangement, with special "family" or "play" rooms, promoted by *Parents' Magazine*, for example, as "don't-say-no" places (although space was too tight in typical '50s starter houses to indulge such psychological luxury).[4]

In Texas, the biggest seller in the mass market of the 1950s was the ranch house, typically a one-story wood-frame structure on a slab foundation with a low-pitched side-gabled or hipped roof and an uncomplicated footprint; in most new postwar suburbs, many of the houses were simple rectangles, incorporating even the garage, of around 1,000 square feet of living space, sometimes without a single stepback, extrusion, or change in grade. The lack of a second floor meant that all the rooms, typically with eight-foot ceilings, had little opportunity for lofty vertical spaces. The houses were usually set widthwise to the street frontage, splitting the lots. In back there was a fenced back yard, where pets were kept, the barbeque was built, and the children played protected from the street. The front lawn retained part of its ceremonial importance, but with a change. Moving the garage from the back to the front of the house turned the driveway, perforce, into a car display area, and made the car part of the house's facade.[5]

Late-1950s ranch house, Dallas

These changes, automotive historian James J. Flink argues, "turned the home into an extension of the street."[6]

In terms of exterior appearance, ranch houses were relatively quiet affairs, with cladding, plantings, and other elements emphasizing a modest horizontality. The look was something between a shriveled prairie-style house and a flattened-out saltbox. Architects in the 1950s were hopeful that postwar America would embrace the modern style that had arrived from Europe a generation earlier. Modernism offered what architect and writer Michael Benedikt might call an architecture of preenactment, a physical expression of the belief that postwar America had arrived in a future of technologically determined bliss. Most people rejected this imagery, however, preferring an architecture of reenactment in which their lives, however novel in terms of social organization, were garbed in the ranch house's split wagon wheels, the colonial house's lamps and painted shutters, the Tudor house's masonry, and other appropriated trappings of nostalgically evoked and therefore authenticated experience.[7]

Builders say they know better than architects what people want in a house, and that they build to suit the market. To a certain extent, this is true; builders generally do more research and get more immediate feedback from a broader segment of the public than their architect rivals. But it is more accurate to say that builders give people what they will accept, rather than what they want. Certainly this is true of the ranch-house style: Clark says surveys showed that many people regarded even ranch houses as too "contemporary" (the phrase used for the builder's-vernacular analogue to modernism, the lowest-price and lowest-prestige option offered to buyers), preferring two-story colonial styles instead. But ranch houses could be produced more cheaply than the older styles; people by the hundreds of thousands settled for ranch houses. Most of the buyers were, after all, just entering the market; to them, even a minimal house represented a vast improvement in economic status and independence. And most buyers, in Texas at least, were young people from rural families who were moving to the suburbs to work in the industrial core of the cities; to them, ranch and minimal-traditional houses portrayed an acceptable amount of stylistic distance from the drafty, vertical, vernacular houses in which they had been raised. But they were, nevertheless, not "dream homes" in the sense of fulfilling all the expectations of buyers.

In fact, the lack of dreaminess is the most striking aspect of ranch-house suburbs of the 1950s. The houses of the 1950s and the streets they lined were attenuated, inexpressive things, with applied decoration reduced to shreds that architects called debased and banal. But then, in the social situation in which they were built, overt expression wasn't much needed. European cities, to which architects appealed in condemning the new American suburbs, were compact and dense because they developed under conditions of scarcity or physical threat; the same holds true for dense, walkable historic American cities. By comparison, in the 1950s in the new suburbs of Texas and other states, a landscape of abundance and confidence for almost the entire population was created, home of a new America, victorious (for the second time in the century) in a war in which all the battles had been fought across the seas. The very banality of the suburban landscape was a tribute to the reign of peace and to the apparent ascendancy of this new society over the problems of previous generations. A growing economy brought jobs and job security and predictably rising family incomes. Cheap oil and a cornucopia of mass-produced technological wonders brought freedom and amusement. Demographic changes in which people married younger, had more children, and divorced less frequently than they had for generations brought a sense of personal and familial security. And more people moved to suburbs, where most of the inhabitants were of the same age, class, and race.[8] More than that, they left other groups behind in the city, so the architectural images previously used to mark territories and assert social standing atrophied, dissipating into the general landscape.

The images of placidity nurtured by this landscape were challenged during the 1960s, despite continued prosperity, by the demographic shock wave called the baby boom. Children born in the late 1940s and 1950s had become teenagers, checking out of the family nucleus to enter a newly created cyberspace, the world of the radio and record player. This was home to the rock-and-roll bands that mirrored the generation's burgeoning economic cohesion and its amplification of the expectations—of freedom, safety, abundance, and self-expression—that had shaped the childhood of its members.

Builders in the 1960s responded to buyers by playing off the I-won't-settle-for-this-anymore feelings of ranch-house owners ready to move up.

2711 Hood Street apartments, Dallas (1963), by The Oglesby Group

The houses they offered for sale were bigger, with more complex spatial divisions; sometimes there were level changes, and sometimes there were clerestory windows and skylights to give extra verticality to the still basically ground-hugging arrangement. Children got separate bedroom wings, and the number of bathrooms increased, sometimes to a one-to-one ratio with the bedrooms.

The period from the late 1960s to the mid-1970s brought the maturation of the first baby boomers to leave home. Where the market had called for detached single-family houses, there was a demand for a large number of apartments near universities and employment centers. Most, like those of Harold Farb of Houston, who made his fortune during this period, were "garden apartments"—two- or three-story stacks of more-or-less identical low-ceilinged, single-floor units arranged around courtyards. Architects found new opportunity to work in the residential market. Commissions to design apartment complexes paid well enough to support a medium-sized office, and such firms as Enslie Oglesby Associates of Dallas[9] and Neuhaus & Taylor of Houston[10] designed complexes that won awards in statewide architectural competitions.

"Swinging-singles" apartment complexes became a social fact, and a new elaboration of the youth culture developed within them. Life in these complexes was a physical analogue to the electronic zone of rock music. Young people of a given ethnic group and income level could live in villages with hundreds of people just like themselves, all free of parental supervision for the first time, all under the same social injunction to think of their homes as centers of fun, recreation, and self-fulfillment.

Like their parents, the young people of the swinging-singles complexes were self-supporting and independent. The difference, for most, was simple: They were not married, and there were no children. The force behind this difference was a new technology, as powerful in its way as electricity and the mass-produced car: reliable contraception. Freed by birth control (usually) from the consequences of sexual activity, the students and young professionals of the late 1970s and early 1980s were given a never-before-realizable power to hold at bay the requirements of adulthood, and to turn their lives into an extended youthful summer of experimentation with the varieties of experience offered by cars, jogging, designer clothes, food, alcohol, drugs, sex, and anything else that appealed to them.

Enough people survived this experimentation with earning power and expectations intact to create a demand for the next new housing type, which developed in the late 1970s and early '80s—the condominium. The condo market began developing as single people with rising incomes tired of or outgrew their rental units, and began looking for houses to buy. But because house and land prices had been rising so fast, two incomes were required to purchase a median-priced single-family detached house by the late 1970s, and all but the most prosperous singles were unable to keep pace.

Condos were created by builders to serve this niche; they were trying to squeeze profits out of an increasingly fragmented and saturated market in which costs for land and construction were constantly rising. Their solution, getting buyers to pay for equity in housing with up to twenty units per acre, was an extension of the "less-is-more" strategy that succeeded with the ranch houses of the 1950s—they found out what consumers wanted but couldn't have in their previous housing, and built it into their projects as a substitute for the things that the previous generation *had* had but that these consumers said they could live without—for example, a large yard and a separate visual identity for each unit. In making this strategy work, developers had to rely on appeals to the culture of the youth market, to indicate that what they were selling was not just shelter, but a better, more sophisticated way of life. More sophisticated than what? Than the life suffered by the buyer's parents, trapped in the old, banal, undifferentiated world of the '50s suburbs, kept by kids and other outdated encumbrances from the fern bars, exercise studios, ski vacations, and foreign restaurants that equaled the good life. While it worked, the national market looked to Texas for leadership.

Thus it was that the Houston architectural firm Kaufman Meeks was profiled in *Professional Builder* magazine in early 1983 as one of the most important design firms in the builder-house field nationwide, particularly for those leaving the rental market for condominiums and densely clustered starter houses. Asked the secret of why his firm's designs sold, Mark Kaufman said, "We have found with first-time buyers that an emotional rather than functional choice is made. Whatever has an emotional impact (cathedral ceilings, large glass areas, good-sized kitchens) will sell . . . quickly. A portion of the functional aspects of a basic unit can be given up for appeal. For example, with the first-time buyer, a large or island kitchen is needed. But the pantry closet does not necessarily need to be in the kitchen, just near it."[11]

And thus it was that Charles Schultz, a vice-president of the Raldon Company of Dallas (the company had been cofounded by Don Dixon, who would later go on to short-lived fortune and long-term fame as the architect of the $1.2-billion failure of Vernon Savings) was profiled as a national trend-setter in *Builder* magazine's issue on Texas in 1983.[12] Schultz was quoted as saying that educated professionals all over the state were ready for innovative housing of the type offered by his firm's hot-selling and densely planned Park Place project. The project's yards were "too small for a Texas barbeque," but were "just right for modern-day hot-tub entertaining," Schultz said, signaling the use of youth-culture hot buttons to replace old-fashioned lot and room size. The same less-is-more substitution was demonstrated by the other high-density projects, designed by Kaufman Meeks, EDI Architects/Planners of Houston, and other Texas firms, showcased in the *Builder* magazine Texas issue. These firms, specializing

Park Place housing project, Arlington, a development of Raldon Co.

in mass-market housing, were treated as authorities on innovative design, at least by builders.[12]

Some of the best-known high-style architects in Texas in the 1980s also made their reputations as well as a sizable part of their livings designing condominiums and townhouses for upper middle-class clients. In Dallas, for example, Lionel Morrison and Susan Seifert designed a series of severe modernist townhouse projects on Armstrong Avenue that were widely admired by other architects.[14] Taft Architects gained national attention for the Grove Court project in Houston, in which units with open, loftlike spaces were clustered around a central entry courtyard, which was, for Houston, a radical innovation at the time.[15] William F. Stern of Houston made *Esquire* magazine's list of up-and-coming architects in 1985, largely for designing a series of townhouse projects, including the Wroxton Street and Albans Street townhouses, that filled in formerly single-family lots in neighborhoods near Rice University and the Texas Medical Center; in them he used traditional house-form exterior elements over street-facing ground-level garages, fusing scenography with elegant planning and sensible ur-

Armstrong Avenue townhouses, Dallas (1986), by Lionel Morrison and Susan Seifert

Grove Court townhouses, Houston (1981), by Taft Architects

ban gestures in a way that came to help define the postmodern style in Texas.[16] The Miami-based firm Arquitectonica opened a Houston office that produced a number of bright-colored, animated townhouse projects, including the Taggart Townhouses, which broke from the explorations of neotraditional house forms explored by Stern and others by mixing Caribbean colors with contemporary adaptations of forms and details derived from the early work of Le Corbusier. [17]

High-style projects like these were designed for the top slice of the market segment that builder condos also aimed to capture: young, high-earning relative to their age group, perhaps cohabiting, but with no children. These projects symbolized the required sophistication through their very density, as well as an uncluttered artfulness indicative of the sanction of architectural taste, as opposed to the hot tubs and woven-bamboo ceiling fans offered in builder projects, with their suggestion of pandering to the lowest common denominator of public taste. Indeed, among builders, townhouse design always had a calculated, corner-cutting quality; this showed in the workmanship and materials of many of the builder condo projects in Texas, which Philip Langdon, author of the 1986 book *Ameri-*

Wroxton townhouses, Houston (1982), by William F. Stern Associates

can Houses, surveyed and found so abysmal that he likened boom-time Texas construction practices to those of the Soviet Union.[18] Among the high-style architects in Texas who took it up, however, the craft of townhouse design was treated more seriously. It evolved, in fact, a whole polemical life, posited in the design studios of the Texas universities and through stories in *Texas Architect*, *Cite*, and even in the national architecture magazines, as a way to build a denser, more modern, more sophisticated city for the future Texas. Given the echoes of Philadelphia, New York, and San Francisco that townhouses evinced, such an association is understandable. But there were also surprising results to the townhouse movement: Richard Keating, then head of SOM's Houston office (which was known for office-building design, not residences) could have built a house for himself anywhere in or near the city; he chose, instead, to build a townhouse-like two-story house with walnut floors, precisely finished cabinetry, and yawning interior vistas, on a small lot near the Museum of Fine Arts, hidden behind a wooden wall like many of the more modest townhouses that lined the streets around it. Explaining the design in an interview after the house won a statewide design award, Keating described himself in terms that made him sound like Robert Schultz's ideal customer: young, unmarried at the time, unwilling to settle for the old-fashioned housing Houston had to offer, and interested in having lots of people over for parties.[19]

The social experiment that these condos and townhouses represented might have taken root; after all, land prices in the most-sought-after neighborhoods were high, leading to increasing densities. But the whole process was based on trying to capture a fragment of a fragment within the market, and it depended on a constantly growing supply of young single people with high incomes. By the early 1980s, however, the demographic peak of young singles was over. Not only that, but, with the collapse of oil prices, the people in the target market were either losing their high-paying jobs or moving out of state to hang onto them. The best-located, best-designed projects, like the Lionel Morrison townhouses in Dallas and the William Stern townhouses in Houston, sold well and retained a relatively high percentage of their value, and a number of new large-scale projects were built in 1989 and 1990 in Houston near the Texas Medical Center and the Galleria area. But mass-market speculatively built condos, particularly those on the suburban fringes, nosedived in value. The economic downturn not

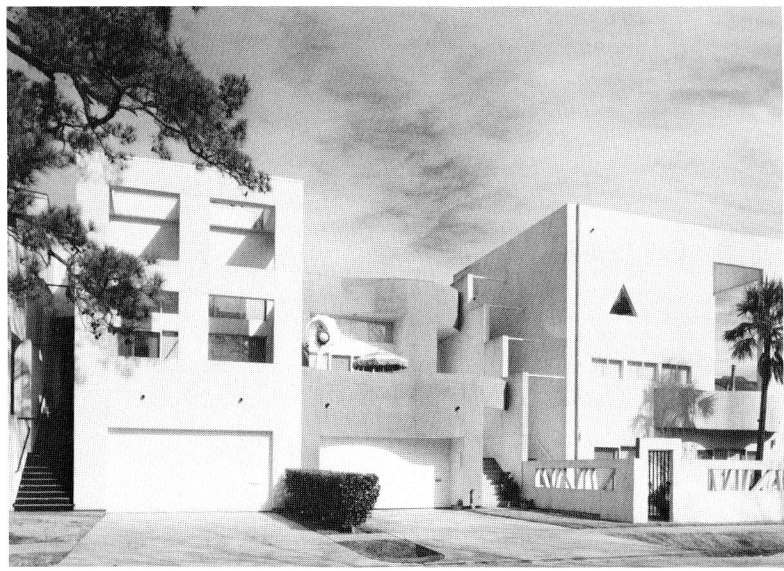

Taggart townhouses, Houston (1984), by Arquitectonica

Keating house, Houston (1983), by Richard Keating

only removed potential condo buyers and thus depressed prices, it exposed a fact that the previous upswing in the market had hidden: From the eaves line out, condo owners were dependent on a communal attachment to their shared spaces, an attachment that was too intricate and too old-fashioned for most Texans to handle and that evaporated the day one or two of their fellow owners defaulted on their mortgages.

What remained was the substrate of the market, single-family houses in the suburbs. And here, by the end of the decade, the passage through the turmoil of the '80s had wrought spectacular changes.

If the ground-breaking house of the 1950s was a starter home, the quintessential '80s house was built for the move-up market, and the first striking feature to be noticeable about these houses was where they were to be found. Although a flood of single-family houses were built all over the outlying suburbs of Texas' cities early in the decade, by the late '80s, as foreclosures and house abandonments multiplied, building activity had contracted to the relatively few "planned communities" around the state. Planned communities are projects where developers powerful enough to control 3,000- to 5,000-acre blocks with multiple tiers of neighborhoods are able to specify everything from the street signage to the size, materials, and architectural style of the houses that smaller building companies are permitted to develop for sale. They even control tree plantings in different sections to signify the price and status of given streets within the overall community. In First Colony, for example, oaks equal high price; pines, low price. After the plunge in value of the rest of the market, people turned eagerly to these developments. In Houston, for example, nearly half the new houses started in 1989 were built in four planned communities: The Woodlands, controlled by George Mitchell; Kingwood and Clear Lake City, controlled by Friendswood Development, the real estate division of Exxon; and First Colony (which alone accounted for 25 percent of the new housing starts), owned and operated by Gerald Hines Interests and Royal Dutch Shell Pension Fund. In San Antonio, planned communities on the northern rim of the city operated by David Ellison sold well, as did Ben Carpenter's residential developments in Las Colinas. The promoters of these projects attribute this demand to the "quality" of their product, which is accurate to an extent. It needs to be said further, however, that the images of quality involved are codes for the sheltering hand of an overlord who has put up economic boundaries and brick walls and hired armed patrols to hold back the tide of decay nibbling at the rest of the city, creating, in a big way, just the sort of defensible space missing from condos. The feudal quality of these "planned communities" is very strong. They are nodes of security within a revived landscape of threat, in which the threat arises in part from the instability of the real estate market itself.

On a smaller scale, the same phenomenon was repeated in a number of the bedroom cities that either started the decade as elite enclaves (Highland Park and University Park, surrounded by Dallas) or were lifted to such status as the rest of the market eroded (Bellaire, West University Place, and South Side Place, all separate cities inside Houston's boundaries). The houses in these communities were typically one-story bungalows or two-story neocolonial houses dating from the '30s and the '50s, set back on relatively narrow lots. Despite some speculation that started in the '70s, they had the most stable property values around, in part because they were close to downtown and medical-center workplaces and the best public and private schools. Doctors and lawyers and other professionals who had continued to prosper throughout the decade bought these houses in the 1980s. Rather, they bought the lots and treated the houses as "teardowns," since the houses were considered too small for the new owners' needs, and of types that offered too little resale value. In place of the earlier houses were built Georgian-style houses that pushed out to every allowable inch of the lot and loomed over the lower-scaled neighbors, where they still existed.

The second striking quality of the '80s houses in the planned communities (and, to a lesser extent, in the elite enclaves) was their aggressive exterior expression, which reinforces the impression they give of confronting some external threat. Because they provide the most profitable form for building on small lots, most of these houses are two stories tall. Most have high-pitched roofs, multiple gables and dormers that penetrate their cornice lines, corner projections, multiple-paned windows (some with Palladian curves), and brick-infill skins with contrasting-colored brick or stone arches over windows and doors. These transformations of structural detailing into misused applied decoration—what Peter G. Rowe in his 1990 book *Building a Middle Landscape* describes as a divorce between the form and

A Georgian-style house that replaced smaller bungalow in University Park

Builder house, Rockwall, ca. 1989

figuration[20]—drive most academically minded architects to despair. Often these houses have garages projecting forward from the front of the house, although the garage doors usually face to the side and the street wall of the garage is fitted with windows to make it look as if there were a regular room inside, a simultaneous acknowledgment and denial of the connection of house to street.

What these houses most resemble, in fact, are the minimal-traditional houses of the '50s, on steroids. Whereas the street had been made a welcome part of houses as early as the 1930s, here houses are throwing out new, defensive protuberances. It is as if each house on the block has muscled up to create a convincing projection of the security of its inhabitants. And why not? The street is no longer the landscape of abundance and confidence that it was forty years ago.

On the inside, the '80s houses regained some of the traditional layers that '50s houses gave up to the street. Having an upstairs where kids could have bedrooms, a game room, and one or more bathrooms away from the parents' master suite helped with this layering of public and private spaces. Still, compression and informality were the dominant traits of the major part of the ground-floor public spaces. Whereas the entry sequence in a '20s-era neocolonial house might have been through porch to hall to sitting room to dining room to kitchen and bedrooms, in the '80s house it was often through a vestigial hall to the "great room," which combined living room, family room and dining room, and which opened directly onto a kitchen, with its cooking island, pantry, and a home-office desk that was big enough for a computer. More likely, family members would enter from garage to laundry room to kitchen. (Houses with formal halls and dining rooms were also built, and they came to be much more acceptable at the upper edge of the builder-house market by the early 1990s.)

One of the two most important interior spaces that characterize the '80s house, in fact, takes its life from this renewed emphasis on layering. This is the master suite, at the farthest, most intimate reaches of the house. Here, tucked away like a secret vice, were the relics of the sybaritic singles life of the condos, but paired: his-and-her electrical outlets for simultaneous blow-drying, his-and-her showers, closets, and sinks, a nook for the exercycle facing the built-in television cabinet, floor-to-ceiling mirrors, a whirlpool bath big enough for two, a fireplace, an outdoor shower, and various other fantastic innovations. Parents could maintain the intimate pleasures of their youth in the master suite, reenacting the rituals in which they toned and cleaned their bodies in preparation for the sexual quest that popular culture had urged on young people in the '60s and '70s. However, in the house's great room, the other major innovation of the '80s, things were much different. The great room, linking kitchen to family room, was like a '50s family room except that it usually featured a two-story gabled or vaulted "cathedral ceiling," and almost all the activities that families shared, from parents helping with homework to Christmas parties, were compressed into its program. Here, families acted out roles much like those of their counterparts in the '50s (recoiling from the roles and activities that the adults would probably have thought appropriate a decade earlier). After coming home from work, Mom cooked at the kitchen island, where she could see the kids as they watched television; Dad was there too, since the separate living room had disappeared.

The openness of the space and the compression of activities in the great room arose partly from a peculiar factor of the market for middle-class homes (well understood by builders and architects since the late '70s), which was that most sales were made on Sunday afternoons, during which a couple would look at five or ten houses, staying in each one only a few minutes. To sell, the house had to have "curb appeal" (thus the use of color and projecting volumes on the exterior), and it had to have "impact" from the front door. To achieve the latter effect, builders put as many of the house's hot-button features within sight of the front door as possible—sometimes even the see-through fireplace leading to the mysteries of the master suite.[21]

But the reason that families responded favorably to these displays has less to do with the thrill of an island kitchen than with the threats families felt themselves facing during the decade. The family of the 1980s was a much different entity than that of the 1950s. Half of all marriages ended in divorce. Most middle-class women worked outside the home to support the family's mortgage payments, meaning that their preschool children were cared for by others. Drugs and crime were everywhere, and the faces of missing kids were on milk cartons and grocery bags. Parents had to work like driven yuppies, missing recitals and baseball games. They had to worry about losing their jobs as downsizing and streamlining swept the corporate world. They had to suffer the nagging emotional ache of enforced separa-

Builder house bath room and master suite, Rockwall

Builder house great room

tion from their children and to worry that loss of contact might leave the kids too much freedom and too little direction, so that the kids would experiment with sex and drugs as the parents' own generation had done in the '60s and '70s. The evening hours provided the one chance that families had to be together between sleep and the world of work, and the great room was their cathedral of togetherness, giving shape to this brief retreat from economic and social pressure. The '80s houses designed with such arrangements were dream houses, in a new, uncomfortable sense: They were places in which the psychological conflicts of the everyday world were reconciled through more-or-less unconscious fantasy.

Builder houses became so expensive in the 1980s that houses designed by individual architects for individual clients became competitive in price. But the gulf in taste and expectations between academically oriented architects and the public was too great to allow architects to escape their marginal status; only a few thousand such houses were designed and built in Texas in the 1980s, compared to perhaps one hundred times as many builder houses.

High-style house architecture in Texas both ignored and was determined by the forms and dreams of housing in the mass market during the 1980s, like a narrow stream splitting to pass around a huge boulder. Many of its practitioners, such as Frank D. Welch of Dallas, Howard Barnstone of Houston (who died in 1987), and O'Neil Ford of San Antonio (who died in 1982), were regarded by their peers as the most important architects in the state, heroes in the struggle to reinstate professional architecture as the proper medium for organizing modern life, even as father figures.

Like builders, academically trained architects sold dreams cloaked in house plans, although these dreams were simpler and more conventionally traditional than those of their builder counterparts, even when they were expressed in "contemporary" architectural terms. The main split between architects and the public, which kept architects at the fringe of the market, lay in their respective readings of what the house should embody. Architects had rediscovered brick, Doric columns, and dormers, which seemed to promise that they, too, were ready to provide an architecture of reenactment. But their designs were off—too flat and too open, as if it were still the 1950s and the street remained a friendly place, and as if the family were not under threat—providing reenactment without an adequate sense of shelter. Worse, they seemed determined to treat design features as elements in a mental game in which they and the clients were in control, instead of the dead-serious market-positioning devices, controlled by invisible and inscrutable forces, that would keep the house saleable when the family could move up or had to move away.

For those few clients with the economic position and cultural training that made high-style architect-designed houses desirable, the dream was that they could possess and inhabit objects whose "quality" (springing from learning and taste, rather than mere economic power) conveyed an elevated cultural status on both building and owner.

For architects, house design was The Grail, the dream that they could find an intellectual and emotional centering point that would keep their professional lives from splintering into arbitrariness and irrelevance. This centering point could be a planning style, a decorative scheme, a constructional technique, a response to landscape or urban conditions, a poetic view of materials, a fondness for horizontal or vertical composition, or a philosophical pragmatism. It could be of any historical or contemporary vintage, echoing or reacting to any antecedent, from Vitruvius to Santiago Calatrava to Pee Wee Herman. Some architects tried to imagine a primal housing condition as their starting point—the primitive hut of branches lashed down for the first time over broken tree trunks, or Adam's house in paradise.[22] Other Texas architects were content to start with houses constructed by eighteenth- and nineteenth-century Spanish and Anglo pioneers of the state, and to mine them for principles that could be applied to 1980s urban and suburban situations.[23] Still others posited modernity itself, the broken condition of tradition and daily experience, as the only psychologically true starting point. Any argument with some connection to building would do. All that mattered was that the starting point seem intrinsic, that it should arise from the logic of the design process instead of from a meretriciously recursive bending to and manipulation of the client's tastes. The hope was thus to find something pure in an impure world, an unassailable foundation on which a superstructure of mental elaborations could be raised.

Armed with such a starting point, architects could embark on the task of house design not as mere tradespeople but as explorers of truth, an attitude of such innate egotism that only clients in possession of educated tastes or considerable amounts of money, or both, could find it tolerable. Such clients are rare, and as it appears, most of the high-style houses of the '80s embodying the fruits of this attitude were designed and built for the architects themselves or for their close relatives.

Many remarkable houses were built in Texas in the 1980s. In the best, the architect tried to deal with house forms, decorative schemes, and materials with long-established traditions in Texas, updating them in similar or at least analogous contexts to those in which the sources occurred.

Two houses in Houston designed for his own family by Houston architect William F. Cannady provide good examples, as well as the clearest possible contrast to the style of builder houses from the period.[24] In the first, Cannady abstracted from craftsman-style house detailing to create a terrace-topped modern house; he later planted an addition with thin pseudo-gable decorations between the house and the street, illustrating the transition he was making from modernism to postmodernism. The second house, a two-story stucco-covered Italianate villa with an L-shaped plan on a much more prominent site facing the Museum of Fine Arts and the Contemporary Arts Museum, shows Cannady's next stylistic step, to neoeclecticism.

Cannady house, Houston (1991), by Wm. T. Cannady & Associates

The house designed by Cunningham Architects of Dallas for Marlene and Morton Meyerson provides another example. Here architect Gary M. Cunningham's starting point was the dowdy neoclassical composure and quasi-civic quality of the industrial building he remodeled for the house, a former electrical switching station on the edge of Highland Park, dating from 1924. For the most part, the building's shell was left unaltered, except for cleaning and sealing its materials. Cunningham treated the interior like a 1920s-era Dallas mansion; on the ground floor there are a hall, a front parlor, a living room and dining room, a closed-off kitchen, even a back parlor-library; there are bedrooms on the second floor; and the entire third floor is developed as an acoustically tuned ballroom-like loft space. But the architects industrialized the physical expression of these interior spaces, turning the house into a kind of museum of electricity as brutal low-tech power supply through the use of the sail-like, delicately pivoting gate, the sharp steel entry canopy, the glazed trench (once filled with buss bars) bisecting the ground floor, jagged openings framed and glazed, rather than smoothed over, and hundreds of other details that proclaim their opposition to the conventions of 1980s house decoration. The massive crane

Meyerson house, Dallas (1988), by Cunningham Architects

in the living room, left over from the house's previous incarnation, is the centerpiece of the treatment.[25]

A gentler but even more poetic blend of industrial materials with traditional forms was created in the Carraro House on a country site near a dry creek in Buda, by Lake/Flato Architects of San Antonio. Here the frame of a long shed from the abandoned Alamo Cement works in San Antonio was converted into three pavilions—for a garage, for bedrooms and offices, and for living room, dining room, and kitchen spaces. Silos, grain elevators, and metal-skinned industrial buildings have been touchstones of a romantic modernity ever since Le Corbusier called them the real American architecture in the 1920s; architects in Texas, trying to reconstruct modernism's roots when the collapse of postmodernism became imminent in the late 1980s, started photographing the remaining structures in Dallas and Houston and in various small towns, studying them in schools, and reusing them for housing and offices. In the Carraro house, Lake/Flato achieved the most successful of these attempts, fusing the industrial frame seamlessly with nineteenth-century stonework to form a building for the main living spaces within the large, screened-in pavilion.[26]

Carraro house, Buda (1990), by Lake/Flato Architects

Mediterranean house, Highland Park (1989), by Frank Welch & Associates

All these architect houses are out by themselves, either physically, like the country houses by Lake/Flato, or socially; the Meyersons, for example, live on the industrial edge of a neighborhood of renters and condo owners, far from people of comparable income and social prestige. Thus, there was little pressure for any of these houses to conform to the neighborhood context, and they were largely polemical undertakings.

Where architects did design houses to meet an existing neighborhood context for clients whose income and attitudes matched those of their neighbors, they tended to be much more respectful (compared even with house builders, who typically replaced tear-downs with overbearing '80s houses).

For example, the Mediterranean house in Highland Park, designed by Frank Welch & Associates of Dallas and completed in 1989, follows the conventions of house architecture along its very prestigious streetscape, with massing and siting that complement those of its neighbors. Nevertheless, Welch rooted his design in the primacy of articulated detail, from the hovering knife-edged, gutterless eaves, to the stripped masses of the brick arcades and walls. Everything about the house seems natural and orderly,

This page: Speck house, Austin (1989), by Lawrence W. Speck Associates

except that it is about to fly apart into weightless planes of spatial delineation. This gives the Mediterranean house both a pleasant animation that its neighbors lack and a kind of out-there polemical edge.[27]

Simple stone farm buildings with metal roofs had become acceptable models to both architects and builders in the Austin market in the late 1980s, and this allowed other architects to pay obeisance to context while experimenting with form. Taft Architects of Houston made the Williams house in Austin fit its upper-middle-class neighborhood, despite its organization in an unconventional eroded-cube arrangement, through simply arranged planes of clapboard siding and local limestone.[28] Lawrence Speck of Austin, in his own house in West Austin, similarly made neighborly gestures to the stone houses on his street by building the house's main family-room volume from limestone. Nevertheless, the architect's polemical response to context is in force: Speck appealed both to vernacular tradition (the mortar is smeared partially over the surface of the stone in a technique used by nineteenth-century German masons) and to what, by the late 1980s, could be called traditional modernism (the roof of the family room is not supported in compression on conventional wood trusses but is instead held in tension between the stone walls and thin steel members under the roof peak, while the bedroom pavilion is surfaced in gray panels made from wood chips and concrete).[29]

Only the Mixon house in West University Place, completed in 1984, really violates the code of same-class suburban neighborliness, however. Here, Taft Architects wrapped the house in a clown costume of brick, split concrete block, painted wood, and roof shingles, yanking the garage volume forward and capping it with a portico more aggressive than anything in First Colony, setting the entry behind a grotesquely elongated front stair of poured concrete, and treating the whole first floor as if it stood on a flood plain that the neighbors had been foolish enough to ignore.[30]

The Mixon house is an extreme case, but (with the possible exception of the Mediterranean house) by the standards of the mass market and the suburban enclave, all of these architect-designed houses, with their flat facades, hard materials, and quirky details, fail more or less at the task of communicating the qualities of shelter and repose that most people in our society expect from houses. Not only do many of them look slightly oddball, most of them are out there in the city, with no servants of a princely pro-

Left and facing page: Mixon house, Houston (1983), by Taft Architects

tector watching a black-and-white monitor at the gates, meaning that their owners obviously believe that such a location is still safe for high-priced housing. Since the market for residential real estate is dominated by forces that require conservatism and standardization within a rubric constructed by nonarchitect builders, it is unlikely that their unique features (created by the architects in pursuit of a dream of primal clarity, for clients pursuing a dream of cultural aristocracy) will contribute to the easy conversion of these houses to commodities. Indeed, it might turn out that none of these high-style houses will be easy to sell if and when the time comes. But that is the risk one takes in attempting to stop the oscillation of architecture between the worlds of money and meaning.

Transco Tower, Houston (1983), by Johnson/ Burgee Architects with Morris Aubry, associated architects

3
'80s Middle-Class Workplaces

The sixty-four-story Transco Tower (1983, designed by Johnson/Burgee Architects with Morris Aubry, associated architects) stands in lonely splendor among the mid-rise shrubbery of Houston's Galleria-Post Oak area.[1] Promoted by its developer, Gerald Hines, as the tallest building in the world outside a downtown, Transco Tower is a beacon that can be seen from miles away, advertising the stature of its lead tenant, the Transco Companies. As Stephen Fox has pointed out, the Transco Tower is a farrago of echoes and inversions, "a ghost image of a skyscraper from the city that Post Oak rejected," using reflective glass in place of the masonry skin of the 1920s art deco towers of Manhattan from which it is derived (the glass is set in smallish rectangles, as stone would be) and using gray nonreflective glass to stand for the shadows that have modeled the surface of the originals.[2] It is also one of the last of a breed. Few large American businesses need or want a tall downtown building any more, and even fewer want a tall suburban building. The problem is that such buildings are built around elevators.

The invention of the traction elevator in the 1880s is considered one of the crucial factors that made skyscrapers possible. Land was scarce in the business centers where early twentieth-century corporations needed to cluster together, and elevators made it possible to build high enough to get all of a company's employees into a single building. The size of the corporation dictated the number of floors needed, thus the building's height, and thus, by extension, its wealth and importance. This gave shape to the skyscraper as the dominant symbol of American architectural culture, equating height with corporate stature. Such an equation still holds true for banks and their ancillary law firms, which, despite dwindling numbers, continue to be the mainstay of the downtown (and even suburban) market for signature high rises. Arguably as important as this positive projection of power is the fact that locating one's offices in a skyscraper signifies a desire for separation from the problems of the surrounding city. Companies from the 1880s on wanted their offices in high rises so that the people in control of the companies could separate themselves physically from the rest of the city, with its constantly nagging problems of decay, crowding, poverty, and crime. The vertical layering of space in high rises, with their controlled ground-floor access and canyonized views, served this purpose. The lower classes connected with each other horizontally on the sidewalks, while the CEOs connected horizontally overhead. The views told the real story: Up high were the people; below there were only ants.

But, for companies that depend for their existence on research and product development, the high-rise building strategy proved to be unworkable, as shown in a series of developments that started in the 1950s and that led to the building of low-rise corporate campuses in Texas in the 1980s for IBM, Exxon, Conoco, 3M, Schlumberger, Compaq, and other such companies. There are many reasons why this is so, some of which derive from what could be called external considerations, and others from patterns of internal organization of American companies.

First, the expense of downtown properties and high-rise construction left most potential tenants out of the market. Second, land was cheaper in the suburbs, and, since cars and ever-better roads made nearly any suburban location as accessible as downtown, almost anywhere would do. In addition, the high-rise strategy had never been very effective at keeping the city at bay; you had to mingle with the ants too much. How much better to flee the city to a glade where the ants couldn't follow, and where there was room to create an entire world, without the distraction of competing images. In sheer volume of office space created, this process dwarfed downtown office construction by the mid-1950s, and it became a major constituent of the myth that the princes of the real estate market controlled the cycle of property valuation and devaluation for the benefit of all.

But the main reason for the shift from high-rise to low-rise construction has to do with the internal organization of American companies and the anxiety they have lived with in recent years. These days, corporations fear that if they were to locate in a high-rise building, their employees, antlike, would get out of their cars in the attached garage each morning, zoom up on the elevator to the floors on which they work with people from their own departments and no one else, whoosh to the ground for lunch, and at day's end scurry away on the elevator to their cars for the homeward journey. This, they feared, would eventually spell the death of the company.[3]

Whence sprang this fear? Partially it arose because, since the 1980s, most American companies have been under increasing threat from within and without. Not only were foreigners grabbing market share and an ever-greater percentage of the money spent on corporate securities, but the invention of junk bonds had touched off a frenzy of mergers and acquisitions that meant that anybody—especially middle managers working for prosperous, well-capitalized corporations—could find themselves out hunting for a job overnight. The atmosphere was captured by a series of television spots for computer systems that AT&T ran in the late '80s, which critic Barbara Lippert of *Advertising Age* magazine dubbed "slice of death" ads. In one called "Banquet," the boss, in front of mortified colleagues and spouses at a black-tie dinner, excoriates a manager named Murphy, who had unthinkingly ordered the wrong computers. "Manufacturing can't hook up with sales. . . . Brilliant, Murphy," the boss says. In another, a middle-aged department manager writhes while a younger colleague, who has obviously been promoted over him in the corporate structure, humiliates him for "blowing his budget on stand-alone" computers. Oddly, nowhere in the ads is it said that AT&T makes equipment that could help one avoid such unpleasant scenes; AT&T apparently decided that they would best be served by emphasizing the chilly gloom pervading the social atmosphere of American business.[4]

As if it weren't bad enough that any misstep could wipe out a career or a company, the fear animating American businesses stemmed from a long-term crisis in office worker productivity.

After World War II, the "service industries," which embrace everything from burger-flipping to medicine and corporate law, but which center on white-collar office work, edged out manufacturing to become the largest sector of the American economy. That share had climbed to 68 percent in the 1970s, and by 1990 it had grown to nearly 75 percent. In Texas, where manufacturing and mining jobs were scoured away by the oil-price collapse, fully 80 percent of jobs are now in the service sector.[5]

The productivity of workers (measured in units of work produced compared to units of cost) in the agricultural sector of the U.S. economy has increased decade by decade for more than a century, and so, until recently, has productivity in the manufacturing sector. When manufacturing productivity began to flatten out in the late 1970s, it was regarded as a terrible crisis, one from which the country is only beginning to recover. But it is the service sector, the fastest-growing part of the economy, that is in real trouble. Office worker productivity has remained essentially stagnant since the end of World War II. A vast amount of theorizing and experimentation has gone into solving this problem, but so far it has been to no avail.

Until just after the Civil War, as Adrian Forty shows in *Objects of Desire: Design and Society from Wedgewood to IBM*, American businesses were usually small in scale, and most offices were arranged like the one depicted in Herman Melville's "Bartleby the Scrivener": A proprietor shared space with one or more clerks, people who held a status analogous to that of skilled artisans before the advent of mass production. The clerks had the responsibility for seeing business transactions through from start to finish. They could influence, if not control, both the pace and content of their work, squirreling papers away in the typical nineteenth-century clerk's desk with its privacy-protecting high back and roll top and the numerous drawers and pigeon holes in its pedestal base.[6]

By the turn of the century, however, manufacturers of farm equipment and household goods, railroads, utilities, banks, and insurance companies proliferated and increased in size, and offices within them became larger and more departmentalized. More important, office work became more like factory work, particularly after followers of the new scientific-management movement, led by Frederick Taylor, began applying to office work the time-and-motion studies and principles of abstraction and repetition they had derived from factory mass-production. According to the Taylorists, all workers were lazy and devious, and they required managers who exerted themselves forcefully. To make this possible, one of the first things the Taylorists did was to redesign the clerical worker's desk, changing it from what Forty describes as "a small private domain. . . [encapsulating] the responsibility, trust, and status given to some clerks," to a flat-topped table with legs instead of pedestals and only a few shallow drawers. This design made the work surface open to inspection, so that, to quote Taylor, "any tendency to defer until tomorrow what can be done today is nipped in the bud"; at the same time, systems of standardization were developed to control each task and how it was performed, down to the place of the pencils on the work surface. Workers were arranged in "bullpens," in which they could be easily supervised from a central point; messengers or mechanical conveyors were used to move files to and from central storage, further decreasing the worker's control over work flow. "The clerk now worked to a tempo imposed by management at a desk that had been designed and organized to prevent its being used in any way as a private space," Forty writes. This alteration, he argues, showed "the change in the status of the clerk from craftsman to proletarian—the employer was buying not only his or her time, but also the right to supervise every movement." The industrial appearance of typewriters, telephones, adding machines, and other office equipment used by nonmanagement personnel during this period, particularly when contrasted to the more "domestic" finishes and materials used in office equipment for managers, also showed a deliberate connection between office and factory.

Frederick Taylor's voice was the most influential in management circles early on, but it was by no means the only one. A "human relations" school of management, which argued for a more enlightened approach in which employees were viewed as basically responsible and creative, developed as early as the 1920s. Historians trace the beginning of the human-relations management style to 1927, when researchers from the Harvard Fatigue Laboratory, in a series of experiments at the Hawthorne Works of the Western Electric Company, found that productivity increased when workers were allowed to design their own working conditions and when they felt that management was acting responsively to their needs.

This style of management, and the somewhat more democratic, less factory-like office environment it fostered, became widespread after World

War II. Partially this was because postwar unemployment was low and the country's growing service industries had either to lure workers with higher pay (they did not: factories paid more on average) or to make the office seem like a cleaner, more interesting place in which workers partook of higher status. Partially, also, it was because businesses were growing and divisions and departments were proliferating, while at the same time more and more members of the work force had the same educations and came from the same suburbs as did the managers. This meant that there was less social distance than before between managers and employees, and it just wouldn't do for managers to treat people like themselves as if they were low-class, uneducated factory workers from the wrong side of the tracks. Floor plans changed, as fluorescent lighting and air conditioning became standard, and the new work arrangements also reflected changes in status. Men typically worked in private or semiprivate offices; women, on the other hand, who were entering the work force in increasing numbers by the late 1950s, but who were regarded as temporary, low-status employees, were typically still relegated to bullpen-like typing pools and to the vestibules of managers' offices.[7]

Underlying all the ostensible good feeling of the time, however, was a fear that the very uniformity of the social situation among America's growing new cadre of office workers concealed a threat of continuing proletarianization. William Whyte's *The Organization Man* and Sloan Wilson's *The Man in the Gray Flannel Suit*, both influential best sellers, were essentially conservative pleas for a return to prewar values, in hopes that middle-class people could somehow steer clear of big, faceless organizations and regain the autonomy enjoyed by lawyers, doctors, and other professionals. The numerically few but influential beatniks of the 1950s and hippies of the '60s and '70s identified an oppressive sameness in American business life as the source of what they perceived as moral vacuity, and they adopted lives designed to escape both.

Since the 1950s, the ideological balance of American business management has teetered between the Taylorist and the human-relations styles, and between the twin fears that, on the one hand, business would snuff out the innovativeness of its workers by imposing too much control, and, on the other hand, that excessive laxity would allow workers to destroy their employers.[8]

One of the markers for the recurring oscillation between these two viewpoints has been in the use of computers within business. Companies with big, centralized computer systems—airlines, insurance companies, brokerage houses—often used them to extend supervisory discipline invisibly, monitoring the exact number of seconds workers spent at their tasks and the number of key strokes performed per hour. These mechanistic measurements were typically then used as the "objective" standards on which raises and promotions for clerical workers were based. By contrast, companies that embraced the use of personal computers after they became widespread in the 1980s often did so with the acknowledged aim of returning a sense of empowerment and autonomy to the workers, who would use them for business planning, writing, and other tasks—creating a new electronic roll-top desk, in which workers could regain control over the pace and content of their jobs.

The amazing thing, given the fact that billions of dollars have been spent on computerizing American offices since the mid-1970s, is that computers have had no measurable impact on the overall productivity of white-collar workers. Productivity levels for a few jobs have increased, but the effect in aggregate has been negligible. It's as if farmers had changed from horse-drawn plows to gasoline tractors and still produced the same amount of grain per day. But that is a misleading comparison. Office workers typically don't produce *things*; instead, they evaluate ideas and make decisions. Nevertheless, measured in units of corporate productivity for each standardized unit of worker pay, productivity among office workers has not changed since the introduction of computers. This may be because, in the increasingly abstract world of business, there are only two real jobs: persuading and deciding. Computers make it easier to gather and analyze more data, and to present information in more coherent ways, thereby appearing to make it easier to perform the mechanics of persuading. But this has had a number of paradoxical effects: making an increasing volume of information equally compelling, despite the inherent contradictions and qualifications of all information; nearly destroying the ability to accept ambiguity, which previously would have been justified by lack of information; throwing the weakness in the available information into higher relief; and creating an appetite for still more information. As a result, deciding becomes more, not less, difficult.[9]

These pages: H. E. B. Grocery Company, San Antonio (1985), by Hartman-Cox with Jones & Kell

Another marker for the oscillation between discipline and trust in American management style has been the portrayal of workers in popular management-advice books and in the business press. In the 1970s, for example, when long hair and recreational drugs moved from the upper to the middle to the working class, business routinely suggested that the nation's fall from industrial preeminence was being caused by a drug-addled generation that had never learned the American work ethic. Not ten years later, however, most such blame-the-workers talk had stopped (although the workplace, due to the climbing cost of health insurance, had become the focus of efforts to control drug abuse and even such legal activities as drinking alcohol and smoking tobacco). Tom Peters, the authors of *The One-Minute Manager*, and W. Edwards Deming were the most influential and popular management theorists of the 1980s. Their message was that too many managers were trying to manage processes that workers could handle better without interference, and that the key to prosperity lay first in discovering and respecting the capabilities and creativeness of workers and then in doing whatever was required to win workers' commitment to the organizational goal.[10]

(Peters, in television shows and speeches for which he charged extraordinary sums, delivered this message in vehement outbursts meant to convey passion, a numbingly false style of "evangelization" that was adopted by salesmen and managerial motivators nationwide.) The members of the baby-boom generation, whose sheer lumpish numerousness has exacerbated every crisis in America from the counterculture of the '60s to skyrocketing house prices in the 1970s to stalled productivity in the '80s, have responded eagerly to the implication that their individualism and creativity are the last best hope for defeating all the problems that American business faces. Such a message probably won't last, however. As the members of the baby boom generation age and as the costs of health care required to maintain them at a peak of individualism and creativity continue to escalate, we can expect to see management putting more and more emphasis on youthfulness, vigor, and competition among workers, and on an unquestioning attitude when one is directed to walk the plank for the good of the ship.

These pages: The Menil Collection, Houston (1987), by Renzo Piano and Richard Fitzgerald & Partners

The corporate campuses built in Texas during the 1980s show physical expressions of both Taylorist and human-relations influences. Some of them are in urban locales—the headquarters of the H. E. Butt Grocery Company in San Antonio, for example (1985, by Hartman-Cox of Washington, D.C., with Jones & Kell and with interiors by Chumney Urrutia), which was built in the adapted buildings of an abandoned army garrison along the River Walk between downtown San Antonio and the King William district.[11] The headquarters of H.E.B., as the chain is known throughout South Texas, must rank with the late-'70s revitalization of the Strand area of Galveston as one of the most important projects of historic preservation and urbanism of the century in Texas.[12] The only project that surpasses H.E.B. headquarters for urbanistic impact is the Menil Collection (1987, by Renzo Piano with Richard Fitzgerald & Partners of Houston), which, with its unpretentious gray-stained wood siding, its straightforward plan, and its exquisite canopy of light-bouncing ferrocement "leaves," is also the single best building of the 1980s in Texas.[13] It may seem strange to think of a private museum as equivalent to a corporate headquarters, but in this

case it makes perfect sense—the main difference is that the H.E.B. headquarters is devoted to the marketing of groceries, whereas the Menil Collection is concerned with creating and disseminating knowledge about a genuine and genuinely catholic integration of world culture from prehistoric Anatolia to twentieth-century art. Additionally, surrounded by the gray-painted Montrose-area bungalows housing numerous employees and providing offices for half a dozen cultural, scholarly, and religious organizations that Dominique de Menil subsidizes, the museum is more than a corporate headquarters; it is a company town, projecting an image of a Houston in which aristocratic taste can become a commercial base, like oil technology.

Such an image is analogous to similar late-'80s cultural developments in Dallas, where, for example, business leaders such as North Park Mall developer Raymond Nasher used the opening of the Meyerson Symphony Center to regale a host of visiting international journalists with the message that Dallas was henceforward to be thought of as a city where culture and education mattered. The Menil's projection of an economic role fit

These pages: Frito-Lay headquarters, Plano (1985), by Lohan Associates

even more closely with the building of the architecturally negligible Wortham Theatre Center (1988, by Morris Architects)[14] as part of downtown Houston's cultural district, which was similarly hyped to the international press as a sign of the city's sophistication and diversified economy. Unlike the Meyerson and the Wortham, however, the Menil Collection was not created in partial hope of shoring up the prices of surrounding real estate. Indeed, it had no appreciable effect on the continuing slide of real estate values in the Montrose area, which started as a middle-class suburb in the 1920s and turned in the 1980s into a neighborhood for the flood of unskilled immigrants from Central America that Houston's new economy secretly required.

Being disconnected from the real estate fortunes of the surrounding city makes the Menil Collection like other corporate campuses of the 1980s, such as the small-scale suite of low-key, regionalist-style office buildings crawling along the edge of a ravine at the Schlumberger Wells Services Headquarters in northwest Austin (1987, by Howard Barnstone Architects and Robert Jackson Architects; the Schlumberger company provides the

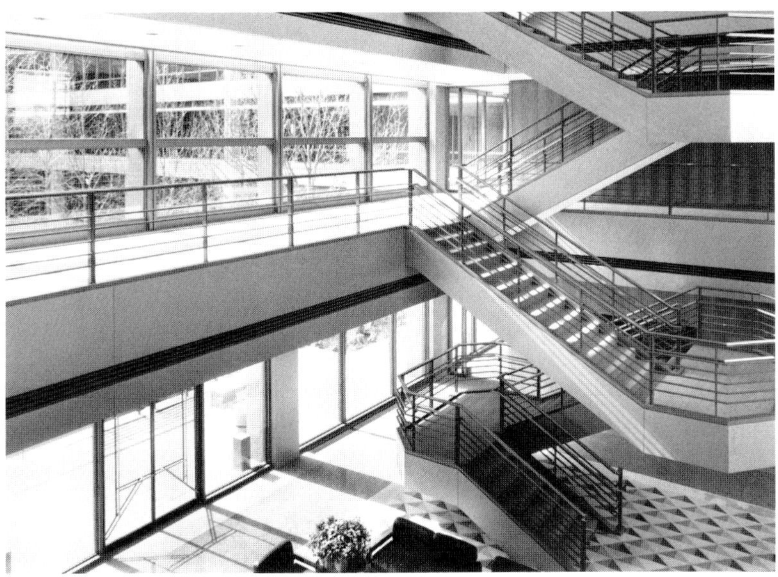

base for the Menil family fortune) and the 3M headquarters (1989, designed by CRSS), a group of enormous office buildings clustered at the edge of another northeast Austin ravine. Both projects are centered in natural scenic areas at the suburban edge of an established city. Still others turn away from the city toward manufactured focal points. The Frito-Lay headquarters (1987, designed by the now-closed Dallas office of the Chicago architects Lohan Associates, the successor firm to Ludwig Mies van der Rohe), a crisply detailed triangular arrangement of steel and glass buildings set around an artificial lake among artificial hills in Plano, north of Dallas, is an example.[15] So are the rhythmically asymmetrical groups of buildings with wide white plastic sunshades at the Conoco headquarters on Interstate 10 west of downtown Houston, also set around an artificial lake (1986, Kevin Roche John Dinkeloo & Associates). And others still, like Solana, which is a special case, are in the middle of nowhere.

All these projects except the Menil Collection have several things in common. First is the emphasis on amenity for employees shown by the presence of jogging tracks, health clubs, and scenographic integration of

3M head-quarters, Austin (1989), by CRSS

workplace and parklike natural or quasi-natural setting. These amenities, which had arisen one by one to become a standard part of suburban corporate-headquarters and research-center development, projected a double message. On the one hand, they were presented to employees as proof that the company cared for them as complete people. Indeed, the health-and-fitness facilities seemed coded with the implication that workers, in using them, were being invited to think of work as a place to perfect themselves in non-job-related ways (ways that had been tinged in popular consciousness with preparation for continuous erotic questing), and thus to think of work as the locus of self-fulfillment that up to then had been associated with the home. But the expense involved in building such facilities was usually justified to management and stockholders in terms of higher productivity and lowered health-benefits costs.

The main similarity among all these corporate campuses, however, is the emphasis on a physical expression of corporate "destratification," the strategy for survival urged on corporations by Tom Peters and his cohorts and forced on them by corporate raiders and competitive pressures.

Conoco headquarters, Houston (1986), by Kevin Roche John Dinkeloo & Associates

Destratification is why corporate campuses were built as low-rise buildings, usually linked by a simple linear circulation path and with elevators used only for secondary movement. Corporations were shucking off layers of management, trying to get decision-making closer to the sources of contact with customers and product development, and in their new buildings these corporations tried literally to compress the vertical distance between the layers that remained. Thus the Frito-Lay headquarters (with three work levels over a ground-level service floor) was designed to fit below the crest of a hill, allowing parking to be concealed on both sides, and arranging the circulation path so that employees entered from the garages and went to work by walking either straight ahead, up one floor, or down one floor. Such horizontal organization was thought by researchers to have a collateral benefit. People who worked within sight of each other or who, in a large building, had to walk by each other daily, were found in experimental situations to talk to each other sometimes, while those whose paths seldom crossed (as in a vertical elevator building) almost never spoke. In addition, the resulting chance conversations, particularly among people who worked in different areas or departments, were thought to spark creative ideas that were valuable to the growth and development of the corporation.

Like the health clubs, the horizontally unified circulation patterns of the new corporate campuses of the '80s in Texas seem to imply the type of contradictory messages that psychologists call a double bind. The *paseo* at 3M Austin, for example, the zigzagging open area that links the office buildings with the cafeteria, is an extraordinary interior space, lit with specially developed Fresnel lens skylights that bring bright daylight into the space without heat gain. Similarly, the office buildings at Schlumberger Wells Services have highly individualized offices for each of the engineer-researchers, in which the interior and exterior walls change to follow the line of the canyon rim onto which they face, and which are linked by an airy, plant-filled "interior street" to the central cafeteria. Considered as pure architectural objects in isolation from their users, both spaces are innovative and effective solutions to the program presented by the client organization. But, in the long run, the underlying contradiction contained in those programs, between freeing workers to control the content and pace of their jobs, and, conversely, extending corporate discipline so that even chance encounters are structured to benefit the organization, undoes the architectural quality of the space. What looks like a belief in worker creativity and commitment masks a higher-order Taylorism. Employees may find that the manipulation of worker contacts in the central circulation spaces is an intrusion on privacy, one that they feel compelled to subvert to maintain their self-respect.

It may have seemed to some architects and clients in Texas in the 1980s that improving corporate productivity was as simple as doing away with elevators. Some corporations no doubt realized benefits from a move to newer, more parklike surroundings. But suburban office campuses are now the norm rather than the exception in American business life, and office worker productivity has not changed. This stasis, despite the money and effort devoted to altering the work places, makes it appear that architects and corporate planners spent their time during the 1980s devising mechanistic and ultimately trivial solutions to a far-from-trivial problem. The corporate campuses of the 1980s in Texas, architecturally pleasing though many of them may be with their well-lit circulation spines and bucolic views, represent a dead end. Indeed, they may soon be seen as tombstones, like the downtown bank towers of the 1980s. This is because the new grooviness of '80s management ideology masked a stagnation in wages for middle-class knowledge workers that produced a *decline* in real wages and family earning power (the latter by 47 percent).[17] Most office workers are earning less, in real terms, than they did in the 1970s. And that's just the beginning. The '90s style of management, continuing the destratifying trends of the 1980s, discards the idea that employees are partners, fulfilling themselves by growing with the enterprise. Instead, employees are excess baggage, to be let go and hired back, if at all, part-time or through employee-leasing firms that slash pay and benefits (particularly for health care).[18] This is a momentous change. The entire mythos of real estate is built on the assumption that middle-class people will have rising earnings, so that they can take their places on the home-buying escalator, shop in the stores, get well in the hospitals, and pay taxes on the infrastructure. If that assumption evaporates, so does most of the real estate system as it is now constituted.

Interior, Loma Park School addition (1987), by Reyna/ Caragonne Architects

4
Schools from the Bottom Up

In the years immediately following the Second World War, a handful of young Texas architects including William W. Caudill[1] and Donald Barthelme[2] rethought school design. They were preparing for the task of educating a new school-age population, the baby boom, in a landscape without precedent in American settlement, the suburban housing developments of the emerging postwar middle and lower-middle classes. There would be no more two-story brick neoclassical or Tudor-style elementary schools, with their double-loaded corridors and fire-hazard stairwells; these were to be replaced with projects such as Barthelme's West Columbia Elementary School of 1951 and Caudill, Rowlett & Scott's Phillis Wheatley Elementary School in Port Arthur of 1952, in which lightweight single-story steel-and-glass pavilions with scientifically tested natural lighting and ventilation were set in flowing asymmetrical arrangements around peaceful courtyards, in harmony with the newly settled prairies. Like Barcelona Pavilions with floor-mounted desks, the schools in the new Texas style were modern, hopeful, economical, and antimonumental, perfect for a period of physical and psychological expansion, in which the classical monuments of previous generations were tainted with totalitarian associations, and in which the future seemed as open and full of possibility as a newly cleared building site. In the process of coming up with these designs, Caudill, Barthelme, and the other young Texans set the standard for postwar school design and construction nationwide, and they put Texas on the architectural map in a way that could never have been accomplished by the office towers of Wyatt C. Hedrick, Alfred C. Finn, and the other reluctant modernists whose firms dominated commercial building. West Columbia Elementary wiped out ten years of jokes about Texans as yokels who were too rich for their own good.[3]

The 1980s also had their monuments of architectural education in Texas, but they were of a different sort. By the early 1980s, the patina of hope that clung to education in the '50s had rubbed away; a deepening sense of failure and fatalism was left behind.

Educational achievement among Texas elementary and secondary students ranked near the bottom of all states in national surveys (which also showed declining scores for almost all schools nationwide). Diffuse societal changes lay at the root of this educational decline. There were alterations in family structure. There were increases in the number of poor students, many of them from recent immigrant families (the problems were worst in black urban neighborhoods and the poor Mexican-American areas of South Texas). There was the emerging domination of private lives by television, particularly the lives of children, for whom television was a low-cost babysitter that rapidly took the place in the nuclear family once held by older relatives in extended families. There was television's contribution to a general decline in literacy as a means for conveying and cementing cultural bonds. And there were failures of educational policy and theory. The reasons were enumerated and debated endlessly; meanwhile, students in increasing numbers were coming out of the schools unable to write coherently, to locate themselves geographically or historically, or to balance their own checkbooks.

There were two basic responses to the educational crisis. One focused on reforming classroom instruction and the systems for educating and paying teachers. The other focused on money.

Reformist critics of the state education agency and local districts maintained that the schools were full of substandard teachers who were protected by seniority. Additionally, they charged, the educational focus of classes had gone awry; instead of getting a good grounding in the basics, students spent too much time on seemingly "relevant" classes that were in fact of little use in preparing for the future. Worst of all, it was said, many schools put more emphasis on football teams and band uniforms than on educational excellence. Experimental programs were tried, and bills setting up state-mandated competence testing and other requirements were enacted by the Legislature, but little changed.

The problems of finding enough money to fund education statewide were even thornier. The State of Texas, in keeping with a provision in the state constitution requiring the Legislature "to establish and make suitable provision for the support and maintenance of an efficient system of public free schools" aimed at producing "a general diffusion of knowledge," spent a considerable portion of the state budget on education; in 1985, for example, this amounted to $4.6 billion, or about 42 percent of all public educational expenditures in the state, with most of the rest coming from local school districts, which collected in property taxes and spent 49 percent of the total educational funds, or about $5.4 billion; federal grants and other sources made up the balance amounting to a total of $11 billion in 1985. The state paid a base rate of $1,350 per pupil to school districts. Even at this level of effort, Texas showed up at the bottom of lists ranking state expenditures per pupil.

The state's cumbersome and antiquated collection of more than fifteen hundred independent school districts (some of them relics of a time when the state was primarily rural, some of them set up as vehicles for white flight from the troubles of urban schools) didn't help. Nor did the wide disparities in wealth available to support the schools in each of the different districts (oil wells, for example, or businesses with valuable property). In 1985, for example, the most property-rich school district in the state had $14 million in property value per student, while the poorest had only $20,000. A statewide study showed that 68 percent of the school districts in the state, which served over 60 percent of all the students, fell below the state average of $250,000 per student. The poorest districts tried to make up for this difference by taxing property at higher rates: in some districts, property was taxed at $1.55 per $100 of valuation, while in other, richer, districts, the rate was only nine cents per $100. The state supplied "equalization aid" to make up for some of the differences, but it was insufficiently equalizing. In 1985, the result of these disparities was that expenditures per pupil (including state equalization funding) ranged from a low of $2,112 in one district up to $19,333 in another. [4]

In an early '70s lawsuit titled *Rodríguez v. San Antonio Independent School District*, a group of Mexican-American families charged that the Texas school-finance system violated the U.S. Constitution's guarantee of equal protection under the law. In 1973, the case went to the U.S. Supreme Court, which called the Texas system "chaotic and unjust," but not unconstitutional; the situation limped along for a decade before another major challenge was mounted.

That challenge came from another group of Mexican-American families in the Edgewood Independent School District of southeast San Antonio, who attacked the crisis on both the educational-reform and funding fronts. Their efforts, shown in buildings designed by Reyna/Caragonne Architects of San Antonio, produced the iconic Texas school buildings of the 1980s.

Formed from the breakup of an earlier district in 1913, EISD was (and remains) one of the two poorest school districts in Texas. Much of its area is taken up by parts of Kelly and Lackland Air Force bases and other property that is exempt from local taxation. Single-family houses and vacant land occupy most of the rest. Industrial and office development is minimal, providing few jobs, and the district has none of the oil wells or other revenue generators found in neighboring districts. The population of the area grew rapidly after 1940, in part because Mexican-American families displaced from San Antonio's west side by federally funded slum-clearance programs in the 1940s and '50s had nowhere else to go; in Edgewood, the houses were low quality, and the area lacked municipal water, sewers, and paved streets. Although San Antonio eventually annexed the area and made major infrastructure improvements, the pattern of low-income settlement remained, and local family incomes were among the lowest in the city. By 1976, when the district's physical plant had grown to twenty-seven schools, enrollment had begun to decline, adding to the district's problems.[5]

Local political activists mounted a campaign to take control of the Edgewood school board, which, despite a largely Mexican-American population, had had a majority of Anglo members, and in the late 1970s they succeeded.

The new board enacted a number of educational reforms aimed at cutting the drop-out rate and increasing the focus on classroom instruction. The most famous of these was the "no-pass, no-play" rule, which required students to have passing grades in all academic subjects if they were to be eligible for extracurricular activities.

In 1984, the no-pass, no-play rule formed the centerpiece of a sweeping package of educational reforms and changes in equalization funding for local districts enacted during a special legislative session at the behest of Governor Mark White and citizen-lobbyist H. Ross Perot. Public controversy over the package focused on this provision; along with the unpopular tax hike required to fund the reforms, it cost White the next election.

In Edgewood, the school board was unhappy with the Legislature's new funding formulas, which, board members said, left Edgewood ISD at the bottom of the heap, unable to meet the state's newly handed-down educational requirements. So, in 1984, together with twelve other property-poor school districts and twenty-five families, the Edgewood board sued state education officials, charging that the funding system denied students in property-poor districts the equal protection under law guaranteed by the Texas (as opposed to the U.S.) Constitution. They argued that their status as property-poor school districts made them a "suspect class," in legalese—people likely to be victims of illegal discriminatory policies, and thus eligible for judicial redress of legislative wrongdoing. The suit resulted, in 1989, in a ruling by the Texas Supreme Court that the state's funding system was unconstitutional. Several regular and special sessions of the Legislature wrestled with ways to fit the court's decree (chiefly by creating regional school-finance authorities with paired rich and poor districts),[6] but as of late 1991, matters were still up in the air. Not only were the poor districts unsatisfied, but the rich school districts had entered the fray, arguing that local control of schools was being disrupted.[7]

In 1982, as these matters were beginning to percolate, Edgewood ISD hired Reyna/Caragonne Architects to plan a program of consolidations and improvements to the district's schools, and later to design the new school buildings. Elías Reyna, one of the firm's partners, attributed the choice in part to his role as an active supporter of the new board chairman. The firm

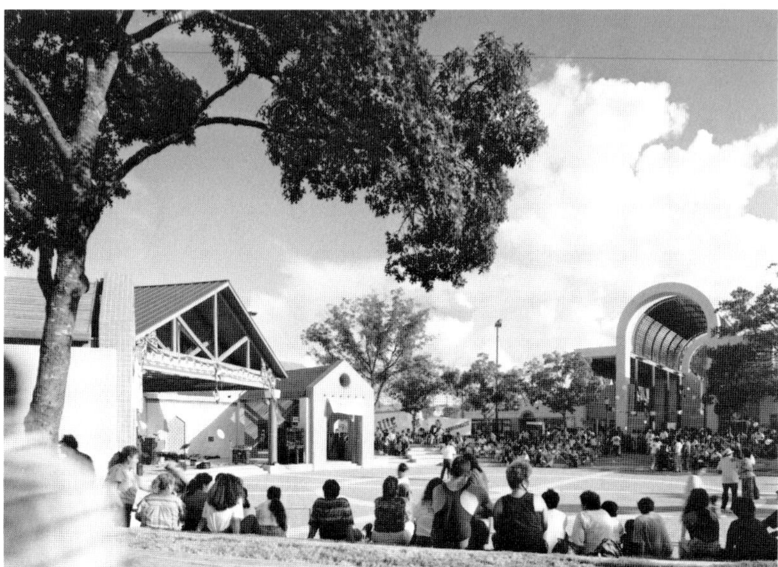

These pages: Plaza Guadalupe (1985), by Reyna/ Caragonne Architects

was also at the time building a strong reputation for such projects as Plaza Guadalupe, a public square and office-theater complex that won both a national award from *Progressive Architecture* magazine and a state-level design award from the Texas Society of Architects; one of the schools designed for Edgewood ISD also won a TSA design award.[8] Such a measure of fame meant relatively little in a shrinking local market, however. Partner Alexander Caragonne, looking for work, opened a California office in 1985, and the firm split up in 1989.

Compared with what was possible within the budgets of some districts, these Edgewood improvements weren't much: a new classroom wing at Loma Park School, a new building for Wrenn Middle School, and new classrooms, cafeteria, and support facilities for Gardendale School, for example. The total budget for demolitions and construction was $10 million, around $55 per square foot. But the architects captured the pugnaciousness of the district's leaders, and the outsiders' stance adopted by architects and clients kept the postmodern stylistic elements of the projects remarkably fresh, even after such elements had been devalued by association and eventual

PLAZA GUADALUPE 1984
1327

Loma Park Elementary School addition

identification with pseudo-public spaces, particularly shopping malls.[9]

Reyna/Caragonne used brightly colored steel, stucco, tile, and concrete block throughout the public spaces, arranged in strongly axial and symmetrical circulation schemes around double-loaded interior corridors. In using these plans, the architects explicitly refer to academic planning and explicitly reject the Texas-'50s-modernist plans of the district's earlier buildings, associated with the past that the new school board was trying to supplant. For emphasis, the entrances are pedimented and exploded into fragments; columns are highlighted, and windows are covered with symmetrical steel grilles. The construction details are uneven (a subject about which the architects were touchy: Caragonne threatened to sue *Texas Architect* magazine for printing a design-awards juror's comment that the projects looked "shabbily built"),[10] so that stucco work betrays thinness where mass was aimed for.

On the whole, however, the elements combine to produce a robust, charged architecture that dots the Edgewood area with landmarks. Whereas most modernist schools recede into the landscape, implying a focus on the

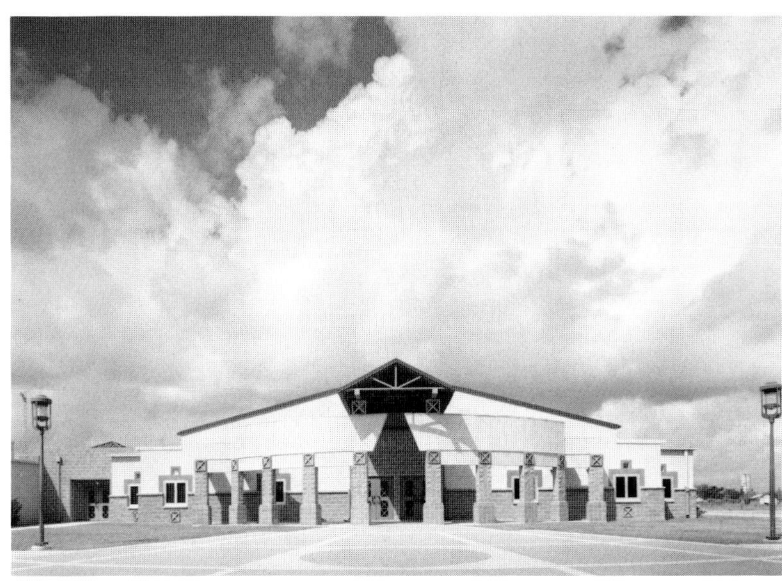

Wrenn Middle School addition

semiprivate world of students and teachers, these schools insist on a public role for education. In this, the Edgewood schools proved to be as influential architecturally as the district's reform program was politically. The newfangled old-fashionedness of Reyna/Caragonne's floor plans gave physical expression to the "back-to-basics" movement that the EISD trustees saw as crucial to their goal of improving educational quality. In designing these schools, the architects were continuing a trend that had started earlier on the East Coast, but they were way out in front of the pack in Texas.[11] By decade's end, other school districts and other architects throughout Texas picked up on the new conservatism implied by the style, and were using the '20s-style plans, pediments, peaked roofs, and other postmodern details of the Edgewood schools to communicate their hope for educational renewal based on a return to old-fashioned pedagogy. The hoped-for effect was not produced, however. Average statewide scores and educational levels continued to slide in the early 1990s.[12]

Architects seldom get to accomplish the goal nearest their hearts, which is to design and complete significant places, shaping the meaning of the

Gardendale School addition

environment through structure and making that meaning accessible to others. Often, the architects themselves fail because they lack talent or concentration. More often, the places they create are robbed of significance when crucial decisions about site, budget, use, and expression are made by others. Even when architect and client work together toward realizing the architect's vision, the resulting projects can be simply swallowed by the cacophony that is the American landscape. And finally, even in the most harmoniously realized projects, all that has been established is *intention*; the ultimate meaning of any given project is decided not by the architects but by the audience, which responds based on a concatenation of histories, contexts, and events that architects and clients often can barely imagine. The Edgewood schools of Reyna/Caragonne are some of the most successful architectural projects of the 1980s, monuments to the emerging will of an ethnic group growing from despised minority to political contender, and to the accommodations in public policy that they have come to demand.

Interior of Dunn Tower, Methodist Hospital, Houston (1989), by Morris Architects

5
Feeling Better about Medical Buildings

In the name of cost-cutting, health-care architects began the decade of the 1980s designing buildings that were the epitome of functionalist design, mere boxes for equipment and beds, so stripped down that, except for their windows, some hospitals had facades resembling those of their own attached parking garages. Patients in these institutions were treated as relatively anonymous supplicants for care, shuttled from place to place on the orders of their physicians, able to stay in the hospital as long as their doctors felt necessary. By decade's end, however, hospital design had become part of the overall mythmaking of Texas real estate. Also, paradoxically, in the name of cost-cutting, hospital architects began designing projects in which they appropriated images from resort hotels, creating places where patients were treated like honored guests, except that they were required to be hustled home at the earliest possible moment.

The story that links these trends in health-care design traces back to the 1960s, to the Great Society programs under which Lyndon Johnson and the Congress, shamed that the poor and the elderly of the richest nation in the history of the world were denied access to health care, set up the federal Medicare program for the elderly and the state-administered, federally funded Medicaid program for the poor. Throughout the '60s and '70s, Congress and the Nixon, Ford, and Carter administrations expanded eligibility and coverage for these programs, as did most states. Even more important, health-care insurance, as a fringe benefit of employment, became standard, at least for those with fulltime jobs. Such insurance often paid 90 to 100 percent of the "first-dollar cost" of care. In Texas, the spread of private insurance joined with rapid population growth and the widening government programs to fuel a spectacular building boom; billions of dollars were spent for construction in the state, and by the early 1980s one of every twelve hospitals in the U.S. was in Texas.[1]

As the decade started, however, the overriding concern among government officials and insurers was no longer access to health care but rising costs. Health care, which had consumed 5.3 percent of the gross national product in 1960, gobbled up 10.5 percent in 1982. In Texas, health-care-cost inflation outstripped even the feverish national pace, rising 155 percent between 1975 and 1980, while the national average rose 122 percent. Partially, these price jumps stemmed from the general inflationary climate in the country. But, for the most part, it arose from conditions within the health-care system itself. The first of these was a growing population: Not only were there more people, but more people were being saved by medical care from early death due to infectious diseases; they then lived on to come down with diabetes, coronary-artery disease, cancer, emphysema, and other long-term, expensive-to-treat conditions. The second inflationary factor was the growing skill and specialization of the medical profession, which was continually evolving better—and more expensive—ways to diagnose and treat diseases that had simply killed people in earlier generations. More people with more illnesses, along with more doctors, more tests, and more possibilities for treatment, all added up to spiraling costs. Finally, with government or private insurance picking up the tab, practically no questions asked, there was little economic incentive for health-care providers to hold down costs; indeed, doctors, under constant threat of being sued for malpractice (an outgrowth of changing legal doctrines of liability, as well as of the growing skill of physicians, who came to be regarded as next to infallible, and thus culpable for every mishap or treatment failure), were pushed out of self-protection to order every con-

Memorial Southwest Hospital, Houston (1976), by S.I. Morris Associates

ceivable test, to use the most expensive treatments, and to encourage the longest possible hospital stays.[2]

Starting in the late 1970s, federal officials and private insurers reacted by trying to control medical costs through a variety of means. Construction was limited through a state-administered "certificate-of-need" review system, and federal and state officials went over every item in the construction or renovation budget of a hospital or hospital wing, squeezing out every nickel. It was during this period that hospitals became little more than stripped-down functional diagrams, garage-like fortresses enlivened only by the application of superscaled graphic devices directing patients from admitting to X-ray to surgical suite. Simultaneously, health-care design came to be regarded, even by its practitioners, as a low-prestige subspecialty within architecture. An example of the style is the Memorial Southwest Hospital (1976, by S.I. Morris Associates) in Houston, which presents to the freeway a blank front of alternating strips of concrete and windows perfectly aligned with its own shorter but visually stronger parking garage.[3]

The certificate-of-need system failed and was abandoned in Texas in 1985. Even bigger changes had been taking shape earlier, however. Starting with its landmark 1981 budget and tax bills, the Reagan administration instituted a new strategy that had been proposed in the 1970s by then-congressmen David Stockman and Phil Gramm.[4] Under this strategy, the Medicare program switched to paying health-care providers fixed payments for typical treatments, based on averages for "diagnostically related groups," in bureaucratic jargon. This "DRG" system was embraced by Medicaid programs in Texas and other states, and was emulated by a number of private insurers. At the same time, the insurance companies began scaling back on the fees they would cover, requiring patients to pay the first $200 or more for treatments. They also charged higher premiums, which led many employers to cut back coverage for employees and to deduct some or all of the cost of the insurance from employee paychecks. The idea behind these government and insurance-company devices was that, for the first time, providers would have an economic incentive to hold down their expenditures; to be profitable, hospitals and doctors would have to find a way to treat patients within the DRG fees. Further, proponents argued, patients spending their own money would be pushed to use health-care services less and to find the most cost-effective providers, bringing competitive shopping to the world of health care for the first time. Hospitals would shrink, as would the percentage of the GNP consumed by health care.

The paradoxical effect of these new regulations was to encourage another building boom. Hospitals, faced with fixed payments, began to "unbundle" their services, creating free-standing buildings for treating patients on a short-term or outpatient basis. New providers, including insurance companies, began to enter the market, constructing clinics for their own cost-controlled health-maintenance organizations, while doctors formed similar provider organizations, with new clinics of their own. Additionally, for-profit hospital companies such as Humana and Health Care International began expanding across the country, and for-profit groups created the decade's only new medical-building type, the minor-emergency clinics, pejoratively called "docs-in-a-box," which proliferated in strip shopping centers and free-standing buildings near freeway intersections.[5] At the same time, the increasingly diffuse suburban population of cities nationwide (particularly in Texas) drove centralized hospitals to turn themselves

A minor-emergency clinic in Dallas, an example of the "docs in a box" building type

into chains of suburban hospitals. Memorial Hospital of Houston, for example, razed its downtown building in 1978 and reconstituted itself as hospitals spread around three of the city's quadrants.

In another sense, the health-care building boom of the late 1980s was inevitable. The DRG system recast patients as consumers, and that brought hospitals into the realm of real estate mythology, where technology still mattered but much less than transactions based on fulfilling fantasies and quelling fears. The first steps were tentative, resulting in hospitals and clinics that were still dominated by their technology (equipment and services used up fully half of the typical hospital construction budget) but were measurably more open and friendly looking than the hospitals of a decade earlier. The Memorial Northwest Hospital in Houston, for example, was reorganized by a new wing addition, designed by Falick/Klein Partnership of Houston, that emphasized the entry sequence so strongly that the building became a kind of billboard for itself to attract patients cruising the nearby freeway. Such other projects as All Saints Episcopal Hospital in Fort Worth and the Rockwall Diagnostic and Surgical Center, both completed in the

Memorial Northwest Hospital, Houston (1989), by Falick/Klein Partners

late 1980s and both designed by HKS of Dallas, use open, expressively clean-scrubbed architectural elements to give the institutions lively, inviting public presences.

There was even talk that the consumer-orientation of the new market would lead to creation of a new hybrid building type, the medical mall, in which medical services would be surrounded by nonmedical retail spaces in an atrium joined to a free-standing hospital. (HKS designed a medical mall for an Austin site in 1985, but ground for it was never broken.)

Despite the stringent application of these modified free-market mechanisms, DRGs failed to control health-care costs. General inflation, which had ranged into the double digits in the late 1970s, was largely squeezed out of the economy by the national recession of 1981-83 and by stable energy prices. Health-care inflation was different. It rose nearly three times as fast as general inflation throughout the 1980s and into the 1990s. In 1990, for example, the general inflation rate was less than 6 percent, but health-care costs went up more than 17 percent, and the government's General Accounting Office estimated that they consumed 11.3 percent of the GNP.[6]

All Saints Episcopal Hospital, Fort Worth (1988), by HKS

The reason for this continued inflation was twofold. First, although they were paying more of their own money than before, patients were not really able to shop for medical care, since, beyond deciding to commit to paying their deductible, patients had neither the expertise nor the power to decide ultimate treatment cost or to terminate treatment based on price sensitivity. Sure, a woman with a sudden headache might go for an examination to a roadside minor-emergency clinic instead of a general-hospital emergency room, thereby potentially saving money. But if, on examining her, the doctor decided that she needed a CAT scan and a biopsy, and the biopsy revealed that she needed brain surgery and chemotherapy and various follow-up blood tests and examinations, that was that. Doctors, not patients, were the people who determined the extent, and thus the cost, of care, and only those who relished the thought of risking death would assert themselves as primary consumers, at least in serious situations. One rule of the DRGs was effective, however: Since patient reimbursement for length of stay in a hospital was rigidly controlled on the basis of national averages for

Ben Taub Replacement Hospital, Houston (1991), by Llewelyn-Davies Sahni and CRSS

a given illness, whatever treatment was called for, patients now stayed in hospitals only the minimum number of days possible.[7]

This change was of little importance in terms of cost savings, however, compared with the second factor leading to health-care-cost inflation. This was the fact that the primary mode of competition among health-care providers was not for patients but for technology. Computerized axial tomographic (CAT) scanners, nuclear-magnetic-resonance imagers, and lithotripsy equipment, along with dozens of sophisticated body-tissue tests for chemical imbalances and genetic predispositions, all started as exotic and prohibitively expensive additions to traditional treatment. New procedures such as kidney, heart, and liver transplants and in-vitro fertilization started the same way. As the worth of each was proven, however, these technological marvels became more common. This brought down individual prices, but it drove the system-wide cost ever higher. A nuclear-magnetic-resonance imager's price (to use an arbitrary example with made-up numbers) might have dropped from $2.5 million to $500,000. But if this increasing affordability and the demand of doctors for the most up-to-date equip-

Veterans Administration Hospital, Houston (1990), by 3D/International and Stone, Marracini & Patterson

ment led a thousand hospitals and clinics to install one of their own (instead of, say, fifty hospitals at the old price), the system had to absorb a massive bulge in capital costs, and that meant raising prices for all patients.

This technological explosion is precisely what drove the health-care inflation of the 1980s, because patients demanded that doctors cure them by whatever means available, and doctors demanded that the facilities they used should have the best equipment at whatever cost. And replacing equipment, or installing new facilities, stimulated the health-care building boom that continued in Texas throughout the 1980s. In Houston alone, between 1985 and 1990, almost $2 billion in medical construction was undertaken. The projects included the new Veterans Administration hospital, designed by 3D/International and Stone, Marracini & Patterson; the Harris County Hospital District's Ben Taub Replacement Hospital, designed by a joint venture of Llewelyn-Davies Sahni and CRSS; and the Lyndon Baines Johnson Hospital in northeast Houston, designed by a joint venture of Llewelyn-Davies Sahni and Rees Associates of Texas, which replaced the county's '30s-era Jefferson Davis maternity hospital.[8] All of these buildings are some-

St. Luke's Medical Tower, Houston (1991), by Cesar Pelli Associates with Kendall/Heaton and Brooks/Collier

what better scaled than their '70s-style counterparts, but they still read as big envelopes stuffed with technology. And their patient-care wings are arranged in '80s-style triangular floor plans, which maximize efficiency in deployment of hospital services, in place of the slabs-radiating-from-a hub plans that were the norm until the 1970s.

Most prominent of all the '80s projects (actually completed in 1990) was the St. Luke's Medical Tower, designed by Cesar Pelli & Associates, with Kendall/Heaton Associates and Brooks/Collier of Houston as associated architects. This blue-mirror-glass building, with its twin, syringe-like towers, has no triangular-plan wings because it is devoted to the doctors' offices and the unbundled day-treatment suites for the adjacent St. Luke's Episcopal Hospital demanded by contemporary regimes of payment and technology. The building provides the Texas Medical Center, a nearly incomprehensible maze of hospitals, research labs, office towers, and schools that has come to be Houston's largest employment center, with a needed landmark, a beacon that stands out on the southern horizon as visibly as Johnson/Burgee's Transco Tower does to the west. As such, it uses architectural flash to do the one thing that hadn't been done by other recent towers, such as the practically anonymous Scurlock Tower (1980, Morris Aubry Architects) and the Smith Tower (1989, Lloyd Jones Fillpot Architects). Clearly, however, the St. Luke's Tower functions as a landmark less for patients than for doctors, proclaiming the availability of first-class technological backup and an easy-to-locate address.

As the economic situation of the '80s clarified, there was a subtle shift in the imagery employed in hospital design. Patients, particularly those with private insurance and the wherewithal to cover their deductibles, became the primary targets (after doctors). These patients were envisioned not as mall shoppers but as hotel guests, and new hospital public spaces, and even some patient-wing spaces, became explicitly hotel-like to attract them. Two buildings from the '80s provide remarkable examples of this trend, and probably indicate a major direction for hospital design for the near future.

The first of these is the luxury floor of the A.W. Roberts Hospital at Baylor Medical Center in Dallas designed by HKS, which opened in 1985; the floor features hotel-like furniture, chandelier-lit elevator lobbies, and suites with kitchens for those who prefer the cuisine of their own chefs to hospital food.

Pedimented facade, Dunn Tower of Methodist Hospital, Houston

But it is the Dunn Tower at Methodist Hospital in Houston, designed by Morris Architects of Houston and completed in 1989, that marks the culmination of the decade's upheavals. The $68-million building is a 600,000-square-foot, 338-bed hospital addition with special-care suites and sixteen operating rooms; its facade is aggressively postmodern, using symmetry and pedimented roof forms to achieve visual separation from its late-modern neighbors, such as the Scurlock and Smith towers. Its ground-floor interiors are exceptionally hotel-like. Besides the lobby furniture, there are tall potted bamboo trees, polished granite floors, a fountain with a nude-on-a-dolphin sculpture, a vaulted skylight, even mezzanine balconies of the kind usually found just outside a hotel ballroom; these lead, in fact, to meeting rooms for visiting groups. Staff members, in business attire, act like exceptionally solicitous hotel functionaries, ready to carry your luggage and fetch you a cup of coffee while you wait for the admitting staff to check whether your insurance policy will be adequate.

The architects have appropriated imagery from vacationland to help consumers part with their money and that of their insurers; to do so, the architects have suppressed all visual evidence of medical technology and doctors. Before, patients relied on doctors to make them well; now, patients were to rely on a concierge to make them comfortable. But beyond the lobby lies the maze of patient-care wings, laboratories, and operating rooms, where things are the same as before. In point of fact, patients have little more effective choice, and they are certainly not like hotel guests in anything but the most superficial sense. But, in constructing a whole environment in contradiction of this simple truth, architecture fulfilled the role assigned to it in almost every building type during the 1980s, that of cloaking reality in anxiety-soothing myth, so that a given institution could set itself apart in the market.

Given current trends in both technology and payment systems, buildings like the Dunn Tower will probably be popping up regularly around the country. It is hard to say what will become of the luxurious imagery in which this building is wrapped, however, if government officials and consumers ever devise an effective means of both providing access to medical care and controlling costs.

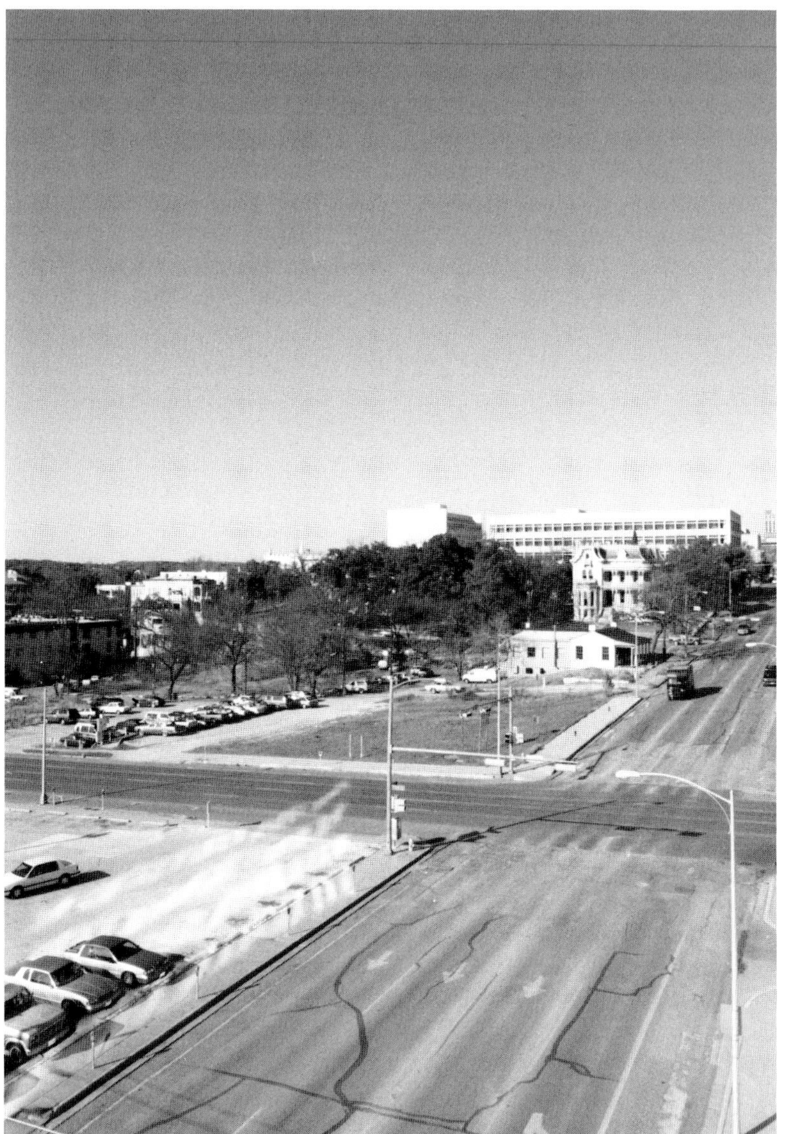

The former site of the Alamo Hotel in Austin, cleared by Lamar Financial and cursed by Tony Hearn

6
Plans and Curses in Downtown Austin

Except for that of J.R. McConnell, perhaps the most emblematic real estate story of the 1980s concerns an unbuilt project intended for a site at the corner of West Sixth Street and Guadalupe in downtown Austin, which was occupied until 1984 by the Alamo Hotel. The hotel, which was inexpensive, was often used by social-service agencies to shelter some of the homeless families that were arriving in downtown Austin in growing numbers. It also had a bar that was a popular place to hear local bands.

In 1984, the Alamo Hotel site was acquired by a subsidiary of Lamar Financial Corporation, the holding company for Lamar Savings of Austin and other savings institutions around the state. Lamar Financial announced plans in July of that year to tear the hotel down and build in its place Lamar Financial Plaza, a $125-million project including a twenty-seven-story tower, designed by architect H.C. Hwang of Houston, and a fifteen-story hotel. Lamar Financial would occupy a third of the tower.[1]

The day the hotel was to be torn down, however, an evangelist named Tony Hearn, operator of the Angel House mission, showed up and circled the site, pouring a blood-like liquid (made of oil and food coloring, accord-

Austin's Sixth Street, 1991

ing to Hearn) onto the sidewalk. Hearn claimed the hotel "in God's name, for the poor to have a place in Austin," and cursed the site, saying that, if the hotel was indeed torn down, the land "will never yield a profit to anyone who holds it."[2]

Despite this warning, the hotel was razed; the lot stood empty and there was no further word on the planned complex until February 1986, when Lamar Financial's chairman, Stanley Adams, announced that Kumagai Gumi, a Japanese construction company, would finance and build the project.[3] There was no reason, at the time, to question the truth of the announcement, although Adams had begun acting in what some saw as an excessively eccentric way, even for an S&L magnate. Not long after the Kumagai Gumi announcement, Adams notified Texas regulators that he planned to open the first savings and loan on the moon. The puzzling news releases continued: In July 1986, it was announced that RDC International of Houston, owned by architect Hwang, had bought the property (along with a high-rise trade center in Canton, China) from Lamar Financial, which would remain a partner in the project. The picture came into focus that

Office buildings on Loop 360, part of the fringe development that gave Austin the country's highest vacancy rate by late 1987

same month, when federal savings-and-loan regulators filed a civil suit against Adams and other Lamar officials, charging them with illegal real estate and stock transactions. (Lamar's later collapse cost taxpayers over $1 billion.) Lamar Financial's headquarters, the feds alleged, was to have been built on the proceeds of land flips and kickbacks, by an institution that had been looting federally insured deposits.[4]

In 1989, Adams was indicted on criminal charges of bank fraud by federal prosecutors. Defying what he said were false accusations, he filed to run in the 1990 Democratic gubernatorial primary, listing his occupation as "alleged white-collar criminal."[5] Later that year, he retained Richard "Racehorse" Haynes to defend him against criminal charges. As his trial approached in 1991, Adams received a letter from Tony Hearn offering to intercede with what Hearn called "the Source" to get Adams a reprieve if Adams would rebuild the Alamo Hotel for use as a single-room-occupancy hotel for the transient poor.[6] Adams apparently refused; in November 1991, he pled guilty to two of the charges.[7] The Alamo Hotel site remains a parking lot, and not a particularly busy one. Most of it is covered with grass.

Sinclair Black's vision of downtown Austin, proposed in 1981

Stanley Adams was not the only person with unrealized visions for downtown Austin. At the start of the 1980s, downtown Austin had a poky kind of vitality that was unique in the state. There was, as yet, little rush to build skyscrapers, but there was a modestly strong base of activity. Sixth Street was a zone of restaurants, night clubs, and artists' lofts, while Congress Avenue, the broad boulevard connecting the State Capitol to the Colorado River, had two old but active hotels, two department stores and several smaller retail shops (including two bookstores), a surprising amount of pedestrian traffic, and several rehabilitated historic structures (including the 1876 Tips Hardware Building by J.N. Preston, restored by Bell, Klein & Hoffman in 1981 for Franklin Savings Association, an S&L that made a name for itself by locating its branch offices in adapted historic houses and nineteenth-century commercial buildings).[8]

Institutionally, the city in the 1980s was riddled with the problems that had surfaced earlier in other Texas cities, including developers besotted with leverage, like the characters who were already visibly creating debacles in Houston and Dallas, schemers willing to treat other people's money as if it poured from a tap. The mythmaking machinery, from the local monopoly newspaper to the paid public-relations companies, kept the public media full of the message that local princes were working selflessly to make the city prosperous for all. The city government was gridlocked by neighborhood-group politics and the flood of money that roared into the city as development opportunities dried up elsewhere in the state. The mayor and city council, elected every two years, yawed between no-growth and pro-growth majorities that made city policy easy pickings for any group of developers willing to work behind the scenes and take a long view.

Such a long view, it seemed, had been reached by city officials and a significant number of developers, in the early '80s, with an apparent consensus supporting a vision of downtown in the future as a low-rise, high-density zone of animated courtyard buildings and pleasant walkways. This, it was hoped, would attract back to downtown the developers who were throwing up glass-skinned mid-rise buildings along the outlying highways, particularly Loop 360 and the northern part of Highway 183, fast enough and with little enough prescience about the market that by the late 1980s Austin would have the highest office-vacancy rate in the country.[9] A low-rise, high-density downtown represented a kind of master-planning utopia to the energy-conservation-activist architects who proliferated in the universities in the late '70s and who worshiped "the sustainable city," an architectural response to the spiraling energy costs of the preceding decade. It represented a similar utopia to their spiritual heirs, the postmodernist architects of the 1980s, who carried on the vision even after energy prices fell, captured by the moral force of its echoes of the supposedly more humane historical city, of the sort that Austin had been so recently.[10]

Architect and University of Texas professor Sinclair Black of Austin had articulated this vision in considerable detail in a feature in *Texas Architect* magazine in 1981, laying out the possibilities for planned growth in the sixty-square-block warehouse district that lines the southern edge of downtown between Fourth Street and the Colorado River. Black proposed zones for government, housing, and offices, all in energy-efficient courtyard buildings.[11] Black's architectural proposals were often kitschy, but at least he was trying to provide a unifying vision that included a public realm to balance the increasingly privatized spaces of the city. As it turned out, almost none

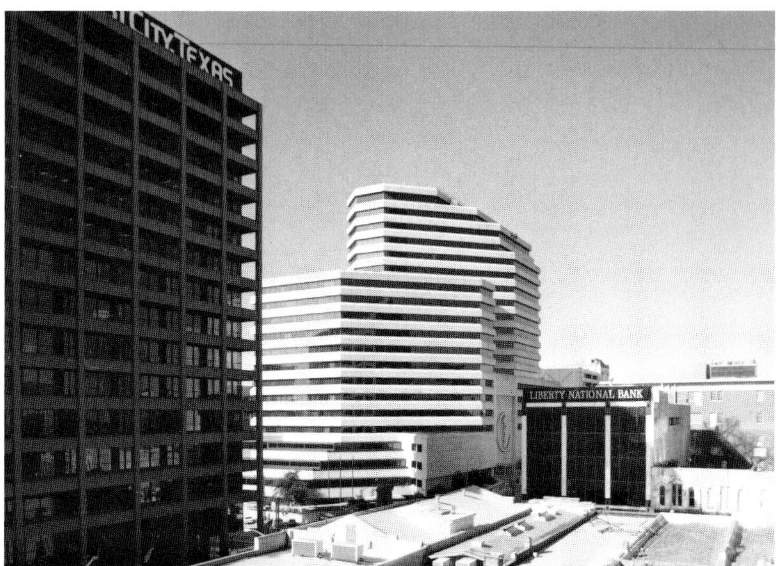

First City Centre (1984), by Holt + Fatter + Scott

of what Black proposed came to be built. Black's firm, Black, Atkinson & Vernooy, with offices in a rehabilitated warehouse, was part of a small movement of theaters and bars into the area, but not enough to create a critical mass.[12]

Black suggested building a complex of city offices that had been planned sporadically since the early 1970s to consolidate city offices spread throughout buildings all over the downtown area. This would save the city $1 million in rent annually, a figure that threatened, at the time, to climb throughout the 1980s. Black's suggested municipal-office complex would be sited, for reasons of civic symbolism, at First Street and Congress. City officials decided that consolidating offices would be a good idea, but they quickly switched sites and began talking instead about building on city-owned property several blocks to the west, adjacent to the current one-story city hall.[13]

In 1982, the Austin city manager sent out requests for proposals for a city-hall design-build package with vague specifications about site, financing, and program, and, at the end of the year, two projects were recommended as acceptable choices to the city council: developer Robert Barnstone's plan, with a schematic design by Austin architect Robert H.

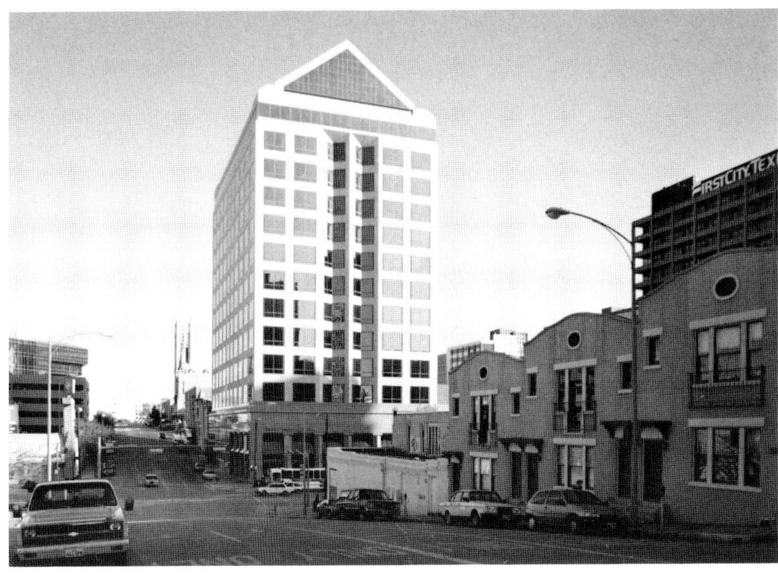

Capitol Center (1983), by Skidmore, Owings & Merrill

Jackson; and a plan by the Watson-Casey Companies, prepared by Austin architects, Holt+Fatter+Scott. These recommendations were thrown out, however, and in September 1983 the city council announced yet another competition, with a first stage to pick a schematic design and a second stage to pick a development team and final design.[14] Black, Atkinson & Vernooy won the first-stage competition in early 1984, and the Watson-Casey Companies, teamed with BAV, was chosen to develop the project later in the year. A land swap was involved, and private development would be used to pay for some of the city's construction costs.[15]

The teaming of BAV and Watson-Casey seemed to take care of most objections. Watson-Casey, one of downtown's most active developers, had worked on a number of projects with Holt+Fatter+Scott, with undistinguished results. Their First City Centre, at Congress and Ninth Street, with its bands of glass and beige stucco, was bulkily horizontal. And it was compared unfavorably to the gable-roofed Capitol Center at 10th and Congress, designed by Skidmore, Owings & Merrill, Houston, and even to Morris Aubry Architects' One American Center at Sixth and Congress, a building

One American Center (1984), by Morris Aubry Architects

Republic Square (1987), by Holt + Fatter, with Rossetti Associates

Model showing staircase of the unbuilt Laguna Gloria Art Museum downtown, by Venturi Rauch and Scott Brown

apparently patterned on the cannister-shaped gold-glass headquarters of the lead tenant, American National Bank (later MBank, later Bank One), two blocks west on Sixth Street (1973, by Lloyd, Morgan & Jones of Houston).[16] BAV, it was thought, would design a more appropriate city hall, while Watson-Casey would have the expertise, the deep pockets, and the political savvy to make the complicated deal succeed.

It didn't work out that way. Negotiations for the municipal-office complex dragged on while the market softened and the city got cold feet—with property values and rental rates falling, it no longer made financial sense, at least in the short run. The city council was looking for a way out of the deal with Watson-Casey by 1986, when the development company defaulted on a payment for First City Centre; the council broke the city's contract with the company and dropped the idea of building the complex.[17]

It happened that Watson-Casey, at the time, was involved in yet another deal with the city; the company was to donate land for a new downtown home for the Laguna Gloria Art Museum, designed by the celebrated Philadelphia architecture firm Venturi, Rauch & Scott Brown; city bonds

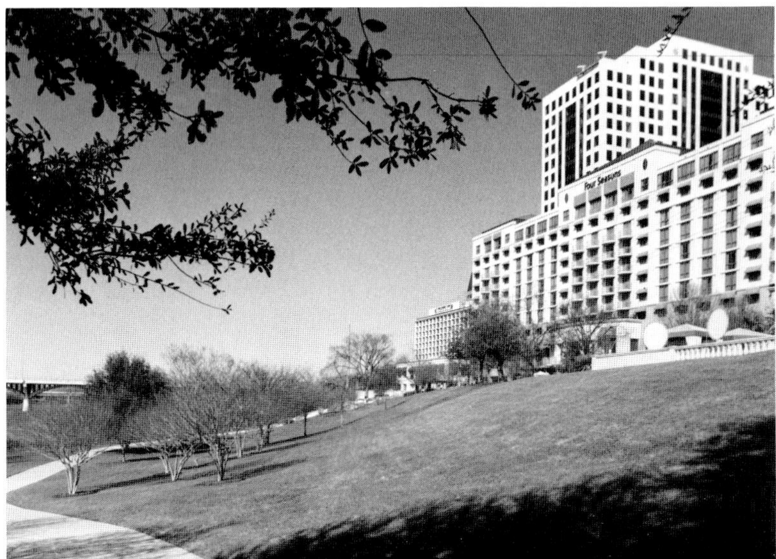

San Jacinto Center (1986), by HKS with the WZMH Group and Richardson Verdoorn

would pay for construction, and the city would pick up some operating costs. VRSB's design, for a quarter-block site facing Republic Square that would eventually be surrounded by tall buildings, went through several versions;[18] all of them echoed such important but small-scale Austin precedents as Cass Gilbert's 1910 Battle Hall on the University of Texas campus and Hugo F. Kuehne and Robert Leon White's 1933 Austin Public Library building. [19]

The new museum and Denise Scott Brown's proposed Barcelona-like *rambla* of pedestrian spaces, which seemed to take off from some of Sinclair Black's earlier suggestions, would have been an amenity for Watson-Casey's Republic Square development (the first phase, with stepped mid-rise buildings in concrete and black glass with red-steel mullions and other accents, was designed by Holt+Fatter with Rosetti and Associates and completed in 1988), something along the lines established by the promoters of the Dallas Arts District, which was to have been raised above the standard market by the Dallas Museum of Art and Meyerson Symphony Center. [20]

Watson-Casey went bankrupt and defaulted on the land to be donated to the museum, however, and the land ended up in the hands of NCNB,

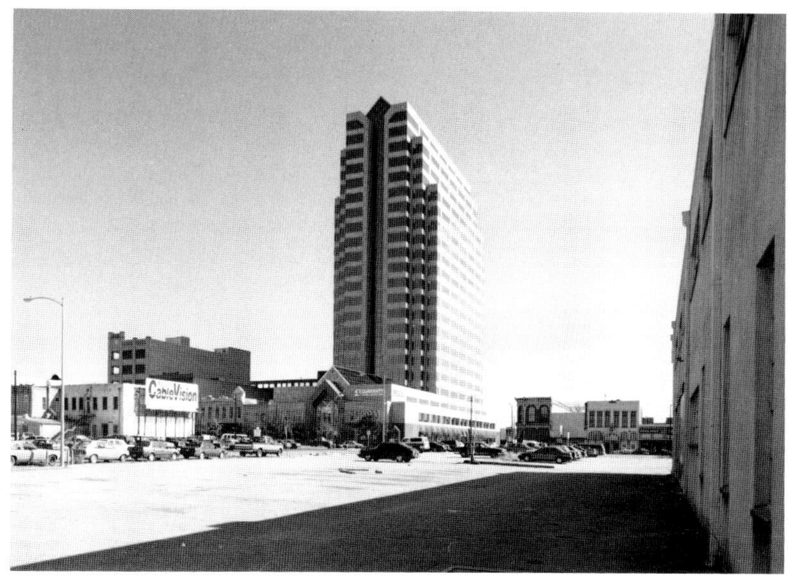

300 Congress (Temple-Inland building, 1986), by Hylton-Dey

which had bought out the failing RepublicBank, lender on the deal. City officials insisted that NCNB drop a clause in the contract governing the Laguna Gloria property, stipulating that title to the land would revert to the bank if the city used it for anything except a museum in a specified period of time. NCNB refused, and the project died in 1990. [21]

Besides Republic Square, the one major project in the warehouse district begun during the 1980s was the Austin Convention Center (designed by the Austin Collaborative Venture, a joint venture composed of Page Southerland Page, Lawrence W. Speck Associates, and Villalva Cotera Kolar, with Lawrence Speck as lead designer). Located in an area that Black had suggested should hold multifamily housing, the convention center nevertheless proposes to reorder downtown into a notional monumentality, creating a triangle of civic nodes with the Capitol and the old city-hall building.[22] The rest of the development in the warehouse district during the decade took the form of suburban-type office towers on or near Congress. The best of these was San Jacinto Center, including the Four Seasons Hotel and its accompanying San Jacinto Tower office building (1987, by HKS

One Congress Plaza (1987), by Taylor/Lundy/HKS

with the WZMH Group of Dallas as design consultants, and the landscape architects Richardson-Verdoorn of Austin). The buildings were largely unoccupied for the first several years; they succeeded better as formal objects because of the project's integration with and privately funded expansion of the public Town Lake Park.[23] Otherwise, the new buildings in this zone are a dismal lot.[24]

The Trammell Crow Company's 300 Congress (now the Temple-Inland building, by Hylton-Dey Architects of San Antonio and completed in 1986) is skinned in subtly colored glass and granite. It has space for shops along Fourth Street (although these were never rented), and its three-story lobby incorporates an entrance to the historic buildings along its northern side. The skylit lobby holds both the street line and the cornice line of its neighbors, while the tower itself is pushed back on the site to protect views of the Capitol. The massing of the tower, with the top floors seeming to fall away from a diamond-shaped crowning central window, which grows out of a strip of clear glass rising uninterrupted from ground level, recalls a fountain. It could also be inscribed within a parabola, a dynamic and interest-

101 Congress (1987), by HKS

ing geometric figure. Together, these qualities give the building a sense of presence. On the other hand, the use of that diamond-shaped crowning element (it's like a square tipped up on one corner) to generate the tower's peaked roofline, repeated over the lobby's entrance and echoed in plan by the columnar projections along the street wall, is a major problem; this is one of the most overused visual devices of the '80s, and proclaims a lack of visual sophistication. At the same time, the building's skin of slick granite panels is visually as thin as wallpaper, and at street level the sealant between the panels is emphasized at the triangular corners that jut toward the sidewalk, so that it, not the granite, reads as the most important element. Vandals or drivers have shattered several of the panels.

The architecture firm Taylor/Lundy/HKS of Dallas gave the nearby One Congress Plaza (now named for its lead tenant, Franklin Federal Savings, an institution cobbled together from the hulks of Franklin Savings, First Federal Savings, and several other failed S&Ls) its ziggurat-like profile in aggressive response to a 1931 provision of the city's zoning code, which requires buildings over two hundred feet tall to step back one foot for ev-

Salvation Army headquarters (1988), by LZT Architects

ery three feet of elevation. With its heterodox shape, the building has a certain presence, and its sunken plaza, with a water-wall fountain, is a surprisingly pleasant space. But, twisted as it is on its site to dominate the visual field south of the Capitol, One Congress Plaza projects a belligerent and small-minded purposefulness, made immeasurably worse, after Franklin Federal moved in, by the installation of garish blue neon piping on each of the building's triangular stepbacks. Up close, also, the poorly worked-out patterning of the granite skin panels is apparent.

The tower called 101 Congress (a.k.a. One Tamale Place, after the tiny tamale stand that occupied the corner throughout the 1970s) was developed by Lincoln Properties and designed by HKS of Dallas. The tower portion of the building resembles an unexceptional suburban high rise (thus without much presence); it has windows in copper-tinted reflective glass mounted flush with a polished-red-granite curtain wall, under a stepping series of peak-roofed floors that give the building a pyramidal quality. But the base of the building, which addresses Congress Avenue and First and Second streets, is more ambitious and more troubled. The ground floor has two projecting wings that frame a landscaped entry court on Congress, like a Palladian villa; the front entry has a central arch, outlined in stone panels over the doors. But the putative stones, if they were real, would crash to the ground under their own weight. One might think this was an attempt at a deliberately anxiety-provoking mannerism, except that the evidence of other mistakes is all around. For example, the corner columns of the windows facing Congress, implied by the design, have been forgotten, and the windows and garage entries on the side elevations, despite attempts at disguise, don't line up. It is in this sense that 101 Congress fails not only evaluations of external quality but the test of its own logic. Having taken the trouble to erect a facade of ostentatiously classical stonework in honor of RepublicBank, which was to have been the lead tenant (perhaps echoing the RepublicBank Center Houston, with its almost convincing stone details), as well as to attract the law firms later lured into the building from older structures by bargain-basement rents, the architects ended up with entries and other elements that contradict the rules of masonry construction and the simplest canons of classical composition.

For long-term social impact in recasting the image of downtown Austin, however, the '80s towers on Congress Avenue are relatively unimportant. The most significant project of the 1980s was, in fact, the new Salvation Army headquarters, ably designed by LZT Architects of Austin within a stringent budget and completed in 1989 facing Neches Street, two blocks west of the elevated section of Interstate 35, between Seventh and Eighth streets.[25]

Before 1986, the Salvation Army was headquartered on Second Street, east of Congress, in a portion of the warehouse district relatively cut off from the rest of downtown by its continuing industrial uses and the flow of east-west traffic. The homeless men who made up most of the mission's clientele lined the streets in the area each morning, offering themselves for day-labor jobs; otherwise, they had little interaction with the rest of downtown Austin. That situation began to change at mid-decade, however. With the Texas economy in collapse, compounded by the effects of the national recession of the Reagan years, which produced unemployment higher than at any time since the 1930s, the number of indigent and homeless people coming to Austin for its relatively numerous construction jobs and its mild weather swelled. The Salvation Army was swamped, and the needs of its clients, now including high proportions of women and children, could no longer be met at its old headquarters. Salvation Army officials approached the city for help, and a solution, including such options as moving the mission into a neighborhood south of the river (vigorously opposed by the neighborhood's residents) was debated for months. Then a businessman swapped the city land for the Neches Street site, the new facility was designed and built, and the Salvation Army moved.

The effects of the move, coupled with the collapse of the overbuilt downtown Austin real estate market after 1986 and changes in East Austin, were dramatic. Homeless people hung around the sidewalks and curbs around the new mission during the day (the building was open to them only at night), patronizing the liquor stores and day-labor agencies that sprang up around it; many slept both day and night under the freeway overpasses with their shopping carts and cardboard shelters, and gradually they claimed the Waller Creek park and the lower end of West Sixth Street as their own. At the same time, building after building on Congress Avenue, vacated by bankrupt banks, S&Ls, jewelry and clothing stores, and hotels, was boarded up; in a strange phenomenon, other businesses used the empty windows as display spaces for bluebonnet paintings, driftwood-and-dried-grass arrangements, and makeover sessions in which women were photographed in feather boas and dresses with plunging necklines. Homeless men moved into the doorways, sleeping and urinating under these new advertising displays. And rival gangs from east of the freeway started occupying the downtown area at night, spray-painting graffiti and spraying each other with bullets, sometimes in broad daylight.

The vision of the early 1980s was that downtown Austin had to be controlled as it shucked off its old-fashioned, slightly shabby wrappings and became one of the second-tier cities that business writers touted as the key to America's future, in the process jumping up a level in density and economic activity, with hordes of new middle-class office workers rambling the rambla, enjoying the therapeutic prospect of civic unity portrayed by the juxtaposition of state and municipal governmental offices, even living downtown.

The irony is that, although there were more people living in downtown Austin in the late '80s than there had been in decades, fewer and fewer of the people using downtown fit the profile foreseen by architects and builders a decade earlier. There were still stores and law firms and offices in the

Storefronts on Congress Avenue, 1992

downtown towers, with thousands of people working in them, but the workers had become less and less of a presence. At any time other than rush hour or noon on a given weekday in 1991, traffic had become so sparse that one could jay-walk with impunity across nearly any intersection in downtown Austin, and be virtually assured of meeting only homeless people in the process. The plans to revitalize the area, like the worst examples of '80s architecture, had either canceled each other out or failed the test of their own internal logic. The curse of evangelist Tony Hearn, placed on the developers of a single site for ignoring the effects of new development on the homeless, had spread to embrace the city's core. After the 1980s, the lenders who had hoped to create monuments to themselves were almost all swept away, and the homeless remained. In the future, the task of rebuilding downtown Austin cannot be achieved unless the homeless are taken into account. That this is also true of downtowns in Dallas, Houston, San Antonio, and other Texas cities makes Austin less a special case—or Tony Hearn better at curses than even he believed.

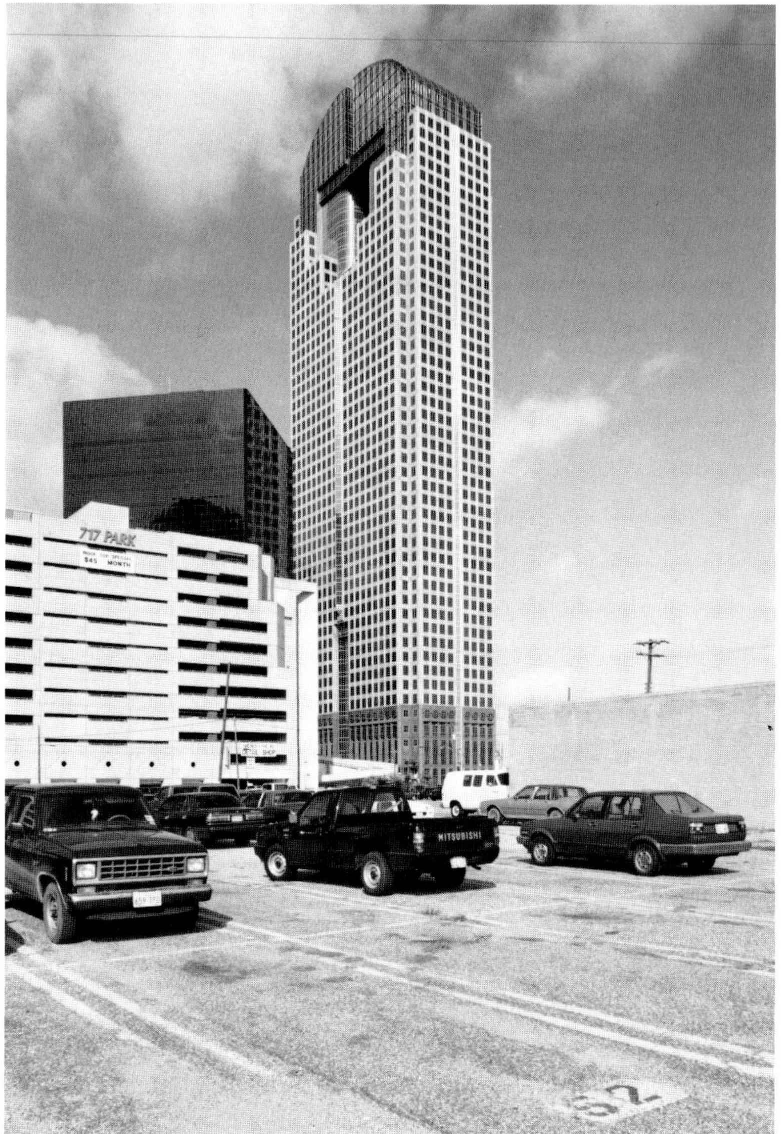

Texas Commerce Tower at 2200 Ross, Dallas (1987), by Skidmore, Owings & Merrill

7
Tower Tops in Dallas

By slicing the roofline of Pennzoil Place (1976), Philip Johnson of Johnson/Burgee Architects made the uniqueness of a tall building's top the primary symbol of the architectural progressiveness sought by sophisticated clients.[1] Modernist style had advanced through a rejection of old-fashioned elements, such as masonry construction, double-hung windows, or representational ornament. The aesthetic of tall buildings came to rely upon a number of technical devices: nonrectangular floor plates; the use of concrete, steel, and glass in ways that emphasized such constructional features as steel's neutrality in dealing with compression and tension, glass's slickness, or concrete's rough texture; the use of cantilevering and other bold structural effects for juxtaposing building parts, usually into asymmetrical compositions; even, indeed, the use of a flat roof.

By the late 1970s, all these techniques had become shopworn, and thus valueless, to Gerald Hines and others among the top tier of Johnson's potential clients. The symbolic role of the top was cemented in public consciousness when Johnson appeared on the cover of *Time* magazine in 1979 holding a model of his split-pediment-topped AT&T Building; although the building itself was not completed until 1983, the image projected by the model (and Johnson's celebrity status) came to stand for what those small parts of the public who cared saw as a breath of fresh air in American architecture.[2] As architectural historian Stephen Fox wrote, this new architecture "made a bid for public awareness, offering itself with surprisingly successful results as a new form of mass entertainment."

Around the same time as Pennzoil Place and before AT&T, Johnson/Burgee designed another remarkable building, the IDS Center in Minneapolis, completed in 1975; its contribution to the skyscraper type was the elaboration not of the top but of the corners. The motif of rippled corners didn't make much of a public impression—it looked like just another of the oddball geometrical abstractions that architects seemed to enjoy—but to developers around the country it represented a new path to competitive advantage.[3]

Air-conditioned, elevator-serviced office buildings typically used to have only four corner spaces per floor, each with the potential for two walls containing windows, to use for offices (fewer if they were "flatiron" buildings, or shared a wall with another structure). The IDS Center, by comparison, had thirty-two corners per floor. In the spatial language of American corporate hierarchy, offices with windows represent a step up in status from a mere cubicle in a building's interior; a view makes an office less like the "cell in a honeycomb" described by Louis Sullivan in the 1890s. And corner offices are reserved for the most important people on any given floor. For the purposes of a speculative developer hoping to attract corporate clients, choosing to construct a building like the IDS Center meant that it could be marketed to corporations in need of many corner windows—those, for example, with the growing number of mid-level managers who were a feature of the late-'70s mania for conglomeration. The arrangement also made the floor space more flexible, so that many tenants, each with a different set of bosses, could have expensive corner offices of their own.

Only a few sawtooth-cornered downtown high rises were built in Houston by major developers for major clients in the 1980s: the 1980 First International Plaza (now the 1100 Louisiana building),[4] for example, developed by Gerald Hines and designed by Skidmore, Owings & Merrill of San Francisco and 3D/International of Houston in rose-colored granite and glass. The style really caught on in suburbs all over the state, where building after building featured a stuttering plan that could house a maximum number of branch managers, law-firm partners, and small-scale entrepreneurs.

The preferred locus for the sawtooth style was downtown Dallas. Here, however, things were slightly different: By mid-decade, when the downtown Dallas building boom was in full swing, there had been a psycho-stylistic shift. The differences between postmodern towers and what Charles Jencks calls "slick-tech" serrated towers were usually described at this time in terms of "style wars"; groups of architects, said to subscribe to different aesthetic principles, were considered to be responsible for each style. The description is true, but sketchy—it leaves out the fact that stylistic differences were upheld by and helped make visible a de facto stratification of the office-tower market.

Buildings for clients interested principally in cost were built with sawtooth edges, and their supporting role on the skyline was underscored by the fact that they were, by and large, designed by local architects.

Thus, for example, HKS designed the Lincoln Plaza for Lincoln Properties (1984), a granite-clad flatiron building on a triangular block with nine projecting bays on its western facade (the building also has excellent landscaping, by Myrick, Newman, Dahlberg of Dallas). And JPJ Architects of Dallas designed the many-cornered Interfirst (now NCNB) Plaza, a gracefully slender building completed in 1985, which, at seventy stories, is the tallest building in Dallas. Interfirst Plaza's mirror-glass facade makes it nearly invisible by day, but it dominates the whole of downtown Dallas at night by means of its argon edging, which makes the central business district look as if it were bathed in the glow of a computer monitor. Sikes Jennings Kelly of Houston designed Pacific Place

Interfirst Plaza (1100 Louisiana building), Houston (1980), by Skidmore, Owings & Merrill and 3D/International

Thanksgiving Tower, Dallas (1983), by Harwood K. Smith & Partners

(1983), a brick-clad mid-rise with flush-mounted windows, which ripples open to an accordion-like glass facade next to the restored Majestic Theatre. Most striking of all is Thanksgiving Tower (1983),[5] designed by Harwood K. Smith & Partners for the Hunt brothers (who were then about to go bankrupt trying to corner the world silver market); Thanksgiving Tower explicitly borrows the blunt-sword profile of the IDS Center. David Dillon, in his 1986 book *Dallas Architecture 1936-1986*, called it "crude" and "expressionless," a "fourth-generation knockoff," typical of a "That's good enough for Dallas" mentality that hurt the city's reputation.[6]

Buildings for the top level of the market, on the other hand, were designed with the symbolism that Johnson had crystallized in the AT&T Building's top; they were conceived more as theatrical set pieces than as spatial arrangements, and the commissions for their design went to out-of-state star architects.

Thus, for example, developer Cadillac-Fairview's Momentum Place (completed in 1987 and named before Momentum Bank, formerly Mercantile National Bank, transmogrified itself into MBank and MCorp, a holding company) was designed by John Burgee Architects with Philip Johnson (HKS of Dallas was associated architect), in a vocabulary, drawn from the early American republic and ultimately from Augustan Rome, befitting a Dallas bank on the rise. The tower has unbroken central bands of glass on each elevation framed by masonry-faced panels with narrow windows and quarter-round stepbacks, all capped by copper-clad barrel vaults (which, like all high-rise tops, conceal a collection of equipment for elevators, air conditioning, and telecommunications). The elevations are blandly colored and lack vertical tension and scale. And, as a "unique" end to a columnar base-shaft-top skyscraper arrangement, the architects' barrel-vault roof seems like a non sequitur; barrel vaults, one is reminded in looking at the top of Momentum Place, are low-scale-building elements that are most expressive as parts of a building's interior and that imply an additional overhead weight; they certainly don't seem to work as the "capital" of a tripartite tower scheme. Repeated over the lobby of the banking hall, however, the barrel vault is constructed in convincingly detailed masonry and makes for a truly grand interior space, unmatched by any other commercial building in Texas since the

Interfirst (NCNB) Tower, Dallas (1985), by JPJ Architects

Far Left: Lincoln Plaza, Dallas (1984), by HKS

Left: Pacific Place, Dallas (1983), by Sikes Jennings Kelly

1930s, except perhaps the architects' RepublicBank Center in Houston. The Dallas office of Houston-based 3D/International designed MBank's offices (except for Johnson/Burgee's building envelope), along with the lobby space, which features a bridge crossing what was billed as the largest securities-trading floor west of Wall Street. The major public spaces and the executive areas were finished in multicolored stone and cherry paneling, with deep-cut moldings that would have done an early-twentieth-century eclectic architect proud. Perhaps unremarkably, when Banc One of Ohio (the holding company) took over MBank in a tax-subsidized rescue operation, its officers reacted with revulsion to this we-are-the-new-Rome magnificence, preferring that the interiors reflect instead their status as home to a mere branch bank. The space leased in the building, which was renamed Bank One Center (the Texas institution was given a "k" in place of the new parent's "c"), was cut back. The bank's own offices were redesigned in a more restrained vocabulary by RTKL Associates, Inc., of Dallas, and MBank's lavish executive dining suite was relinquished to the landlord. Most interestingly of all, the place of honor in the building's top floors was taken over by Bonnet Resources, the "junk bank" created by federal regulators to manage and liquidate MBank's remaining "nonperforming" properties.[7]

Lobby, Momentum Place (Bank One Center), Dallas (1987), by Johnson/Burgee, interiors by 3D/ International

The buildings that best show the role of the building top in creating architectural distinction, however, were designed by the Houston office of Skidmore, Owings & Merrill, headed by architect Richard Keating. The office, despite its relatively provincial location in Houston, had used a quick embrace of the postmodern style to leapfrog into the ranks of architects worthy of prime commissions, at least from the Trammell Crow Company, which was beginning to embrace high-style architecture for the Dallas market. The

Momentum Place

LTV (Trammell Crow) Center, Dallas (1985), by Skidmore, Owings & Merrill

three buildings SOM Houston did in Dallas in the mid-1980s are certainly theatrical, but more interesting is the fact that their scenographic aspects were blended by the architects with market-related features that bridge the gap between the top level and second tier of bankers, lawyers, executives, and other potential renters.

The first of these was the LTV (now Trammell Crow) Center, a fifty-story tower in dark gray granite and flush-mounted glass, completed in 1985. LTV Center was treated in the architectural press as proof that the client, the Trammell Crow Company, previously best known for working only with architects who would "draw the plans" to fit the formulas set by the company's iron-willed and leaden-handed founder, had joined the followers of Gerald Hines and embraced high-style architecture as a marketing tool.[8] This change was ascribed to Harlan Crow, who took over management of the company's real estate developments in downtown Dallas from his father in the early 1980s; LTV Center was his first big project. Family habits die hard, however: When interviewed by Jim Murphy of *Progressive Architecture* magazine after LTV Center was completed, Harlan betrayed some nostalgia for the good old days. "Rick Keating designed the building," Harlan said. "I'd love to say we designed it and he drew it, but the building is to his credit, not ours." LTV Center attracted the right tenants, he added, "because of what we [brought] to the table."

LTV Center was the first commercial building in the Dallas Arts District, and it has a pyramidal top, a first in what David Dillon has called "Dallas's crew-cut skyline." The top projects the power of the lead tenant, the LTV Corporation, in pharaonic terms, and it actually makes visual sense—a relatively rare achievement—given the overall obelisk-like form

Pavilion, LTV Center

seen from the nearby freeway belt. In fact, LTV Center is a more complicated building than it seems from a distance; it is a shallow cross in plan, so it has eight corner spaces per floor. And each facade has four projecting triangular bays, which reinforce the tower's verticality and give it sixteen more corners. Any hint of second-tier architecture associated with these bays, however, is thoroughly obscured by the building's plaza and lobby spaces. The plaza, which resembles a Renaissance theorist's fortified city in plan, has nice hedges and flower beds (landscaping was by Myrick, Newman, Dahlberg of Dallas) and a startling collection of bronze statuary, including works by Maillol, Bourdelle, and Rodin. A stairway, split by a dark but cheerful-sounding fountain, leads from the building to Flora Street, which is fronted by a gable-roofed pavilion for exhibitions and performances. The lobby of the building is finished in brass, African hardwoods, and marble, and has a Rodin sculpture under a central dome; around this and the elevator is arranged a two-story rotunda with cafes and stores. Despite the glitziness of the space, the lobby is the building's biggest disappointment, since, despite the formality of the spatial arrangement, these high-renting retail outlets are allowed to crowd in on the building core and there is neither open horizontal space nor soaring vertical space to complete the experience of arrival. LTV Corporation, one of the 1970s conglomerates for whom the many-cornered big office building was best suited, went bankrupt not long after the LTV Center opened, collateral damage of a decade in which big corporations were bought by raiders so that their pieces could be sold off. The building was renamed Trammell Crow Center, and it continued to rent well.

SOM Houston also designed Renaissance Tower, a remodeling project for LaSalle Partners of Chicago and the real estate arm of Prudential Insurance, completed in 1987.[9] Renaissance Tower was previously known as the First International Building, usually called Interfirst II, designed by Hellmuth, Obata and Kassabaum and Harwood K. Smith & Partners and completed in 1975. Interfirst II was also called the Dos Equis building in Dallas, because the structural cross-bracing under its gray reflective glass cladding was outlined in incandescent lights by night, forming stacked X shapes. SOM replaced the curtain wall (the incipient failure of the reflective glass was the principal reason for the remodeling) with new reflective glass in different colors, adding a pattern of vertical stripes and criss-crossing diagonals that exhibited the structural pattern by day. The architects simply improved the modernist boxiness of the building, instead of updating it by applying historicist details. The biggest change was made on the roof, where the architects both rationalized and whimsified the rooftop clutter. It was turned into a kind of erector-set city, with pyramid-topped towers framing a pyramidal arrangement of equipment houses (one is reminded of a number of '20s-era towers, and of Michael Graves's proposed rooftop aediculae for the celebrated Portland Public Service Building), topped by a tall central tower, also with a pyramidal top. There is another pyramid at street level, a gleaming glass-skinned space frame over an underground food court to the west of the building's base. By reskinning the building and, most of all, by adding the rooftop elements and the ground-level amenities, the owners and architects took what was becoming a class-B office building and converted it into class-A space, at a fraction of the cost of new construction.

The last of SOM Houston's big-top '80s buildings in Dallas (and the last major project before SOM Houston was dismantled because of the

Texas real estate collapse, with Keating and part of the staff moving to Los Angeles and other partners such as Craig Hartman moving to Washington, D.C.) was Texas Commerce Tower at 2200 Ross, developed by Trammell Crow and completed in 1987.[10] Texas Commerce Dallas is an unforgettable building, mostly because it is so strange. What the architects had done with minimal means in Renaissance Tower and with a practiced if heavy hand at LTV Center becomes at Texas Commerce Tower a kind of exuberant garishness; the tone was perfect for a city desperately denying that it was being engulfed by a debacle.

Renaissance Center (Interfirst II), Dallas, resurfacing (1987), by Skidmore, Owings & Merrill

LTV Center had set a pattern for addressing the street with parklike spaces (which, along with the garden at the Dallas Museum of Art, the landscaped space around Lincoln Plaza, and the waterworks of Allied Bank Tower at Fountain Place, had helped transform Ross Avenue into one of the nicest urban walks in the state), and Texas Commerce Tower takes this landscaping pattern even further,[11] to a point of slightly febrile compression. The tower is separated from the street by a 1.5-acre plaza with a broad lawn, set with six ground-level fountains, that slopes down a water-wall fountain under street level (where there was supposed to be a station for the Dallas Area Rapid Transit subway, which never materialized). Several of these fountains are very striking—they recall yoni-lingam fountains found in Hindu temples to Siva. The lawn is framed by topiary hedges (predicted to grow to a height of twelve feet) carved by paths and heavy concrete seating areas. At the northeast corner is a 17,000-square-foot domed rotunda in blue-green metal and glass, planned for a restaurant but as yet unused. A walkway from the street is framed by concrete flag-pole pylons (like those at Pei's City Hall), leading to the glass-domed entry. Curving stairways rise

San Jacinto Tower, Dallas (1983), by John Carl Warnecke & Associates and Beran and Shelmire

to blue-green domed entries on the second-floor corners of the front elevation; these are intended to invite pedestrians to use the skybridge links to neighboring buildings.[12]

The two-story base of the building itself extends this excess, with its angled columns, different-colored stone, window patterns, and rondels. The rose-gray granite-clad shaft of the building, with its deeply notched side elevations producing eight corners, is more sober, and it includes a number of elements that tie it to its context, such as triangular piers rising toward the roofline, and a vertical stripe of glass on the side eleva-

The Crescent, Dallas (1986), by Johnson/Burgee and Shepherd + Boyd

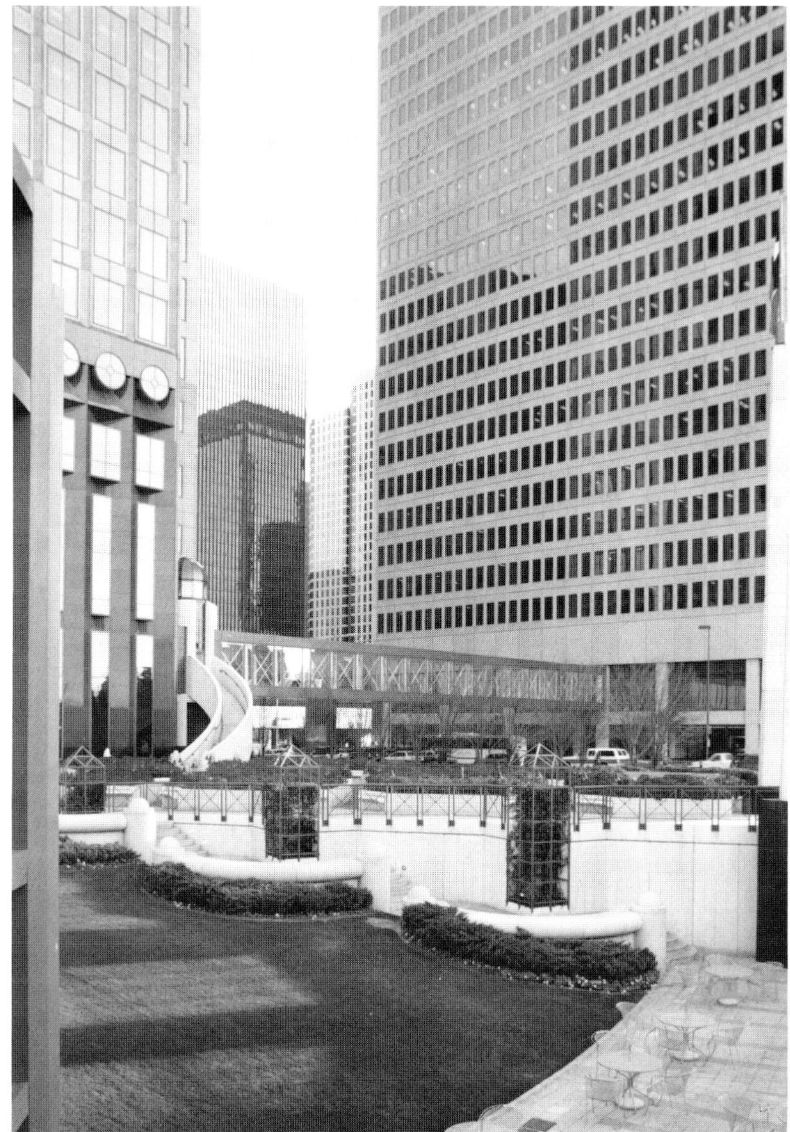

Texas Commerce Tower, Dallas, plaza and base

tions, recalling the bays on the LTV Center; window proportions that harmonize with the adjacent San Jacinto Tower (1983, an adaptation, by John Carl Warnecke & Associates of San Francisco with Beran and Shelmire, of the Embarcadero Center in San Francisco); and even an apparent reference to The Crescent hotel-office complex, across the freeway, in the facade's concave glass strip above the main entry.

Then there's the top, which in elevation makes Texas Commerce Tower the most penis-like public building in the state, built confirmation of feminist complaints about phallocentric culture. This is surely inadvertent. . . or maybe not—perhaps the orifice and those yoni-lingam fountains in the plaza are intended as a metaphorical balance. Leaving aside the anatomical readings, the profile would be enough to make the top "unique" in the marketing sense, but there is the additional complication of the 74-by-27-foot keyhole cut in the center of the upper stories (metaphorically again: a subincision?). Other architects had been experimenting with classical and Gothic references in their postmodern tops; SOM went for a more viscerally entertaining effect, somewhere between the 1960s Japanese metabolists and sci-fi fantasy, like its unsuccessful flying-saucer-as-diamond-ring entry

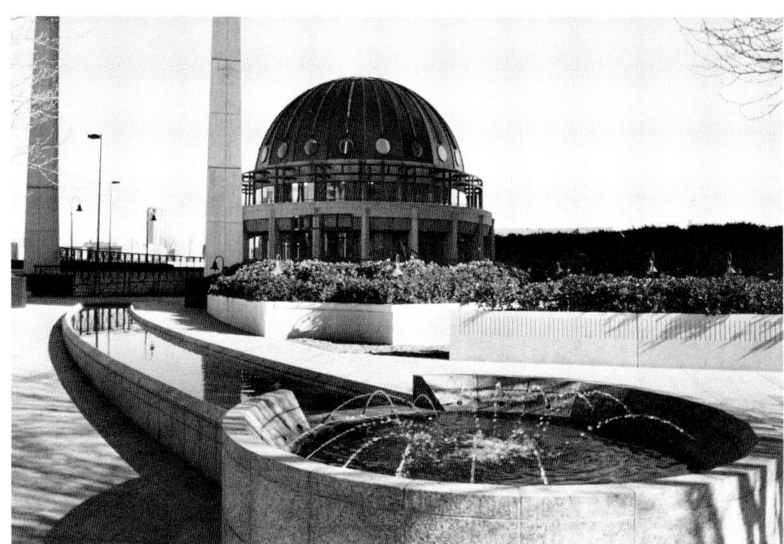

Fountain in plaza, Texas Commerce Tower, Dallas

in a 1982 competition to design the world's second-tallest tower for Houston's Bank of the Southwest, an institution that began to fail immediately after the competition and was sold with the blessing of federal regulators to Mercantile Bank.[13]

Again, the remarkable fact about the hole is not its picturesqueness, but its pragmatism. The hole at the top of the building, as SOM's engineers had demonstrated mathematically in the 1970s, reduces the building's wind load. By elaborating it, with the trickily detailed stone-and-glass segments of the upper stories, the architects are making a big idea out of what is essentially a profit-enhancing measure for the developers—lowering the wind load reduces the size and cost of the structural system, while the skylobby in the keyhole reduces the number of lower-floor elevators. The top of Texas Commerce Tower is thus the farthest thing from the arbitrary artiness that the *Wall Street Journal* derided while it was going up.[14] Instead, it gives a high-style expression to the tactics that speculative developers have always made central to their business—holding down "first-dollar costs" and maximizing leasable space. SOM had found a new way, generated by the logic of construction itself, to combine cost cutting with theatrical image-making.

It's an image we're likely to be seeing for a long time, too. Texas Commerce Tower may be a monument to last a hundred years, since there may never, in the lifetime of anyone around today, be another boom to obscure or replace the downtown towers of the 1980s. First of all, there are no more Texas banks that need to build monuments to themselves. Then there is the fact that the focus of corporate building has shifted almost entirely to the suburbs. Finally, there are population trends. As Clayton Stone, a former vice-president of Hines Interests (who worked on such well-known Hines projects as Interfirst Plaza, Texas Commerce Plaza, and RepublicBank Center in Houston, United Bank in Denver, Norwest Center in Minneapolis, and Ravinia in Atlanta), told a business luncheon in 1983, absorbing the office space built in Texas between 1975 and 1983 was going to take thirty years, and the rest of the country would be similarly overbuilt by the end of the decade. "They booed me then, but I was right. We ignored the most basic population data and business trends," Stone says. "It was the availability of money that drove the market, not underlying need."

Allen Parkway Village, Houston

Housing rehabilitated with the assistance of the Enterprise Foundation, Dallas

8
Public Housing and Welfare

The debate over race relations, political and economic equity, and governmental activism inherited from the 1970s crystallized in the 1980s around questions concerning publicly subsidized housing, particularly in the large, government-run housing complexes on the margins of the country's inner cities. The matrix of antinomies, split along liberal-conservative, urban-suburban lines, ran as follows:

Is a public housing complex part of society's safety net, or a monument to persistent racial and economic segregation? Shelter for the temporarily destitute, or a permanent trap that funnels poor families into underfunded schools and social services, denying poor people access to jobs and all but guaranteeing their destruction?

Do the people who live in public housing constitute a community whose mutual support has helped them withstand impossible conditions and whose political cohesion offers the only hope for equitable treatment? Or do they want nothing more than to escape to better lives? Are they victims of a society that keeps them trapped in circumstances from which they won't be allowed to escape? Or are they morally warped by and thus deserving of their poverty?

Do politicians who support public housing speak legitimately for the disenfranchised? Or do they help keep people dependent on life in a "liberal plantation" only to perpetuate their own careers? Are those who oppose continued funding of public housing the prophets of a new paradigm of equal opportunity? Or are they new-fashioned racists, covering for white America's wish that the urban poor would cease their importunings and disappear?

While these questions bounced around in public-policy debates, the numbers of the poor were increasing, and the demand for public housing grew: A study by the federal Department of Housing and Urban Development (HUD), unpublished but quoted in *The Dallas Morning News* in 1985, estimated that although some 3.7 million households lived in publicly subsidized housing of some kind in 1984, more than 80 percent of those eligible for housing assistance received no government help, and the percentage was growing. The number of apartments available to lower-income households was shrinking by the thousands each year, and new apartments coming on line were priced too high for an increasing number of renters. At the same time, low-income families were forced to devote more and more of their income to rent; according to the U.S. Census Bureau's annual housing survey for 1985, 22 million American households, mostly renters, were spending more than the benchmark figure of 30 percent of their pretax income for housing, while an additional nine million households lived in substandard or overcrowded dwellings. At the same time, the number of homeless people living on streets and in temporary shelters was thought to be growing at 10 percent per year; officials of the U.S. Department of Housing and Urban Development estimated that there were 250,000 homeless people in the U.S. in 1985, while studies funded by big-city mayors and others consistently posited a figure ten times higher.[1]

The underlying problem, according to housing analysts, was that the purchasing power of working-class households was dropping while their housing costs were rising. Working-family incomes fell almost 19 percent between the late 1970s and the late 1980s; working full time for minimum wage had come by the 1980s to supply only 74 percent of the poverty-level income for a family of three. Meanwhile, rental rates rose nationally an average of 16 percentage points more than the general rate of inflation. The rising tide of the Reagan years swamped a large number of boats.[2]

The Reagan administration, ideologically opposed to public housing from the start, cut HUD's budget authority for direct housing subsidies from $30 billion in 1980 to under $14 billion in each of the next eight years. Their aim, officials said, was to replace the programs for constructing and rehabilitating dwelling units with a more-cost-effective program of vouchers that could be used to rent free-market apartments of the tenant's choice, ideally away from the public housing ghetto. The voucher program, however, was funded at a tiny fraction of the need. The administration also experimented with a program of selling off properties to tenants (although, by mid-decade, only a fifth of the twelve thousand units available for sale in the pilot program had actually sold, and administrators testified before Congress that they hadn't figured out how to make the program work).[3] Each year, the Reagan administration proposed cutting the budget for housing subsidies to $8 billion, then $5 billion, then $500 million; when the funds were restored by Congress, officials under HUD Secretary Samuel Pierce, Jr., embarked on a building campaign (still at less than half the funding level of 1980) that resulted in corruption and mismanagement in which both Republican and Democratic party officials were implicated, typified by the payments to former Secretary of the Interior James Watt to grease the wheels for HUD funding of a private developer's project.[4]

In Texas, the debate over public housing focused on the West Dallas Housing Project in Dallas and Allen Parkway Village in Houston, both of which were administered by entrenched local housing authorities, operating on HUD grants.[5] To be sure, all the nation's local housing authorities were forced to cope with rising demand and shrinking operating funds. The authorities in Houston and Dallas, in fact, won awards from HUD for managing portions of their programs. But neither fulfilled its mandate to provide decent, desegregated housing for the needy, and both were the subjects of controversy.

In Dallas, the controversy centered on a federal civil-rights suit aimed at reopening and desegregating thousands of abandoned units in the 3,500-apartment early-'50s West Dallas housing complex (three adjoining public housing projects that make up the country's largest low-rise complex). The suit attracted attention among specialists nationally. A number of well-known architecture, planning, and financial consulting firms studied rebuilding the projects as apartment complexes with tree-lined walks and

West Dallas housing complex

clearly defined private and public spaces, and proposed restoring the area's infrastructure, which had declined along with the projects' population. In 1989, Federal Judge Barefoot Sanders ordered the local housing authority to demolish all but 1,200 of the complex's 3,500 units, to rehabilitate the rest, and to build new dwellings "in areas where minorities are not now concentrated." To date, however, none of the required work has started.[6]

In Houston the controversy over Allen Parkway Village has been even more protracted and more public, perhaps because the issue was not housing but big-dollar private development, a much sexier topic. Allen Parkway Village, on the western edge of downtown Houston, was built in the 1940s as San Felipe Courts, a 1,000-unit whites-only complex. Designed by a joint venture of Houston's architects, led by MacKie & Kamrath, the complex exemplified New Deal attempts to help the urban working class (even in its segregation). By the early 1980s, when it was listed in the National Register of Historic Places, it remained the largest of Houston's public housing complexes, and it remained segregated, its residents now being almost all black or Indochinese. The project's location made it uniquely valuable, and housing authority officials began considering a succession of schemes to sell it off for large-scale private development; in the process, they stopped maintaining units, allowing them to become uninhabitable one by one until by the late 1980s fewer than a hundred apartments were occupied. The last residents, led by Resident Council President Lenwood E. Johnson, filed legal challenges aimed at forcing the authority to reopen the abandoned units.[7]

The situation was at an impasse until early 1990, when a consortium of developers led by Cullen Center and American General Insurance announced that they wanted to gain control of and redevelop the six hundred acres between Cullen Center's properties at the western edge of downtown Houston and the American General corporate campus, nearly a mile away on the bank of one of the city's few scenic amenities, Buffalo Bayou. The project, to be called Founders Park, would include not only Allen Parkway Village but the Fourth Ward, which in turn included the Freedmen's Town Historic District (settled by former slaves in the 1860s and the center of community life in black Houston until the 1940s; it was declared a National Register historic district in 1984). Like Allen Parkway Village, Fourth Ward had become one of the city's most blighted areas in the 1980s, its narrow streets, shotgun houses, and bungalows uncared for by either absentee owners or city authorities, who rushed to raze all unoccupied buildings to prevent their use as crack houses.

Proponents of Founders Park said it would bring growth and needed tax revenues back from the suburbs and save Houston's downtown from strangulation by a widening band of slums and an increasingly wasteful pattern of sprawl development. Critics, including neighborhood residents and a group of architects and preservationists writing in *Cite* magazine, charged that Founders Park would kill the remnants of a once-thriving black neighborhood and destroy some of the city's most important historic fabric.[8] Whose city is this, they demanded: the people's, or the developers'?

The plan for Founders Park called for clearing away Allen Parkway Village, the Harris County Hospital District's vacated Jefferson Davis Hospital, and almost all of the housing stock in Fourth Ward. In their place, the developers would build some 2,500 units of new housing, 440,000 square feet of retail space, and 1.3 million square feet of offices and retail space. The preliminary planning concepts for Founders Park were developed by

Part of the Founders Park proposal for replacing Freedmen's Town with new middle-class housing, by Carr, Lynch, Hack & Sandell; Sikes, Jennings, Kelly & Brewer; and Walter P. Moore Associates

Houston architects Phillips & Brown in association with EDI Architects and with Miami-based Andrés Duany as consultant. These concepts followed the planning ideals of the pedestrian-scaled, hierarchical, neotraditional urban village (itself one of the few seemingly populist-progressive achievements of 1980s postmodernism) pioneered by Duany, his partner Elizabeth Plater-Zyberk, and Leon Krier at the Town of Seaside, Florida. They called for a new middle-class neighborhood, modeled on colonial Savannah's mosaic of public squares, with close connections to a central business district. (Duany quit soon after the project was announced, and Sikes Jennings Kelly & Brewer of Houston became lead architects for the project, working with Carr Lynch Hack & Sandell of Boston.) But making such a place marketable, according to proponents, would require moving almost all of the five thousand present residents out, and it would require further public assistance in the form of the city's authorization to create a tax-abatement district to finance replacement of the area's infrastructure (the Texas Legislature passed a specially crafted bill in 1989 to permit just such an authorization) and the right to seek condemnation of property for acquisition.[9] In exchange, the developers said, they would dedicate a third of the revenue generated by the special tax district (estimated at $120 million) to creating twelve hundred units of public housing. Of these, two hundred would be in Founders Park, while the rest would be distributed as "scattered-site" housing in other neighborhoods. In addition, selected historic buildings would be moved to a small park, and a local school building would be converted into a museum of the area's black heritage, an idea suggested previously by community groups.[10]

Opponents have stuck to their earlier suits and have worked to prevent the housing authority from selling Allen Parkway Village. The historic designations of both Allen Parkway Village and Freedmen's Town give opponents an additional means to tie the project up in litigation, causing delays that might force the developers to turn to other, more conventional projects.

The tide seems to be running against the community activists, however; their opponents have deep pockets and political clout, and many of Houston's black leaders, including most of the black city council members, have decided against siding with Fourth Ward residents. Previously, Fourth Ward community activists had an ally in Congressman Mickey Leland. But with Leland's death in 1989, former State Senator Craig Washington was elected to represent the district, and Washington, who until his election to Congress served as legal counsel to the housing authority, cosponsored the bill in the Texas Legislature that made it possible for Founders Park to qualify for designation as a tax-abatement district. The 1,200 units of public housing promised by Founders Park proponents would be built in Washington's district, and he said that he sees this not as a loss but as a net gain for the community.[11]

The most significant factor working against supporters of Allen Parkway Village (and the West Dallas housing complex as well), however, is the evaporation of support for public housing in general. Activists can continue to argue, with justification, that they are working to uphold society's safety net, the only hope of a viable community for bettering itself and gaining political equity given existing circumstances. But fewer and fewer people want to listen. Despite opposition in Congress, the Reagan and Bush administrations have been better representatives of the American majority's Malthusian feeling about the poor—that they most need the scourge of their own poverty because destitution is evidence of moral failure, and that any public money spent on housing is wasted. The majority is supported in this view, after all, by hard evidence of the HUD-funded public housing system's failure.

The middle class in Texas in the 1980s had been reduced by the swings of the real estate market and the contraction of its income and purchasing power to a single set of concerns: preserving and replicating itself and its favored environments. There is nothing wrong with such an impulse, except that where any group that didn't serve such purposes gets in the way, they must be swept aside. The plight of poor neighborhoods in the 1980s, particularly those where public housing was clustered, showed what might be called middle-class insatiability. Either they were ignored, or a bureaucracy of developers and bankers and architects got together and appointed themselves guardians of the future for land that other, less important people held. "Look," they said. "We are envoys for the prince, and we're going to turn this substandard neighborhood into the most wonderful thing in the world—middle-class workplaces and houses. Everyone prospers."

Those benighted lower-class stick-in-the-muds who didn't buy into the myth typically reacted to such blandishments by organizing themselves politically to resist. It happens that a number of civil suits leading to tougher federal enforcement of voting-rights laws had reshaped Texas municipal politics by the 1980s, decreasing at-large representation on city councils while enlarging the power of neighborhood groups to bring pressure on district council members. These changes made it easier for inner-city residents to win temporary battles. But in the long run it threatens disaster.

Municipal government had once been the locus of handshake deals between upper-crust businessmen-politicians, like the ones that put D/FW Airport next to Ben Carpenter's family ranch, or those that in the 1920s gave the Stemmons family control of the Trinity River bottom land west of downtown Dallas, allowing them to evict the area's black tenants and begin developing what is now the Dallas Market Center. These evictions were among the proximate causes of the building of the West Dallas housing complex, showing a connection to the pattern by which private capital pushes long-term problems onto the taxpayers, a pattern reenacted at a much grander scale in the late-'80s S&L bailout.

In the 1980s, with minority inner-city residents more vocally represented at the city, state, and congressional levels, things suddenly got much messier for dealmakers. Some, like the Founders Park backers, made the necessary accommodations to work with the new political forces. Others—Ben Carpenter, for example—reacted by declaring themselves shocked to discover that politicians were involved in backroom agreements and self-serving decisions. Politics, they declared, was bad; only the economic sphere, where people acted rationally, was valid. This viewpoint, which served the interests of most of the princes working the suburban real estate market, was adopted as home truth by the majority of suburban middle-class homeowners. It had a powerful effect, allowing its adherents to divide cities into realms of light (the economically determined, free suburbs) and realms of darkness (the politically enslaved, redistributionist inner cities). In such conservative, suburb-dominated cities as Dallas and Houston, only the legal inertia of public housing and the electorate's general apathy have kept the programs from being wiped out. The fact that activists in Houston have been reduced to fighting proposed evictions by using historic-preservation designations—among the flimsiest devices in the legal system—is a measure of just how tenuous their position has become. And each battle over public housing stoked the gathering crisis of legitimacy of Texas cities in the 1980s.

The tragedy of it is that, while housing activists have been reduced to fighting already-lost battles, the middle class was undercutting its own long-term interests. The decade saw many of the suburban working-class neighborhoods and lower-middle-class neighborhoods that make up so much of the fabric of Texas' cities whittled away. Falling family incomes, decaying infrastructure, absentee ownership, crime, industrial incursion, and other destructive forces pushed houses, blocks, streets, and neighborhoods from decline to decay to abandonment throughout the 1980s; each increment of loss meant both bigger problems and decreased resources for the officials trying to hold their cities together.

Some small-scale experiments at neighborhood stabilization were tried. In Houston, the housing authority sponsored a "scattered-sites" house-ownership program, in which abandoned suburban houses that had returned to HUD in foreclosure were sold to public-housing residents who passed an extensive screening and training program. This program was bitterly resented by groups in many of the target neighborhoods, however, and while it was clearly a success for the several hundred people served, it was a drop

El Mercado del Sol, Houston

in the bucket compared with the tens of thousands (many of them actually too poor to be eligible) who needed help.[12] Other paint-up, fix-up programs were tried, but were similarly swamped by the size of the problem; officials estimate that between five and ten thousand dwellings in Dallas, for example, had slipped from poor to substandard condition during the 1980s.

The most important change in neighborhood stabilization to come out of the 1980s, however, was almost invisible. This was the growth of a movement to create Community Development Corporations (CDCs).

The first CDC was conceived in the Bedford-Stuyvesant area of New York City during the 1960s by the Ford Foundation. Intended as tools of what writer Neil Pierce has called "corrective capitalism," CDCs are small nonprofit agencies shaped from the membership of existing community groups working on housing and other social services. Because they are heterodox creations, their access to funding depends on adherence to a high hedge of regulations; their advantage is that they are bottom-up development vehicles, investing in their own neighborhoods and able to assess needs close at hand. Since the 1960s, CDCs have

Harrisburg Plaza, a CDC project in Houston supported by LISC

been formed in 2,500 different neighborhoods around the country, and have been responsible for construction or rehabilitation of tens of thousands of housing units.[13] New York, Boston, Baltimore, Philadelphia, and San Francisco each have dozens of CDCs; in Boston, CDCs were responsible for 80 percent of the new low-income housing created in the late 1980s.

CDCs only got going in Texas in the late 1980s, however. Before then, banks were too busy with the real estate boom to worry about areas in need of community redevelopment; indeed, according to housing analysts, the Texas banks and S&Ls actively red-lined working-class and poor neighborhoods, since they were thought to represent such risky investments. A group of volunteer organizers from the Ford Foundation-affiliated group called Local Initiatives Support Corporation (LISC) began working with community groups to set up CDCs in Houston, and the Enterprise Foundation, a similar nationwide CDC support group created and run by retired festival-market developer James Rouse, set to work in Dallas. But little was accomplished at first.[14]

In part this was because there was little experience with community development in Texas, and most of it was bad. The best-known examples of community development gone sour were in Houston. First there was El Mercado del Sol, an enormous enclosed retail mall created from a group of abandoned warehouse buildings at a cost of over $10 million; the new mall was supposed to serve its largely Mexican-American neighborhood and to simultaneously draw shoppers from the office buildings of Houston's CBD, from which it was separated by an elevated section of IH-59. The second project was Palm Center, a renovated '50s-era shopping center in a mostly black area of southeast Houston. Actually, although both El Mercado and Palm Center were undertaken with federal community-development funds, neither could properly be described as a community-development project. Rather they were public-works projects, created by the availability of federal funds and the need to make a show of serving the constituencies of influential city council members rather than by any requirement of the community. Both were also based on the mistaken notion that rent subsidies would be a major factor in the profitability of small retail businesses, when rent typically represents less than 15 percent of a retailer's costs. Lack of customers, which proper attention to market surveys would have anticipated, doomed both projects. Both generated widespread negative publicity for community development in the city, and they contributed to considerable animosity among CDC activists, lenders, city officials, and others who might have been allies.[15]

Despite this background, one of the first CDC projects in Houston undertaken with LISC assistance was another retail center, the Harrisburg Plaza, built on the site of a former Sears store in a predominantly Hispanic neighborhood east of downtown, developed by Weingarten Realty for the East End Progress Association CDC. Here, the bottom-line discipline of the CDC style, focused on demonstrable need within the community, paid off: The project has been fully rented and profitable since it opened.

The visibility of Texas CDCs to the lending community and their ability to undertake projects took a dramatic turn for the better in 1989, although the change had less to do with the accomplishments of CDCs than with a new toughness among banking regulators. In 1989, federal officials in the Texas region announced that they would begin enforcing the Com-

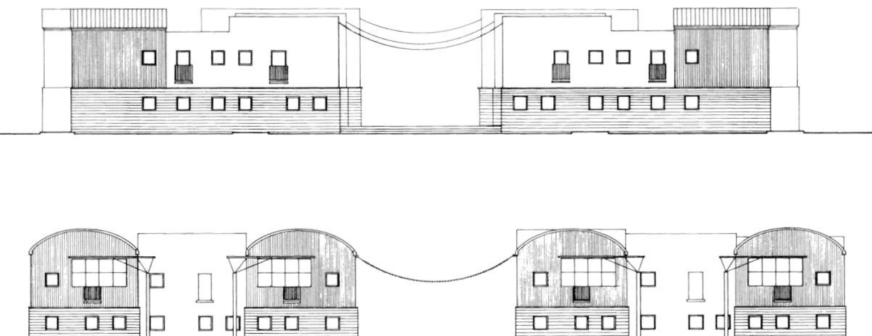

Housing project, Houston, organized by the AAMA CDC, designed by Cisneros Associates

munity Reinvestment Act (CRA), a 1970s law requiring banks to stop redlining. The CRA had been a force in community development in the Northeast since the '70s, but it had been ignored by both institutions and regulators in Texas. The financial institutions became really serious about the CRA when Congress in 1989 passed the S&L bail-out legislation, which contained a provision requiring all institutions to make their CRA-compliance records public; suddenly forced to find vehicles for community-development loans (or have their ability to expand challenged by community activists armed with this new access to previously concealed information), banks and S&Ls discovered that CDCs present not only chances to comply with the law but good, carefully monitored, low-risk investment opportunities. [16]

Since then, half a dozen groups have begun projects for housing in Houston neighborhoods, while the Enterprise Foundation is nurturing a dozen more in Dallas.

While the actual contributions of CDCs in Texas are minuscule, their potential stems from the opportunity to solve the political and social impasse of the 1980s over public housing. They represent a convergence of '60s-liberal ideals of community control and '80s-era neoconservative jargon of "empowerment," particularly the type of empowerment that gets people out of housing complexes for which the government is footing the bills each month. Publicly subsidized housing, tied firmly to local markets, could be given new political life by CDCs.

For that to happen, however, policymakers will have to solve the problem of scale that has always troubled CDCs: Focused so closely within neighborhoods, CDCs are good for creating fifty-unit housing complexes and small economic-development projects that help stabilize threatened neighborhoods, but it is difficult to imagine them turning into a vehicle for providing the million or more new publicly subsidized low-income housing units that reliable projections say are needed nationwide.

That may change. Enterprise Foundation founder James Rouse, it happens, headed a congressional task force that reexamined federal housing policy in the late 1980s, the recommendations of which formed the basis of the Gonzales-Cranston Housing Act of 1990. In it, a considerable chunk of federal housing funds are set aside for CDCs. Additionally, a group of major charitable organizations announced in early 1991 that they were raising over $500 million for CDC-developed housing projects nationwide, and that the Federal Home Loan Mortgage Corporation had pledged $100 million in low-interest housing loans to CDCs.[17]

Where is architecture in all this? Everywhere and nowhere. Commentators have been foolishly conflating public housing policy and contemporary architecture ever since Charles Jencks chose the destruction of the Pruitt-Igoe housing complex in St. Louis as a symbol for what he called "the death of modernism."[18] Repeated by postmodern theorists with amazing regularity, this canard became a handy club with which to beat architects throughout the 1980s; the Prince of Wales dusted off a version of it when he embarked on his antimodernist campaign in the late 1980s. Jencks wrote erroneously that Pruitt-Igoe was given an award by the American Institute of Architects, arguing that this made all American architects somehow complicitous in the project's failings. But of all the factors that contributed to the breakdown of Pruitt-Igoe, the deficits of circulation and space-planning cited by Jencks are surely among the least significant. What the housing authority that paid for Pruitt-Igoe wanted was a place to concentrate poor people and their problems, and that's what the architects designed. The resulting social situation and the complex's flimsy construction and atrocious management made the project untenable. Architecture was one aspect of the failure, but to call it the principal one only serves to let the real culprits off the hook.[19]

The CDC movement offers architecture a chance to ameliorate the toxic effects of big bureaucracy and the thinking that elevates economies of scale over community cohesion. It offers the opportunity to work in a potentially less oppressive social situation to those architects willing to accept the small commissions that community-development projects promise. The resulting architecture—good, bad, or indifferent—will develop project by project.

By the lights of 1980s development in Texas, then, CDCs offer nothing exciting. They assemble tiny increments of change in struggling environments, barely perceptible except to those within the community who care. There is none of the flash and drama that would have animated the activities of, say, condo-builder Danny Faulkner, S&L chairmen Stanley Adams of Lamar Savings and Raymond Hill of Mainland Savings, Houston developer J.R. McConnell, or the other high-flying heroes of the free market who helped create the Texas real estate boom of the 1980s. But then, it is well to remember that, according to U.S. Census Bureau figures, the sum of federal funds expended on subsidized housing in Texas during the 1980s was $1.334 billion.[20] That's only a little more than it will eventually cost to bail out Lamar Savings, about as much as the cost of Mainland Savings, and only about a fifth as much as the takeover of RepublicBank by NCNB cost taxpayers. In aggregate, in fact, it amounts to less than one percent of the cost to the national treasury of the total Texas real estate bust, the pinnacle of American middle-class socialism.

Entry court at Solana (1989), by Legorreta Arquitectos with Leason Pomeroy Associates, with landscape design by Peter Walker Martha Schwartz

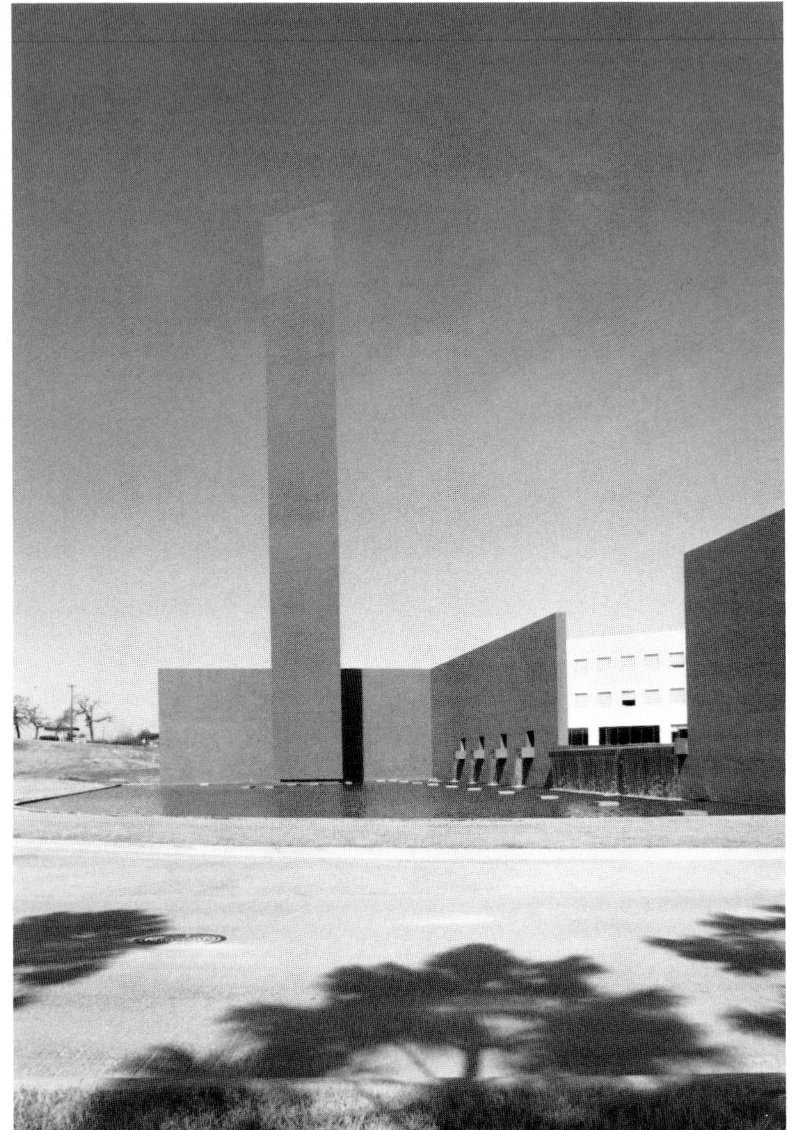

9
Solana, the Electronic Hacienda

Roads for motorized transport have been creating the urban form in Texas since the 1920s, when the relatively compact city of the progressive era began stretching out along Main Street, on to the "miracle miles," beside the highways, and eventually on to what Douglas Harvey has called "the 51st state: the Interstate." With each decade, people were able to travel farther and faster. Each increase in general mobility brought a new set of shocks as the boundaries and physical relationships of Texas cities proved more and more elastic. Each layer of roads created bigger clumps of development, with bigger parking lots, leading to local increases in density along with lower densities citywide. There were the quaintly diminutive motor courts from the 1930s and '40s, like those still to be found on South Main in Houston or South Congress Avenue in Austin; these were followed by enclosed shopping malls, such as Gulfgate in Houston from the 1950s and NorthPark in Dallas from the 1960s, as well as such mixed-use residential, office, and commercial developments as Houston's Sharpstown and Dallas's Park Central. In the 1970s, the state's cities were encircled by eight- and ten-lane freeway loops, creating new opportunities for shopping centers and office parks that competed with downtown; the Houston Galleria was one of the most notable, and the trend continued throughout the 1980s in the creation of office parks and malls on LBJ Freeway in Dallas, Loop 410 in San Antonio, and Highway 360 in Austin. Indeed, it could be said by the mid-1980s that the center of any given Texas city was no longer in its central business district but in the area defined by the interstate ring highway.

But the opening in 1988 of Solana, a nine-hundred-acre office park projected to grow to seven million square feet of office space, straddling the tiny townships of Westlake and Southlake (combined population: four thousand) located just over twenty-two miles northeast of downtown Fort Worth, introduced something new.[1] Since the 1950s, growth has been generated by freeways; for Solana, by comparison, freeway access was necessary but not sufficient. Developed by a joint venture of the computer-maker IBM and Los Angeles-based Maguire/Thomas Partners Ltd. (which has been one of the development firms most interested in using high-style architecture to create a "point of difference" for its projects, and which was ranked as the country's largest developer in 1988), Solana was brought into being by proximity to Dallas/Fort Worth Airport, fifteen miles to the east, one of the prime east-west connectors in the U.S. air-travel market.

IBM officials decided in the early 1980s to move the company's key marketing operations from Westchester County, New York, to the Dallas-Fort Worth area because of its economic vitality, low land prices, pleasing terrain, and giant airport. (Some of IBM's other local Dallas offices were located for a time at Williams Square in Las Colinas, the office park that presaged Solana in drawing on airport proximity.) They wanted a place where international prospects—"the Iacoccas and other big clients, especially from Latin America," according to one of the architects—could fly in, and, after a short drive, hear a concentrated sales pitch without the complications and distractions of an urban setting.

Even ten years ago, such a regional headquarters or marketing center might have been set up in a city or close-in suburb, and the urban ambience through which the potential customers would have passed would have contributed to the image of technical sophistication and business savvy that IBM wanted to project. But few companies these days are interested in projecting images of urbanity derived from loftiness and legibility. Today, only virgin countryside will do. As a creation in such a landscape, Solana portends an upheaval of scale in the physical geography of North Texas as dramatic as that represented by the first freeway malls forty years ago: What recently were cattle pastures and sorghum fields have been transformed into an air-travel hub connecting the U.S. with Central and South America in a borderless market.

As a physical presence, Solana is remarkable. It has more visual variety than a dozen typical suburban office parks, along with buoyant resonances of scale and detail that make the entire project work as an exceptionally cohesive whole. Perhaps the most remarkable aspect of the project is how Mexican it looks.

Solana was designed by a constellation of star architects and landscape architects, which included, at various stages, Ricardo Legorreta Arquitectos of Orange, California, and Mexico City; Mitchell/Giurgola Architects of New York; Peter Walker Martha Schwartz of San Francisco and New York; Barton Meyers Associates of Los Angeles; Leason Pomeroy Associates of Orange (listed, for contractual reasons, as architect of record for much of what Legorreta designed); the Los Angeles and San Francisco offices of Skidmore, Owings & Merrill; the Dallas offices of CRSS and PHH Neville Lewis; and HKS of Dallas. Consultants included Gerald McCue of Harvard University, Tina Beebe of Santa Monica, and hosts of others.

Developer Robert Maguire said in an interview just after the project opened that he and IBM wanted "a Southwestern design, and the historical Mexican influence in the region was something that seemed to tie it together"; he said also that in assembling the team he looked for people who would mesh with Ricardo Legorreta. Mexico's best-known architect, Legorreta describes himself as a disciple of the late Luis Barragán; his earlier work, including offices and factories for IBM in Mexico and several well-known resort hotels, is animated by his firm's modernized and supercharged versions of Mexican vernacular forms and colors. Maguire's choice of Legorreta is exceptional because Mexican architectural influences have almost always been denatured and ghettoized in Texas. The historical Mexican influence in the region is still routinely denied by the Anglo majority, perhaps because demographic change is making Mexican-American influence a growing threat to the majority's grip on political and economic power. It is doubtful that a Texas developer would have committed to Legorreta; most would probably choose to follow the path taken by Ben

Freeway underpass, Solana

Carpenter, who wanted Las Colinas's design to reflect a spurious "Spanish and ranching heritage." Certainly, Mexican-derived imagery had been treated as a sanctioned high-design style for a serious business entity nowhere else in Texas. Like Las Colinas, Solana is a landscape that recreates a history without the past one hundred years of Texas urbanism, but it audaciously links it to a design language that, for the first time, makes Anglo design style pay fealty to a competing Mexican tradition. The building of Solana may, in fact, mark a cultural turning point, providing a first signal that Mexican-Americans are no longer to be treated as outcasts in the world of business.

That said, however, it is nevertheless plain that Solana is a collaboration. Peter Walker of Peter Walker Martha Schwartz is credited with the project's biggest idea, an extraordinary deference to the landscape (while the plantings and water features of the landscape are the most truly poetic aspect of the entire project). Legorreta and Romaldo Giurgola worked out the treeline height limit that unifies all the buildings, along with the coordinated palette of materials and the scale of walls and openings that give the buildings such presence. And the two lead architects, Legorreta and

IBM National Marketing Center, Southlake, by Legorreta Arquitectos with Leason Pomeroy Associates

Mitchell/Giurgola, created complementary ways of bringing urbanity to the suburban office landscape.

A visitor's first glimpse of Legorreta's building ensemble is the Solana entry court, a square of dark stuccoed walls opening over the roadway and slicing into the turf of the underpass that marks the intersection of the project's looping central road with the state highway. This entry court, with its echoes of European and Mexican plazas and gates, announces that the typical relationship of road to project to landscape has been upended.

In the northeast corner of the entry wall, a tall purple triangular pylon stands in a pool of water. The composition, like the walls, is both stark and serene, paying homage to Barragán's famous residential courtyards. A narrow watercourse feeds the pool, drawing the visitor's eye to a cluster of low-scale, sand-colored buildings. This cluster is the IBM National Marketing and Technical Support Center, tucked among the irregular small clearings of Southlake.

The Marketing and Technical Center has a crawling floor plan and slanting wing walls that hide numerous surprises. These begin as one steps into

Entry hall, IBM National Marketing Center

the covered walkway from the visitor's parking lot, under a squared-off tower lit inside by a single punched opening five stories up. Beyond the walkway is a forty-foot-tall vestibule, its every rough-stuccoed inch saturated with a rich electric-blue color set off by light from the square windows at the top of the wall and contrasting with the sandstone-paved floor. To one side, visible through glass doors, is a "mist garden" for ferns and other tender plants. Beyond is a flight of wide stairs opening to a deep-yellow corridor, leading in turn to the back-office spaces, which are linked by deep arcades, dramatically shadowed corridors, vibrantly colored screen grids, and quiet pools.

Variations of the same strategies of slanting walls and startling interior vistas are used in two speculative office buildings and a new Marriott hotel in what is called the Village Center, just to the other side of the highway intersection from the Marketing and Technical Center. The Village Center is announced from the road by two pylons, one square and yellow, one cylindrical and pink, along with a tall, red-gridded purple pigeon roost. Here Legorreta has created an urban space that refers explicitly to the Mexican plaza form.[2] However, he uses office buildings, a parking garage, and a hotel[3] where traditional planning would have supplied a church, a city hall, and an arcade of shops. In a way, it's a shame the development didn't stop across the road. The plaza, with its thick planting, its pergola-covered parking shielded from the road by a concrete wall, and its thousands of brick pavers, is lavishly detailed. But it ends up looking like the disconnected model that it is, evoking not the joyous life that Legorreta obviously intends but an aching loneliness, reminding the visitor more of de Chirico than Barragán. A square formed by speculative office buildings in Texas,

Plaza, Village Center, Solana

barring some supernatural visitation, can never be what Legorreta makes it look like. People have complained that Legorreta's forms and colors are alien, meaning too Mexican-looking. A neighborhood group, whose members knew, even if the architects and developers denied it, that Texas' laws of cultural relations were being transgressed, unsuccessfully sued to get the colors toned down. Solana *is* a foreign element in the North Texas landscape. Beyond that, the real problem at the Village Center is not colorfulness but emptiness and functional neutrality. Legorreta's interiors qualify as successful adaptation, but his urban gestures can't escape the status of scenography. This is less the fault of his design than of the social poverty of the institutions designed for.

The suite of office buildings for IBM on the open prairie of the Westlake side of the project designed by Mitchell/Giurgola Architects (HKS of Dallas was associated architect) fit somewhat better. This portion of the project—six five-story office buildings, two parking garages, a computer building, and a cafeteria building—constitutes phase one of a three-phase, four-cluster group collectively referred to as IBM Westlake. The buildings

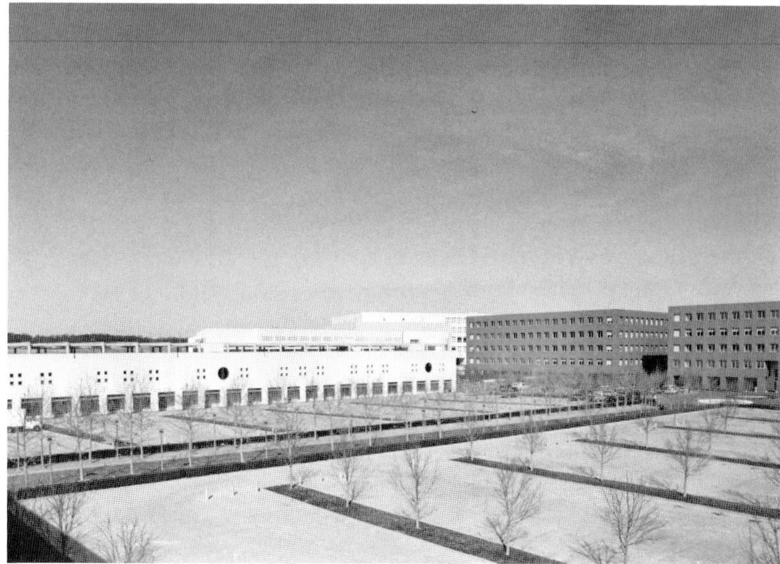

Parking garages, IBM Westlake, by Mitchell/ Giurgola Architects

of phase one, with their reddish-brown-stucco punched shield walls, sit regular and toughly upright on the land, in contrast to the slanting forms used by Legorreta. "We had to unify a project with different architects on different sides of a highway," says Paul Broches of Mitchell/Giurgola. "We came up with the idea of doing hard-edged precincts independent of the land, built of easily comprehensible additive elements, so that they could be phased in, and yet. . . become more of the same thing instead of different things."

Mitchell/Giurgola's concern with establishing hard edges shows in the innovative treatment of the parking areas. Partner John Kurtz of Mitchell/Giurgola says, "We made the parking as compact as possible to keep it from dominating the area, to the point of putting up to 66 percent of the parking into structures. The willingness of the client to go along with that was a key aspect of being able to retain the quality of the landscape." The L-shaped garages of phase one, with their strong stucco walls and painted grids, which echo the punched openings of the building windows, frame the ground-level parking and a proces-

Courtyard, IBM Westlake, by Mitchell/Giurgola Architects

sional avenue to the center of the complex, creating a strongly contained space out of the open prairie.

The buildings of phase one are dark and hard where they face outward, but they are faced in a lattice of white precast concrete and clear glass where they turn toward each other. Here an interior courtyard is linked by colonnaded walkways and pergola-covered fountains. The courtyard leads to the cafeteria building, with its curving facade of panels edged in contrasting joint sealant, ceremonially poised over a reflecting pool that separates the office buildings from the largely windowless computer building.

The use of stucco is one of Solana's strengths, allowing creation of intense colors and unifying forms with enormous impact from a distance. But up close stucco is also Solana's biggest problem. In traditional Mexican building, stucco is applied over masonry. Here it is for the most part plastered over insulating board framed in metal studs, and the difference in effect is inescapable (appearing most glaringly on the pylons at the entrance). What should appear solid is punctuated with expansion joints (standard practice in Texas construction to control cracking in stucco surfaces),

Marriott Hotel, Solana Village Center, by Legorreta Arquitectos with Leason Pomeroy Associates

along with small but perceptible ripples and puckers in surface planes, which make everything look thin and hollow. Max Betancourt of Legorreta Arquitectos says that his firm tried to talk the builders into constructing the walls of the complex in a modification of the way it would have been done in Mexico: smearing a coat of stucco on the base (without expansion joints), waiting for it to crack, then applying the finish coat. But the builders, as required by building codes and insurance coverage, attempted to create Legorreta's massive-looking walls using incompatible construction techniques. The resulting conversion of massiveness to ill-executed planarity, like the emptiness of the Village Center, gives a tragic quality to Solana; while it is unquestionably the best office park of the 1980s in Texas, it is also a failure, undercut by its very materials.

Solana has many virtues that, if they were copied in future developments, would improve the run of suburban office-park development, including superb strategies for ameliorating the impact of cars on the landscape and an audacious enlargement of the range of imagery available for office buildings to include Mexican precedents.

In most other respects, however, Solana is bedeviled by the problems of typical suburban office-park development, which its architects and planners had sought to rise above: It is impossible to get from place to place within the development except by car, and there is nobody home. From the visual cohesion of the complex to the tight security arrangements employed, corporate control of the space is so complete that the people required to make the Legorreta-Mitchell/Giurgola tableau come to life are reduced to ciphers. When Solana opened, nobody was home in a more literal sense as well; IBM's employees were commuting to the project from all over the Dallas-Fort Worth area, and residents of Westlake and Southlake had almost no connection to the development. That is changing. Developers, led by the Perot Company, have started a number of housing developments in the area, promising (according to brochures) to recreate the lifestyle of Virginia's hunt country for lucky residents.[4] (Nearby, the Perot Company is also developing Alliance International Airport, the first industrial airport anywhere, which offers additional evidence that air transport is the engine that will drive the growth of North Texas for the foreseeable future.) This coalescence of economic powers, from IBM to Perot, gives Solana, as a work center ringed by new mini-suburbs, a strongly feudal aspect, providing a reminder of the power of the real estate ritual in people's lives. The princes of the market have worked out the arrangements necessary for the workers' future, and everybody lives happily ever after. And, as in a real downtown, the office buildings provide the civic landmarks.

William Blake wrote: "Eternity is in love with the productions of Time." That may be hard to prove for those of us lacking Blake's visionary powers, but an analogue of Blake's formulation is shown at Solana: The diffuse city of the '80s is in love with the forms and human qualities of traditional urban spaces. It seems to have escaped Solana's planners, architects, and builders, however, that such qualities are inherent in the physical expression of social arrangements that the diffuse city is wiping away.

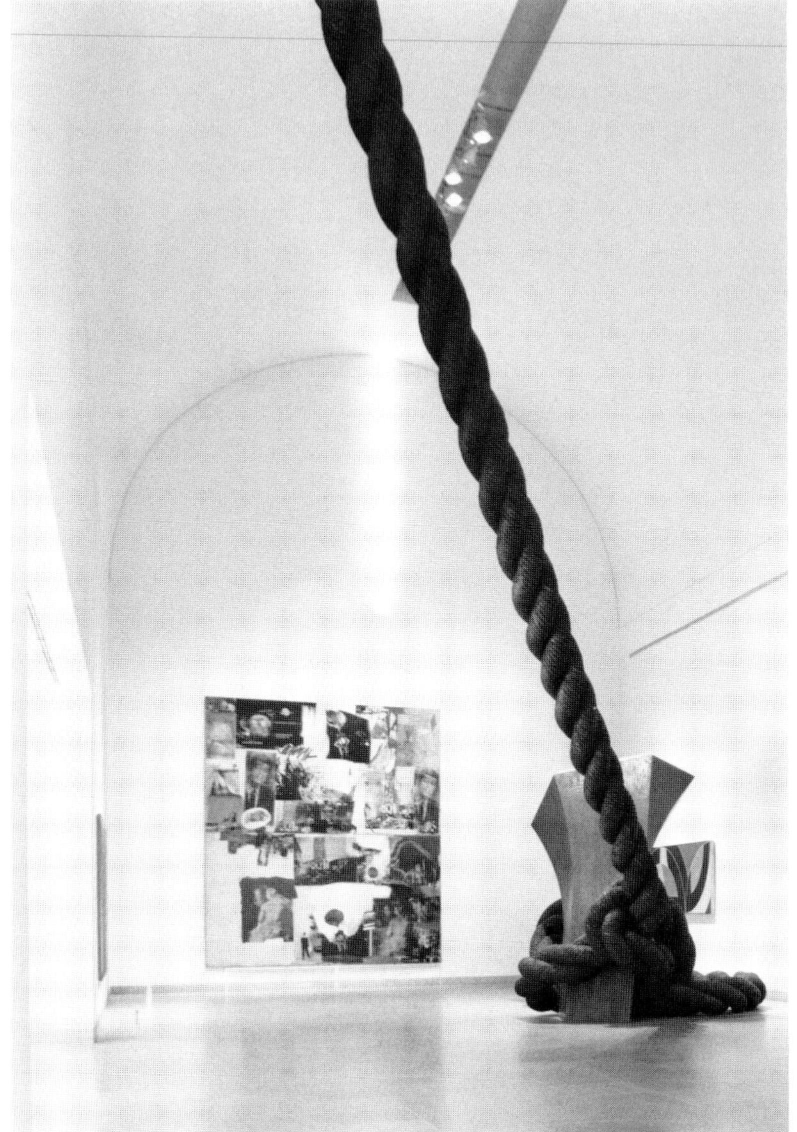

Interior of the central vault, Dallas Museum of Art (1984), by Edward Larrabee Barnes

10
The Dallas Arts District: The Last Ditch

The Morton H. Meyerson Symphony Center in downtown Dallas, designed by I.M. Pei and Partners and completed in 1989, is more than a distinguished modernist concert hall. It is the last sally of the 1980s in a rearguard action—using big-budget cultural institutions to shore up the attractiveness and thus the real estate values of Texas downtowns.

The trouble began in the 1950s, when suburban shopping malls took over the role once held by retail stores in the cities' central business districts. Change accelerated in the 1960s, when low-rise manufacturing and commercial structures moved en masse to the suburbs, leaving vacant warehouse districts on the municipal tax rolls, and when such mixed-use developments as Sharpstown in Houston and NorthPark in Dallas took away more retail activities and began to erode the virtual monopoly on commercial office space formerly held by the CBDs. In the late 1970s and the 1980s, visually arresting buildings containing millions of square feet of office space were built in Texas downtowns, but much more office space went up at the nodes of the radial freeways and ring roads in each of the cities. Shrinking market share left downtown landowners (along with city officials) with a sense that their CBD holdings—tall and memorable, but plagued by parking problems, and, worse, the presence of the urban poor—faced a future of dropping from class A to class B office space. The only way to prevent this, planners and developers agreed, was to redefine downtowns as centers of things the suburbs couldn't have, such as culture.

This formulation was set as early as the 1960s; in Houston, the Jesse H. Jones Hall for the Performing Arts (1966, Caudill Rowlett Scott) and the Alley Theatre (1969, Ulrich Franzen Associates with MacKie & Kamrath) were built to start a new cultural district near City Hall. The strategy didn't stop the exodus of office space to the suburbs—with gasoline and suburban land cheap and plentiful, nothing could—but it had a demonstrable local effect. The northern end of Louisiana Street adjacent to the Alley and Jones Hall became the premier location in the city in the late '70s and early '80s, site of Pennzoil Place, Texas Commerce Tower, and RepublicBank Center. Even such mediocre properties as the Lyric Center (1983, Darrell Comeaux and Associates with Richard Fitzgerald & Partners), with its music-playing "sculpture," gained cachet from its location.

In Dallas, with its long-standing and exemplary tradition of cooperation between private interests and municipal planners, a similar but much more coordinated and ambitious scheme took shape in the early 1980s. The city's art museum, opera company, and symphony would move from their outgrown quarters in Fair Park into new facilities in sixty mostly empty acres in the northeast corner of the CBD. The area, designated as an arts district, was given regulations specifying that new buildings should have ground-level retail space along their street frontages and setting height limits at the center of the district, with restrictions relaxing at the district's edges; a landscaping plan was also developed by Sasaki Associates of Watertown, Massachusetts. Most important, the City of Dallas committed over $75 million for construction and public improvements. The Dallas Arts District was projected to be the site not only of big institutions but of galleries and artsy shops near the new museum, restaurants near the new concert hall, and a quarter with studios and living spaces for the city's artists and arts groups, a Dallasite left bank. Private commercial development in the district would generate tax revenues to pay the city back, so the city would have world-class new cultural institutions at virtually no cost, and the whole of downtown Dallas would get a shot in the arm.[1]

Dallas Museum of Art, entrance on Flora Street

The first major project finished in the new district was the Dallas Museum of Art (1984, by Edward Larrabee Barnes & Associates), a lanky, almost windowless 195,000-square-foot low-rise structure. The DMA has a waterwall and sculpture courts facing Ross Avenue and five pavilions stepping in and out on the St. Paul Avenue side, each of a different height but tied together by a banded limestone skin. Its one vertical component is a forty-foot-tall barrel vault facing Flora Street, the center of the arts district.[2] By the time the museum was occupied, as David Dillon reported in *Progressive Architecture*, speculation in arts-district real estate had driven land prices to more than $150 per square foot, effectively ending all hopes of having an artists' quarter within it.[3]

The Dallas concert hall, to which the city eventually committed some $41.5 million, was to have been completed soon after the museum, but instead of the projected two years, it took nine, and it ended up costing some 64 percent more than the original estimate. Fund-raising for the project, coming on the heels of requests from the DMA, even taxed the resources of the city's numerous philanthropic foundations. Chief fund-raiser

Dallas Museum of Art, water wall on Ross Avenue

Morton H. Meyerson, a former president of EDS (the data-processing company that billionaire Ross Perot sold to General Motors in the early 1980s), brought in $12 million from Perot (on the condition that the hall be named for Meyerson) and another large donation from Margaret McDermott (widow of one of the founders of the Texas Instruments electronics company), and construction started.

The architectural program for the symphony center was anything but modest. It explicitly called for creation of a building that, in a single stroke, would make Dallas a world-recognized center of musical culture to rival not just New York but London, Paris, and Vienna. That such a claim could be contemplated is a measure of the near irrelevance of symphonic music to the overall life of Dallas, a young city with little cultural history and no real connection between the community at large and the world of high culture. It implied that a single structure could supply what in other cities had evolved over many generations, and that Dallas's tiny group of symphony-goers should be content to know that internationally recognized performers liked to play in Dallas.

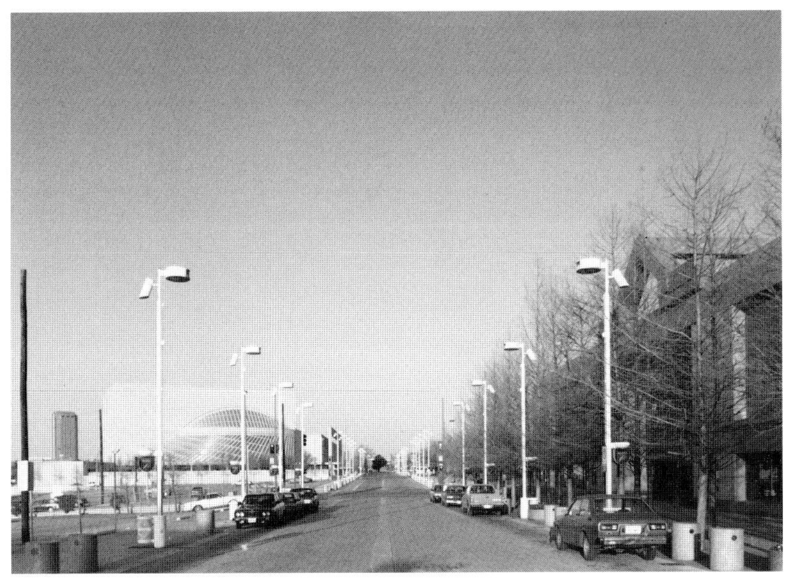

Flora Street, center of the Dallas Arts District

Pei's design was modernist, meaning that he would not engage in the direct appropriation of historicist visual images that other architects were caught up in during the early 1980s. Instead, he and acoustician Russell Johnson of Artec Consultants took the chief remaining route: They treated the issue of excellence in the hall as a technical matter, choosing to appropriate the acoustical style of such historical rivals as the Paris Opera and Vienna's Kunstvereinsaal.[4]

"A symphony hall is essentially an air-tight, light-tight box," with a lobby and support spaces around it, Pei said in an interview shortly before the center's completion. "[The hall itself] would be a shoe-box shape to create the best sound, roughly two cubes in volume. So that was a given."

It was also a given that the building would have a heavy concrete frame (for its sound-damping qualities) and a limestone skin, responding to the precedent of Barnes's DMA. A tall box set in a podium that faces the street squarely, covered in such materials, even with lots of sharply detailed glass added, could have been visually inert. Pei said he saw his task as animating the composition. "In the old days, that was easy, using the classical orders," he said. "Now it's vastly more difficult."

Meyerson Symphony Center's conoid wall

Pei's solution was to introduce circular elements: The three glazed "lenses"—shaped like sections cut from cones—rise from the lobby's roof to the wall of the concert-hall box, softening the angularity of both. Pei complicated matters by twisting the concert hall within the ensemble, turning it toward the heavily traveled Olive and Pearl streets to the west. This gesture is dramatized by the "conoid" glass wall at the base of the western side, a remarkable and remarkably expensive exercise in curtain-wall artistry (no two panes have the same shape or angles), which looks as if it had been stretched by the rotation of the concert hall. From a distance, the resulting massing is complicated but austere. In keeping with a building housing an isolated institution, the center is difficult to read in terms of metaphors that relate to nearby buildings, except as a warehouse into which a spaceship has crashed rather jauntily. From a block away, the building's shapes and the transparency of the window walls create a beckoning, even welcoming, effect, although this is undercut by the fact that the street-level entrance is tucked under a dark carport beneath the lobby volume, and thus hard to recognize. Most patrons, after all, walk up from the under-

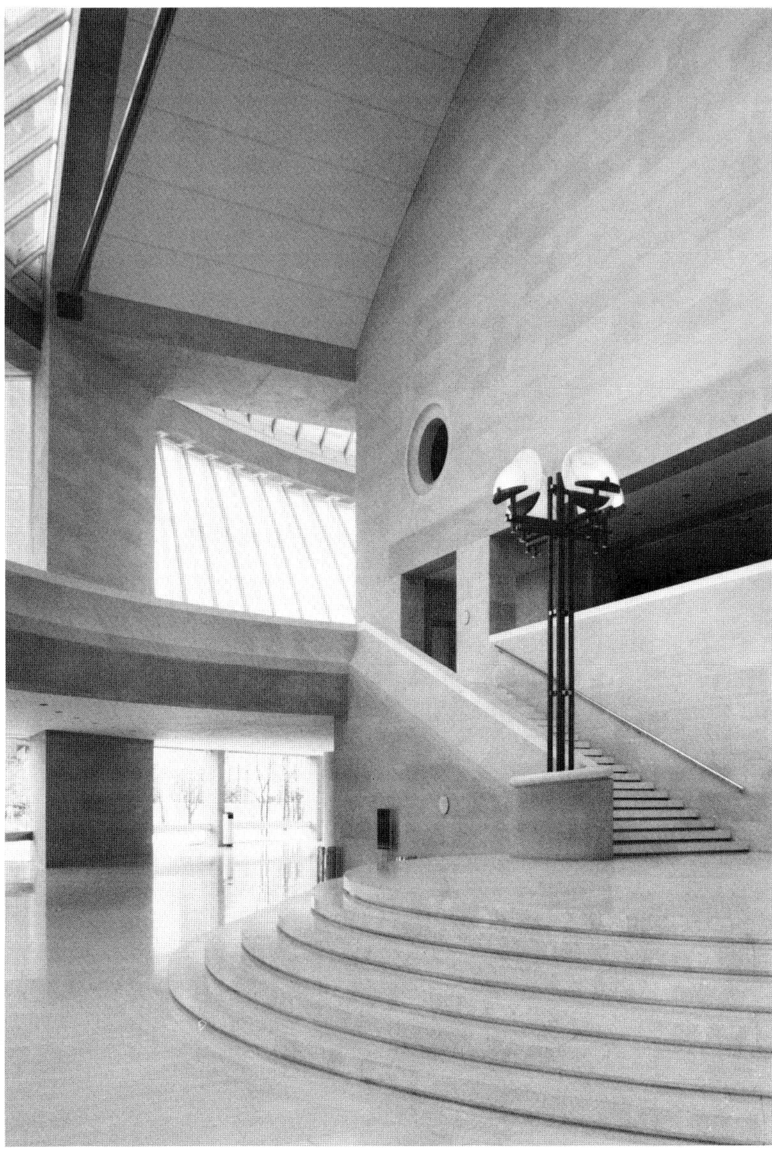

Meyerson Symphony Center's grand stair, under its tied ring beam

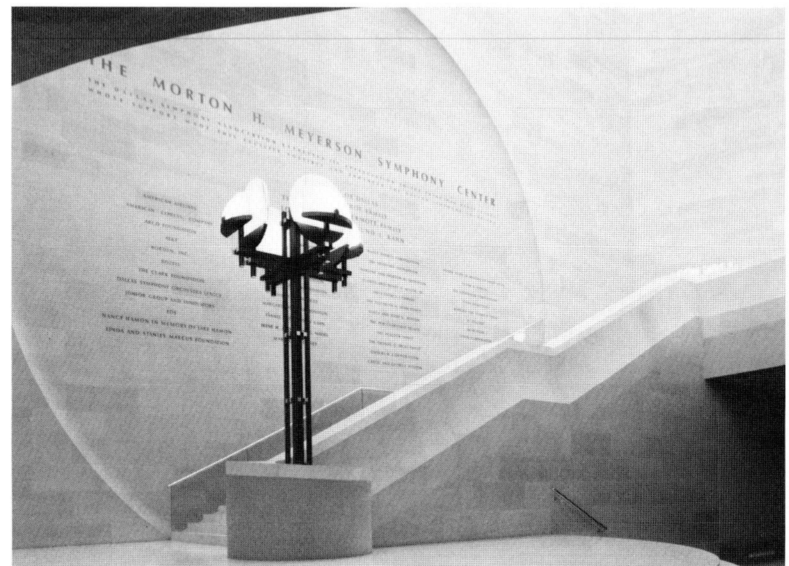

Meyerson Symphony Center, entry from the basement parking garage

ground parking garage; as Stephen Fox points out, the entry sequence resembles that of a suburban shopping mall, a situation that rather undercuts highfalutin comparisons to Vienna and Paris. [5]

Inside, Pei's stratagems produce considerable complexity. Entering by the curving staircase from the basement and walking obliquely toward the central grand staircase, one encounters the lobby's layers of rotated curves. Each of the surfaces stretches out of sight and turns light in a different direction, creating a sense of enclosed endlessness, which Pei said came from emulation of the underlying technique of baroque architecture.

The lobby's openness contributes strongly to its monumentality. Pei and engineer William J. Faschan of Leslie E. Robertson Associates minimized the number of columns in the lobby by supporting the lenses overhead on a ring beam, a circular tension structure of steel and concrete almost twelve feet deep, which springs from the concert hall's side walls and rests on two sharp-edged triangular columns that frame the main staircase to the concert hall (some of the stresses are also transferred to trusses in the roof of the concert hall by tension members in the lenses). To further highlight the tensions at play in the structure, Pei tied the arch formed over these columns by the upper curve of the central lens, using twisted steel cables. This dramatic gesture was one of the most criticized aspects of the center, particularly among the foreign journalists who attended the opening ceremonies. Louise Rogers of the British *Architects Journal* quoted another critic as calling the center "a beautiful and totally logical sum which is ruined by a glaring mistake in the last line."[6]

Despite such cavils, the Meyerson's lobby spaces, with their interlocking curves and shaded vistas, floored in travertine, meticulously finished concrete, and deeply modeled limestone, have been a critical success. Paul Goldberger said that the center shows that Pei, "more than anyone else practicing today, has managed to achieve a viable modernist monumentality."[7]

The 2,062-seat Eugene McDermott Concert Hall has enjoyed the same success, even though it is remarkably different from the spaces that wrap it. The concert hall is part Frank Lloyd Wright, part Olbrich, and part atmospheric theater, featuring gridded, rich-toned cherrywood walls, brass accents, two massive Chinese-looking columns, a red terrazzo floor, and backlit onyx panels set into the upper balcony fronts, all under a sky-blue ceiling and a movable acoustical canopy. Behind the scenes, cloth panels and movable concrete doors opening into ceiling-level reverberation chambers, designed by Russell Johnson, work with the canopy to shape the sound. Charles T. Young, an associate partner in Pei's firm who had primary responsibility for the hall's architectural design, said when the hall opened, "We tried to give a sense of architectural order to what Mr. Johnson designed as optimal acoustically. When we disagreed, we gave in wherever a change would have had a negative acoustical effect." The architectural intrusions were felicitous, particularly compared with Johnson's original design for the hall, shown in an early rendering as a scaleless place, like a narrow Hyatt lobby, dominated by Johnson's massive, uninflected canopy. (Pei disparagingly referred to this as "the tongue" up to the time of the opening.)

Johnson's acoustics and the Pei firm's architectural embellishments add up to a space of acoustical liveliness and visual sumptuousness. The flotilla of international critics who descended on Dallas for the opening duly reported the builders' ambitions and the hall's success. So the goal of getting outsiders to pay serious attention to Dallas as a cultural center was achieved.

These pages: Interior, Eugene McDermott concert hall, Meyerson Symphony Center

But whether the Meyerson Symphony Center can make neighborhood real estate attractive (forget about seeding a viable artistic enclave) remains to be seen. The LTV Center and Texas Commerce Tower were built in and near the arts district; other projects, including designs for twin-towered complexes by Fujikawa Johnson of Chicago and Kohn Pedersen Fox of New York, were awaiting tenants and financing as this was being written. In terms of the future of downtown Dallas, however, the pertinent connections to the Meyerson Center are not with Europe but with northern Tarrant County, where companies owned by Ross Perot are developing Alliance Airport and housing to serve Solana; with Plano, where Perot's Legacy office park has drawn Frito-Lay and other former Dallas-based companies to relocate; and with Richardson, where Perot-owned land is at the center of a burgeoning new manufacturing-research area dubbed "Telecom Corridor."[8] Perot's suburban real estate ventures, which sprawl at a scale that obviates the idea of a city center, are thriving, particularly compared with downtown Dallas. It is good for the city that he cared enough about its downtown to donate millions of dollars for a cultural center. It is obvi-

MCI headquarters (1990), by Hellmuth, Obata & Kassabaum, in "Telecom Corridor," Richardson

ously good for Perot, who, with his gift, boosts himself above the line dividing high from low in cultural stature. Still, it might have been better if he had instead thought of a way to create jobs in Dallas, not just in the already affluent suburbs—although, admittedly, such activities as job creation are accorded little or no cultural value in our society. But, with the split created by his enterprises and his benefactions, Perot's charity may have been in vain: Downtown Dallas may be dead before the Meyerson ever generates any of its intended benefits.

In a time in which poverty, crime, disease, and illiteracy mar the lives of millions of Texans, it might seem like displaced anxiety to be worrying about the prices of downtown properties and the fortunes of those who live off them. The elite that once ruled downtown Dallas was largely displaced by speculators from the East Coast and Canada in the early 1980s, so there is little to be nostalgic for. But nostalgia has nothing to do with it. The logic of urban development implies that, without an active city center that serves commercial interests, the lower orders of the city—most of us—will be cut adrift by the moneyed classes, and the spiral of urban decay

Alliance Airport, in northern Tarrant County

will pick up speed. As the Dallas Arts District and its institutions show, the gulf between culture, commerce, and the people of the city widened during the 1980s, forming a void that may never be bridgeable again, at least in the terms of contemporary urban development in Texas. Dallas is more likely to become the new Newark than the new Vienna.

Palm room, Lucile Halsell Conservatory (1988), San Antonio, by Emilio Ambasz with Jones & Kell

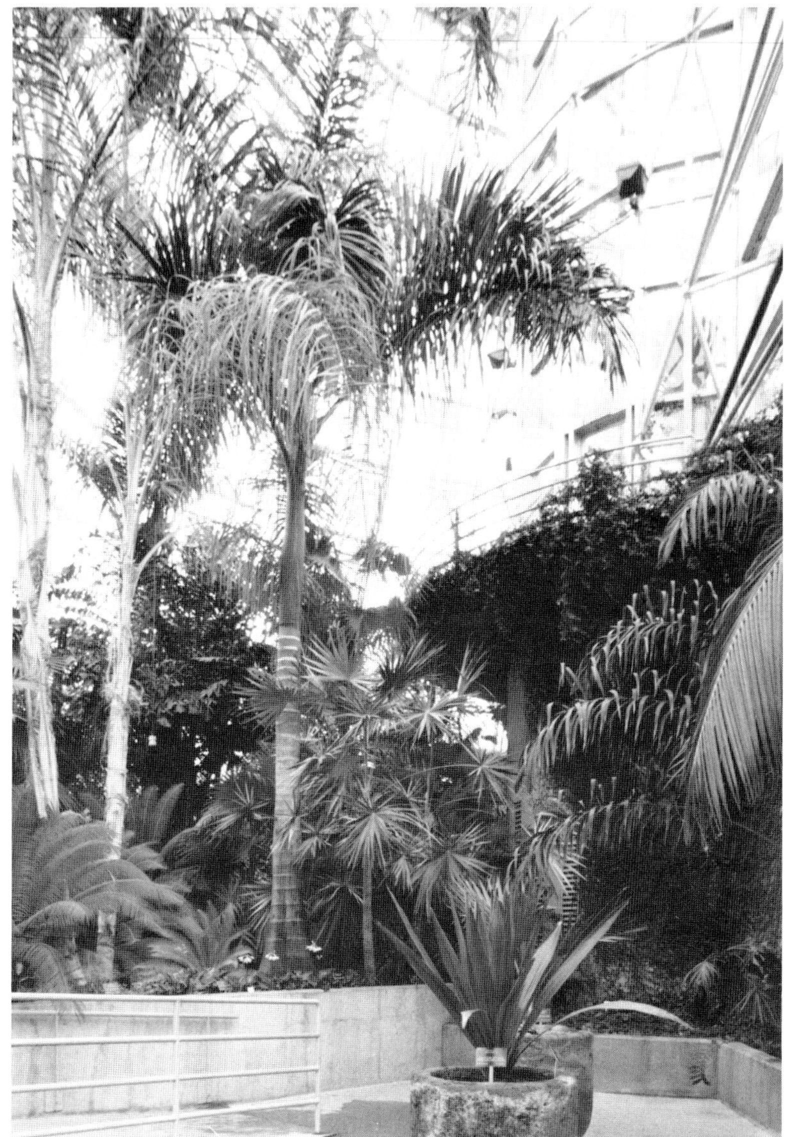

11
Creating More Perfect Landscapes, '80s Style

After postmodernist architecture came to Texas in the late 1970s, it was increasingly common for architects to appropriate historical imagery as a way of wrapping their projects in an aura of cultural legitimacy, thereby giving them enhanced commercial value. Two projects of the 1980s, both revolving around landscape design, tried to go much further. Both strove to redefine not only the buildings on the ground but the ground itself. The Moody Gardens project was an attempt to capture the spiritual meaning of gardens throughout history, by literally planting them at the edge of a mud flat on Galveston Island. The Lucile Halsell Conservatory in San Antonio tried to recreate a presence for untamed nature within the city, redefining the underpinnings of Texas history in the process. But both projects were subverted by the cultural legacy of their surroundings.

A 90,000-square-foot sequence of half-submerged buildings in a small park on the near northwest side of San Antonio, the Halsell Conservatory was completed in 1987 at a cost of $6.7 million. It was the first finished work by Argentine-born architect Emilio Ambasz, who practices in New York and Bologna. Ambasz's earlier roles as writer and curator of design at the Museum of Modern Art in New York made him influential as postmodernism crystallized.[1]

Ambasz was hired by lawyer-rancher-philanthropist Gilbert Denman, who serves as chairman of the board of the San Antonio-based Halsell and Brackenridge foundations and who is an important patron of the San Antonio museum of art in his own right—a perfect above-the-line client. Denman wanted San Antonio to have a botanical center with a conservatory "that would shake up architectural circles." Working with the Halsell Foundation's grants officer, Bob Washington, Denman set up a nonprofit San Antonio Botanical Center corporation with two other charities; then he arranged for the Brackenridge Foundation to donate land and for the Halsell Foundation to fund a design for the conservatory. Ambasz was the third designer chosen.

Frederick Groos, a Denver architect with San Antonio connections, was hired first, but his work was cut short by a fatal heart attack. Next, Denman hired E. Fay Jones, whom he had met at a conference in Arkansas. Jones, too, had a heart attack. He recovered, but resigned the commission. Washington says that one evening weeks later he and Denman were thumbing through a book on the Mexican architect Luis Barragán as they discussed their next step. The book was by Ambasz, who, they found, was working on a plan (never realized) to unify a mixed-use complex in downtown Houston called Houston Center. His design included a huge mist garden with a maze of hedgerows and a glass-walled, cathedral-size shopping center and arboretum.

"We thought as long as he was working on a really big project in Texas, he wouldn't mind coming to San Antonio for our little job," Washington recalls.

Touring the site with Denman and Washington, Ambasz pointed out that a "Crystal Palace"-type glass pavilion wouldn't work given the summer heat. Instead, he proposed "troglodyte" buildings, buried to their roof lines in the insulating earth, with glass roofs. It was an image that he had used before, in an unbuilt design for a house in Spain, and would use again, in an unbuilt project for the Schlumberger headquarters in Austin.[2] The final design was produced by Ambasz's New York office. Jones & Kell of

San Antonio, the architect of record, produced the construction documents and undertook construction administration.[3]

Bob Washington recalls that, when Ambasz first unveiled his model for the design, it showed the glass roofs of the conservatory rising from a vast green lawn. Viewing the model, Washington remarked that he was reminded of the green landscape of Mars, punctuated by crystalline structures, described in Ray Bradbury's *The Martian Chronicles.* "Then you have discovered my source," Ambasz replied. The actual context, however, includes a garden center on one side and a street lined with rundown rental properties, which one drives past to enter the complex, on the other.

Considerable work remained to be done after Ambasz unveiled the scheme. A soil analysis, for example, showed that the site was too unstable to build the project as the single building Ambasz envisioned, so Jones & Kell designed each of the project's rooms as an independent enclosure, floating in its berm of dirt. This adjustment and others contributed to delays in construction; the conservatory opened almost two years behind schedule.

Seen from afar, the Halsell Conservatory is an enigmatic collection of conical and pyramidal glass roofs, sliced and truncated in various ways and oriented to admit the smallest amount of summer sunlight possible. The rooms below them, with concrete walls all but dematerialized by the grass-covered earth piled around them, are arranged around a central courtyard that focuses on an irregular lily pond, and they form a vaguely zoomorphic pattern—there is something like a head and a torso, and ramps suggest legs.[4]

The entry sequence sets the hieratic tone. Visitors first cross a semicircular courtyard that focuses on a passageway through a concrete wall, cut into what appears to be a low hill. Just beyond is a small circular open-air courtyard with a palmetto at its center (replacing a planned bronze tree sculpture that proved too expensive). This space leads to a low-ceilinged passage with a single waist-high exhibit built into the left-hand wall: an alpine habitat display, in which tiny mountain flowers are kept in cold air and blown around by a wind machine. Ambasz's plans show that originally this space was to have been a ticket window. Beyond is a second, slightly larger circular courtyard showcasing garden flowers and housing the project's toilets. Here one encounters for the first time the conservatory's glass roof.

Lucile Halsell Conservatory, viewed from the gazebo

It is composed of a tubular aluminum space frame with spherical connecting nodes. The configuration was generated with the help of a sophisticated computer analysis of the stresses involved. Clipped to this light framework is the green glass skin, which, in a system never tried before in the United States, is held in place by nothing more than its space-age silicon sealant, without the usual mullions. Some of the glass panes are openable, and they can be controlled by a computer to release heat and keep out rain as required. Inside the frame there are movable white cloth shades, and large fans set into the walls pull air rapidly through the space to cool it.

One next passes through a porch with a curved row of tapering triangular concrete columns (their modernist-vernacular "capitals" are swellings that engage the sloping wall behind them) into the courtyard of the conservatory's main section. Turning to the right, one follows a concrete-roofed arcade, stepping from it through glass doors set into a severe concrete wall. The doors lead to two other glass-roofed rooms, one for desert plants and the other for tropical plants. One may turn into the courtyard to the edge of the lily pond, but most visitors stay in the shade at the perimeter. At the head of the courtyard, opposite the entrance, is the temple-

Lucile Halsell Conservatory, entry

Lucile Halsell Conservatory, desert room

like palm room, the largest in the complex; here towering palm trees climb toward the tall conical roof, and the horizontality of the rest of the complex is broken by a ramp that takes visitors up into the crowns of these stately trees. Leaving the palm room, one again passes through the concrete-roofed arcade and under a pergola where fruit trees grow in large pots cut from porous Mexican *adoquin*. Through a low doorway is the circular fern room, obscured by mist generated by watering equipment (mist machinery also operates in the palm and hot rain-forest rooms). Ferns, orchids, and other plants from temperate rain forests climb "rocks" that were shaped from fiber-glass-impregnated concrete. Leaving this room and passing through the remaining potted fruit trees, one comes to a ramp that leads out of the courtyard, to a trail that winds up and around the final piece of the composition, the gazebo. Originally, this gazebo, which overlooks the rest of the complex, was to have been a domed structure supported on concrete columns, and it was to have housed a collection of carnivorous plants with their own mist generators. Ambasz said that he wanted it to remind children that "there was a serpent in Eden." As built, the gazebo is a lattice-

Lucile Halsell Conservatory, fruit trees (far left), and fern room (left).

topped structure faced in painted wire mesh ringed with fragrant herbs. It's a low-key link to the botanical center's Texas native plant areas, which lie beyond.

In this short sequence, from entry court to gazebo, the usual expectations about the Texas landscape are turned upside down.

San Antonio dates from Spanish colonization of the eighteenth century, but the wave of settlement that produced today's Texas started in the nineteenth century, when settlers encountered a land almost emptied of its earlier Indian inhabitants. This openness facilitated creation of the Texas cowboy mythology; even today, the western half of the state is practically empty, and Texas remains the psychological center of America's western frontier.

The state's emptiness in the nineteenth century had another effect: Pioneers, whether from Virginia or Moldavia, were able to project onto the landscape of the new territory qualities of the intensely cultivated country from which they came, including a sense that the physical world, inhabited and cultivated by humankind, reflected a cosmic orderliness.

But the land of this new world turned out to be less Edenic than promised to the earliest settlers. Working the land was a physical and economic struggle. Crops grew badly, or sales prices were low, and even in good years the orderliness of the manipulated landscape was always being corroded by the entropy of nature, which could sweep a life's work away in a single flood or windstorm. The growing efficiency of farm machinery and chemicals meant that fewer people could raise more food; inhabitants of country towns and rural areas began leaving for the city a century ago, and the process continued into the 1980s. As it has come into the present, the rural landscape has a characteristic pattern: A zone of order extends as far from the farmer's house as prosperity allows. The edge of the zone is marked by rusting equipment that stands where it broke down while weeds grow up through its wheelwells and tiller blades, because the effort required to remove it would produce nothing, and the farmer's time and energy are desperately short. In Texas' cities throughout the 1980s, individual private properties flourished (although some only briefly). At the same time, much of the public realm—the streets, the civic and political spaces, the symbols of community—declined, neglected in the great speculative splurge, like so many broken-down tractors. This is the analogue of that inherited agrarian landscape, evidence that Texas' cities are regarded by their inhabitants as extensions of the rural landscape, rather than alternatives to it.

In most of the San Antonio Botanical Center, one can see the construction of the rural social and economic reality recapitulated in the homely work of gardeners. In the conservatory, however, the experience is singularly different. One stands in the shadows, looking at plants that are elevated to eye level or higher and bathed in cool, diffuse light from above. At the same time, one is constantly aware of the operations of machinery, whose function is not to make use of the plants, but to serve them.

Ambasz's underground plant museum is the sacred precinct of a new-old pantheism. In these altar-like spaces, plants are not things to be manipulated, but beings with an independent claim to existence, representing forces that extend beyond human control, in a time, emerging from the mists of the present, that is simultaneously archaic past and utopian technological future. Just as Philip Johnson staked claim to seventeenth-century Holland for his design of RepublicBank Center, Houston, Ambasz has tried to rewrite the Texas landscape to legitimate the urban present, creating a place in which agriculture never

The approach to Lucile Halsell Conservatory

had a claim, where the relations of people and plants are reduced to air-handling and mist-making.

It's an amazing performance, made all the more impressive by the deadpan modernist architectural detailing used throughout. But it doesn't quite work. Like a farmer beside the highway whose old tractor broke down between his house and the road, and whose life of order and industry will henceforth be framed by decay, the Halsell Foundation and Ambasz created a little bit of Mars, only to have it framed by the hulking substandard rental properties that line the approach. Ambasz tried to create a landscape before agriculture; instead, the project is a distillation of Texas' flash-and-trash urbanism in the 1980s, which echoes the rural landscape from which it coalesced.

The botanical gardens project at Moody Gardens in Galveston, which promised when it was announced in 1987 to be one of the wonders of the world, would seem to be the most poetic building venture of the 1980s in Texas, the very model of the above-the-line plenum of joy, intended by its patrons to prove that their wealth was ennobling, if not divinely bestowed.

Instead, Moody Gardens is a false plenum, a frivolity wrapped in an impossibility and veiled by an absurdity. Indications are that the project will never match its original design; any eventual success will come about as much despite as because of the ongoing interventions of its patrons. And those members of the Moody family who backed Moody Gardens initially, and who might have hoped to see it carry their names into the future as beneficent visionaries, will instead find it reflecting an image of them as capricious people who happen to control a foundation with a $415-million endowment.

The story of the Moody Gardens starts with Robert L. Moody, who in the late 1970s and early 1980s served as a trustee of the Moody Foundation (along with his older brother, Shearn Moody, Jr., and his aunt, the now-deceased Mary Moody Northen). A scion of Galveston's most prominent family, Bobby Moody also owns a number of enterprises, including the Moody National Bank in Galveston (which he had acquired on excellent terms from the foundation after becoming a trustee); National Western Life Insurance company, based in Austin; and Gal-Tex, a hotel construction and operating company that owns historic properties in San Antonio and Washington, D.C. The three trustees funded theaters and classroom buildings at colleges across the state (most of which were named after one of the trustees), along with historic preservation (primarily through the Galveston Historical Foundation), and medical research. The Art Deco Santa Fe Building at the foot of The Strand in Galveston was a typical project; rescued from deterioration to house various county agencies, it was renamed Shearn Moody Plaza for Bobby Moody's father.

Bobby Moody's son Russell suffered a disabling head injury in a jeep accident in the early '80s, as the staff of Moody Gardens will tell even the most casual visitor. While seeking the most effective treatment for his son, Bobby learned that programs allowing patients to work with horses, other animals, and plants had remarkable rehabilitative effects, and he learned that no such program was available in Galveston. At his behest, the Moody Foundation funded creation of Hope Arena, a horse-contact-therapy program on a plot of land leased for forty years from the city of Galveston, next to the Galveston municipal airport.[5]

The administrative offices of Hope Arena, designed by Morris Aubry Architects of Houston, opened in 1986; near the offices is "The Garden of Life," a contemplative water garden created by the Houston-based landscape architects Smith Locke Asakura (for which the firm won a national award from the American Society of Landscape Architects in 1986).[6] As the planning for this work began in 1983, Shearn Moody reportedly became interested in the project, and matters took a dramatic turn. Shearn hired horticulturist Peter Atkins, and together they began to think big.

Shearn convinced the rest of the board to consider creating a really important work of landscape on the site. Atkins, with the board's blessing, flew to England to meet Sir Geoffrey Jellicoe, who was by then more than eighty years old and world-famous for his encyclopedic writings and his gardens, including those at the seventeenth-century English estate Sutton Place,[7] which used landscape in unparalleled explorations of contrasting psychological states. Offered the chance to create the biggest, most important work of his life, Jellicoe came to Galveston to look at the site, on a salt marsh facing Offatts Bayou next to the airport. On seeing it, he refused the commission, saying the Moodys must be "crackers." But the clients pressed Jellicoe to continue, and (after learning about the devastating 1900 Galveston hurricane) he responded with a design of fantastic complexity and bleakness based on a passage from the Roman poet Lucretius's *De Rerum Natura* describing humankind's insignificance before the forces of nature.[8] Building the garden would have all but consumed the foundation's endowment, however, and the plan was rejected.

Jellicoe then designed a scheme, unveiled publicly in 1987, for a three-part series of gardens. The first would be a wetlands nature preserve, with triangular walkways; the second would be a campus of tourist attractions, including restaurants, a tropical rain forest "biome" and other facilities drawn from a design by BIOS of Seattle, more animal-contact facilities, a convention center, a dock for passengers arriving from The Strand on the foundation-funded paddlewheeler *The Colonel*, and even a Vietnam Veterans memorial; and the third would be what Jellicoe described as the crowning achievement of his career, the historical gardens.[9]

In this area, the landscape would be laid out (tourists could visit first by boat and return on foot) as a journey through the ways people have interacted with gardens throughout time, from a primeval forest through the

Offatts Bayou, Galveston

Garden of Eden (its sixteen-foot-tall apple sculpture and serpentine earthwork exemplifying the punning tricks of scale employed throughout the project), passing into a sequence of formal gardens in the styles of ancient Egypt, classical Rome, fourteenth-century Islam, medieval Europe, Renaissance Italy, Baroque France, and Victorian England, and winding through a series of irregularly shaped English, French, and Russian romantic gardens that lead (after a boat ride under a "mountain range" topped by a Mughal garden) to Chinese gardens featuring a monumental statue of the Buddha, and culminating in a Zen rock garden and a return to the primeval forest. Such a brief description makes the project sound ridiculously cartoon-like, but Jellicoe's other works are so convincingly syncretistic that there was hope that he could succeed in his aim of creating a place that would impart subtle lessons about relationships between the East and the West, the conscious and the unconscious mind, and the physical and the spiritual worlds of human experience.[10] The Moody Foundation committed $118 million to the project and contracted to hand it over to the City of Galveston on completion; the foundation's officers, like Jellicoe, would be

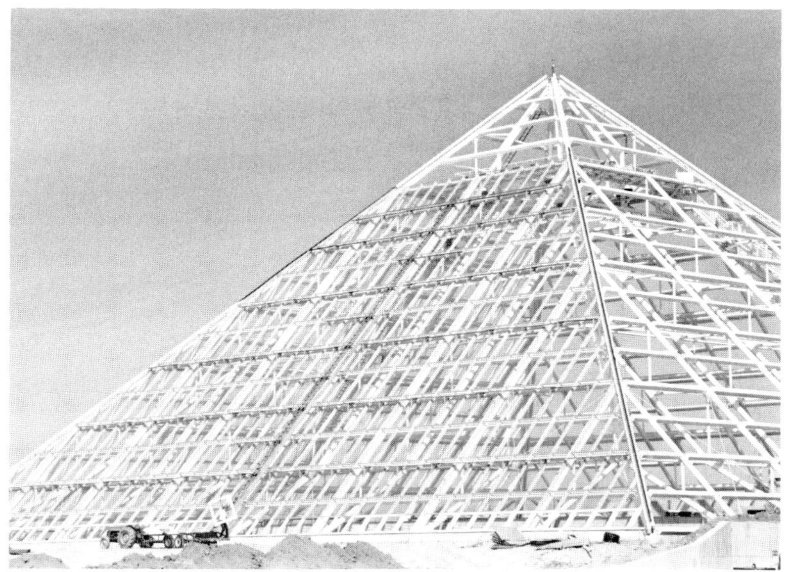

Moody Gardens, biome pyramid under construction, by Morris Architects

cultural heroes in the next century, bathed in the glow of aristocratic connoisseurship and beneficence that this bold application of their wealth had made possible for the first time.

What most coverage of the announcement omitted was that, by 1987, the Moody Foundation's credentials of old-money nobility were in serious disarray. Mrs. Northen had died in 1986, and Bobby Moody replaced her as head of the foundation. And Shearn (the subject of a 1987 feature in *Texas Monthly* entitled "The Sleaziest Man in Texas") was standing trial for allegedly defrauding the Moody Foundation of $1.5 million (part of some $3 million in payments, prosecutors said, arranged by Shearn and some associates supposedly to aid the Nicaraguan contras; the funds were allegedly kicked back to Shearn to pay expenses from his long-running bankruptcy case). He was convicted on these charges in 1987, and, in 1989, of bankruptcy fraud; Shearn appealed the first conviction and won a new trial, but prosecutors decided not to retry him on the charge, since he had already been sentenced to five years in the bankruptcy-fraud case. At the time of sentencing, Shearn and his brother Bobby faced a civil racketeer-

Hope Arena animal-contact therapy center

ing suit filed by the executor in Shearn's bankruptcy case (alleging that they had hidden assets from creditors), a second criminal indictment for mail, wire, and bankruptcy fraud, and a suit by the State of Texas in which Shearn was accused of defrauding the policy holders of the insurance company he owned, Empire National Life.[11] The state suit against the insurance company was closed in 1988, and the second criminal case has yet to come to trial. But in early 1991, just after Shearn was released from prison (having served eighteen months), Robert and Shearn were found to have "conspired with malice" to divert assets that should have gone to pay Shearn's creditors; the case was appealed.[12]

In Shearn's absence, things had not gone well for the Jellicoe plan. There had been talk from the start of having the project bring in some money, but, with investigators turning over rocks looking into foundation affairs as Shearn's troubles escalated, foundation officials began to focus in earnest on making the project pay for itself. And, despite continued public commitment to Jellicoe's plan, staff members and others began to wonder privately if a boat ride through a salt marsh under the Texas sun to see a re-

Hope Arena animal-contact therapy center, interior

condite condensation of world history through landscape—however appealing it might have been to Shearn in his salad days—a project that would require millions of gallons of circulating water and armies of landscape workers, among other high-expense items, would really be the sort of thing that would draw paying visitors away from competing amusements such as Houston's Astroworld or even the Galveston beaches. And how could the plants of ancient Persia, medieval Europe, and nineteenth-century Russia be made to coexist in a marsh prone to flooding and constantly drenched in blowing sand and salt spray from the nearby Gulf of Mexico? It would take magic, not just research. After a series of disagreements over the pace of progress and the future of the project, Peter Atkins left, along with Smith Locke Asakura.

While these questions percolated, the foundation pushed ahead with development of the parts of the project designed to produce revenue, including Palm Beach (imported white sand surrounding a chlorinated pool, marketed as a family alternative to the insecurities, litter, and general grubbiness of Galveston's real beaches), Seaside Safari (the second animal-con-

Moody Gardens bathhouses, by Morris Architects

tact treatment center, marketed as a petting zoo), and a new Galveston Convention and Conference Center (a replacement for the old one on the Seawall near downtown, with *its* insecurities, litter, and general grubbiness, built by W.L. Moody, Jr., in 1956 as a privately owned center, which was eventually unloaded on the City of Galveston). Excavation was also begun on the ten-story-tall rain-forest biome (its architecture designed, like that of the previous parts of the project, by Morris Architects).

Some of these facilities were less than ideally suited to generating revenue: A small building between Palm Beach and Seaside Safari contains hot tubs and rooms for a masseur and a masseuse, built evidence of Bobby Moody's belief that it would be nice to have a place where visitors could soak and get a rubdown. It now stands unused.[13]

If Bobby Moody sometimes seemed to lack a vision of how to steer the project's philanthropic aspects into sustainability, however, his business acumen remained sharp. The new convention center, far from the hotel-lined Seawall, needed a hotel to make it more attractive to conventioneers; Moody's hotel company, Gal-Texas, was hired to build it; completion is

Entry to animal-contact area and petting zoo, by Morris Architects

due in 1993.

Building at Moody Gardens could end after construction of the biome and the hotel, especially if the Texas Department of Transportation goes ahead with a scheme, announced in 1990, to build a giant bridge through the center of what would have been Jellicoe's gardens.[14]

Thus, what started as a modestly scaled therapeutic center veered into the realm of high art at the urging of a man convicted of defrauding his own family foundation, only to turn by decade's end into a chance to bring business to an enterprise of another foundation trustee, both of whom were judged to have conspired to divert funds from creditors in a bankruptcy case. It might even, most poetically, fall victim to a highway-building project. In the future, if the bridge plan can be killed (Moody Foundation officer Douglas McLeod says he is working on it) and if cheap nuclear fusion can be invented to make total climate control possible, Galveston may see the creation of Sir Geoffrey Jellicoe's masterwork. But the Moody Foundation will probably take up other causes before then, and Moody Gardens will become just another

Palm Beach

Convention Center at Moody Gardens (1989), by Morris Architects

The old Galveston Convention Center on Seawall Boulevard

slightly schizophrenic tourist attraction on Galveston's West End, proof that even old money sometimes can't make its controllers into the spiritualized figures we need to lead us toward a better future, and that the line dividing some people from the rest is a fiction.

Kimbell Art Museum (1972), Fort Worth, by Louis I. Kahn

12
Saving the Kimbell for Philadelphia

Who owns a work of architecture? For most buildings, that question has an unambiguous answer: The owner is the client, the person or group that paid to build or purchase the structure. And what is ownership? It is the right to use or dispose of a building however the owner pleases. Such rights have been exercised with unquestioned vigor throughout Texas for as long as anyone can remember. The current anything-goes standard of decency was established in the 1960s, when a Protestant congregation in Houston sold a church on Westheimer Road for use as a nightclub, with the former sanctuary as a bar; the building is now a shoe store. Such transformations had become commonplace by the early 1980s, when Dallas architect Gary M. Cunningham redesigned a former church in the Oak Lawn area for his firm's offices (now shared with Hermanovski Lauck Design); a nearby church, covered in sprayed-on stucco, became Dallas's Hard Rock Cafe.

The significant historic-preservation fights of the 1980s—the Pillot Building in Houston,[1] the Majestic Theater in San Antonio, the central library in Fort Worth, to name a few—waged by do-gooder groups seeking to stop owners from exercising their rights to alter or destroy buildings only

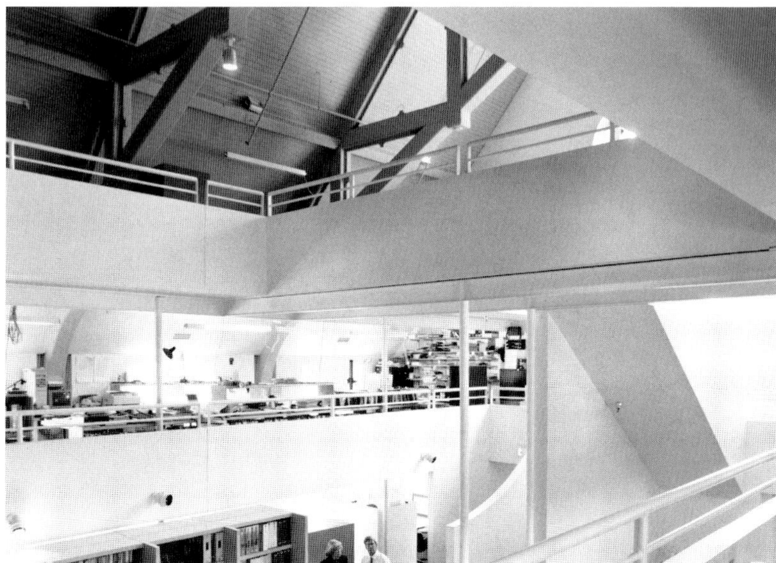

Offices of Cunningham Architects and Hermanovski Lauck Design, Dallas

proved the rule. These efforts either failed, or they succeeded only in making ownership more attractive through financial incentives or enhanced salability. The standard rights of ownership were confirmed even by attempts to thwart them.

In 1989, however, a plan to expand the Kimbell Art Museum in Fort Worth was announced, and the resulting controversy produced an event unprecedented in Texas architectural history: Control of a building was wrested from its owners in the name of cultural preservation.

Completed in 1972, the Kimbell Art Museum is the only Texas work by the Philadelphia architect Louis I. Kahn. It is composed of a series of bays approximately twenty feet wide and eighty feet long, arranged in a classically centralized composition of three bays, punctuated by a lively interior arrangement of galleries, courtyards, support spaces, and circulation areas. The construction is ambiguously modernist, using beautifully finished reinforced concrete for the structural columns and walls, along with concrete beams of heroic length, for example along the entire unsupported base of the wall set above the museum's east entrance. The walls are faced,

Hard Rock Cafe, Dallas

most of the way to the ceiling, in travertine. Wood floors, glass, and precisely detailed stainless steel hardware are used throughout. Each bay containing gallery areas is topped by a cycloid vault (actually a beam in the shape of the arc of a point on a rotating circle) separated by a strip of glass at the module ends from a segmentally arched concrete panel.[2] At the top of each vault is a light monitor in curved perforated stainless steel, which bounces natural and incandescent light onto the walls, Kahn's reworking, according to architect and critic Lawrence Speck, of the clerestory windows atop the cattle sheds of the nearby Fort Worth Fair Grounds.[3]

The overall impression given by the Kimbell is one of unmatched harmony, from its carefully crafted materials to the way it sits on its lawn, to the poetic quality of its interior lighting. During the 1980s, a nationwide consensus developed that Kahn was the best late-twentieth-century American architect, and, along with the Salk Institute in California, the Kimbell came to be seen as the pinnacle of his artistry, the holiest—that is, the most culturally elite—shrine of architecture in Texas.[4] A trip to the Kimbell became a new haj for the architects of Texas, who were pleased to find themselves, for once, in aesthetic agreement with architects and critics from the centers of culture on the East and West coasts.

The public also received the building and the art it housed warmly, coming in increasing numbers to see not just the blockbuster shows that the museum brought to town but the institution's own collection. The newest star in the collection was a Caravaggio painting discovered and authenticated by Edmund Pillsbury, the Kimbell's director since 1980. Pillsbury had also served as director during planning and construction of the Yale Center for British Art, also designed by Kahn but completed after the architect's death in 1974.[5] (Kahn was then at work not only on the government buildings for Bangladesh[6] but on a museum for the Menil Collection in Houston.)[7]

The staff and board of the museum began thinking about possible ways to expand, and began quietly interviewing architects; in early 1989, word leaked out that they had chosen architect Romaldo Giurgola of the highly regarded Philadelphia-based firm Mitchell/Giurgola Architects,[8] who had taught with Kahn at the University of Pennsylvania and who had written a book that helped to boost Kahn's reputation posthumously.[9] Paul Goldberger had called Giurgola "personally as well as professionally Kahn's heir" in 1981.[10] During the early 1980s, Giurgola had moved to Australia to head the office of a joint-venture firm called Mitchell/Giurgola & Thorp, which designed the new Australian Houses of Parliament in Canberra. The Australian parliament project lies mostly under a hill, and when word of Giurgola's selection leaked out, there was some speculation that he would propose an underground addition to the Kimbell under the broad green lawn facing the Amon Carter Museum to the west.[11]

Instead, Giurgola proposed a scheme that looked perfectly self-effacing: The available gallery space of the Kimbell would be doubled simply by adding wings all but identical in massing and finish to Kahn's original galleries—the height and width of the vaults, the lighting scheme, the concrete construction, even travertine panels from the same quarry, everything the same. To indicate that the additions were not part of the original building, Giurgola proposed setting them off simply with twenty-foot-wide, flat-roofed, clerestory-lit "links." The visitor's experience of the new gallery interiors would have been almost indistinguishable from that of the original. The main change would have been to the landscape (the wings would fill the width of the site, requiring the removal of both parking and green areas, and an amphitheater with site-specific sculptures by Isamu Noguchi would have been moved to the west) and to the circulation pattern (parking areas under the new wings, with a light well and stair, Giurgola said, would draw visitors away from the east-facing staff entry to the west entry, as Kahn had intended).[12]

Questioned for a magazine story about the proposal, Kimbell director Pillsbury emphasized that he and Giurgola were "bearing in mind our responsibilities to this great building." He and the Kimbell board hoped to avoid the controversies that had erupted over planned additions to the Guggenheim and Whitney museums in New York, he said. And, at a later lecture at the University of Texas, Pillsbury said that he realized that undertaking a building addition was one of the things most likely to cost a museum director his or her job. But how could things go wrong? The board was solidly behind him and money for the addition would be no problem: $8 million was pledged by board members and others before the plan was announced in July 1989.

By September, however, just the sort of controversy that Pillsbury feared had erupted. Marshall D. Meyers of Philadelphia, the original project architect of the Kimbell and the head of the firm that succeeded Kahn's practice, began talking to critics and influential architects, directing support to block the plan. Paul Goldberger questioned Giurgola's scheme in the *New York Times Magazine* at the end of September.[13] Kahn's widow, Esther I. Kahn, and daughter, Sue Ann, wrote to the Kimbell trustees and to the *Times* urging that the expansion be halted.[14] *Oculus*, the newsletter of the New York Society of Architects, published a series of letters attacking the addition,[15] and David Dillon condemned it in an article in the *Dallas Morning News*. [16]

The real trouble started in November, when Kenneth Frampton and well-known museum architect Richard Meier sent a letter to the Kimbell trustees condemning Giurgola's plan as "mimicry of the most simple-minded character," that "Kahn himself would have abhorred." A who's-who of high-style architects added their signatures to the letter, including Arata Isozaki, James Stirling, Philip Johnson, James Ingo Freed, and Frank Gehry, along with museum director Phyllis Lambert and art-history-institute director Kurt Forster. Henry I. Cobb and Robert Venturi and historian

Mark Gunderson, AIA

These pages: model of Romaldo Giurgola's proposed Kimbell addition

Vincent Scully sent separate letters, as did Marshall Meyers and George E. Patton, the Kimbell's original landscape architect. Fax machines buzzed and telephone lines chattered; Pillsbury's motives and qualifications were dissected; sure, he worked at the Yale Center, it was said, but he had fought Meyers every step of the way, so he had clearly misunderstood Kahn's intentions there as well.[17]

Giurgola joined Pillsbury and members of the Kimbell board in Fort Worth in late November for a sparsely attended presentation of the addition model and a discussion of the central question: What would Kahn have wanted? Giurgola was visibly troubled by the controversy. Pillsbury was combative, describing his quest to preserve the unified museum-going experience that Kahn had created. What would his critics have him and Giurgola do, he demanded—pervert Kahn's intentions by building an underground gallery illuminated with artificial light so that the troublesome collection could be removed from the Kimbell and the building could be appreciated on its own? Pillsbury was similarly combative the following January at a public meeting on the plan in New York, sponsored by the Archi-

Mark Gunderson, AIA

tectural League, highlighted by denunciations from not only Esther Kahn but Anne Tyng, Kahn's former long-time associate.[18] Later, in Texas, a group of Dallas architects circulated a letter asking the Kimbell's board to reconsider, and a group of architecture students from the University of Texas at Arlington picketed the museum.

Local opposition, of course, made no difference, but, soon afterward, Pillsbury announced that Giurgola would drop the plan for additional wings and would explore reusing some of the lower-level office spaces in the Kimbell (set around a little-seen but spectacular courtyard) as galleries. The critics were unmollified. In February, Pillsbury announced that the board had voted, for the time being, to halt all expansion plans.[19]

Did the Kimbell's board ignominiously cave in to pressure? Or did they come to their senses and stop a flawed project? Was Giurgola's plan good or bad architecturally? Would any other configuration have made for a better addition? These are interesting questions, worthy of continuing debate.

But other questions lurk behind them. Why was so much heat generated in a debate that was absolutely aesthetic, with no moral component (with the exception, Pillsbury implied, of the gall of architects from Venturi to Meier to I.M. Pei's partners Freed and Cobb, who have been involved in splashy and controversial additions to other museums)? And how did it turn so quickly into a private conversation among Philadelphians, with a few other East Coast characters in support?

The answers have to do with cultural authority and the ways that money and social class determine authority in controlling architectural meaning. To most of us, buildings are economic objects; if they can bear some of the burden of recording history and culture while serving their primary function, so much the better. But if a building's owner, for economic reasons, needs to alter or destroy the cultural aspect of a building, that's too bad. We in this world live below the line that separates building from architecture.

There is a world above the line, however, and the controversy over the Kimbell expansion shows its intersection with the workaday world. Above the line are people with old money who constitute America's aristocracy. They pay for buildings—museums, clubs, libraries— whose primary function is cultural, rather than economic, which is to say that the buildings serve chiefly to express the sacredness of fortunes that are lived off, rather than pursued. As the Kimbell controversy shows, the paradoxical effect of being above the line in this elevated social class is to enforce a kind of powerlessness in the face of architectural authority. Architecture is necessary to maintenance of the line, so it can't be tampered with unless one has the blessing of the aristocracy of taste (which clearly resides somewhere outside Texas). For those above the line, buildings are not simply things that individuals own and use. Instead they constitute an estate that owns and uses individuals in service to their social class.

What the Kimbell expansion flap dramatized ultimately was the fact that local cultural authority in Texas has been driven to the edge of extinction. Just as banks in California and North Carolina had, by the late 1980s, gobbled up Texas institutions laid low by ill-timed expansion, so the culture lords of American architecture had retaken control of Texas' holiest shrine. They descended from the East to save the Kimbell from the boobs and yokels on its board of directors—people who, up to that time, had been valued peers. The independent architectural authority of Texas, granted in the 1950s, extended in the boom of the '70s and '80s, was yanked like a bad teenager's driver's license.

The coincidence of the collapse of Texas banking and of the halting of the Kimbell expansion is so well timed that it can hardly be ignored. Again, the Kimbell flap was a contest without a moral basis and without readily discernible consequences; its losers still have their millions, while the winners carry away nothing more than inflated reputations. But the situation is a dark portent. With the elitest elite of Texas culture apparently arbitrarily pitched overboard by Easterners, who remained for the developer community in Texas to envy and emulate? Texas society at all levels is porous, and other groups may come forward to fill the gap. But it is equally possible that without the sting of envy, developers can be counted on to kiss the city good-bye. The Kimbell controversy forebodes an acceleration of disaster for all Texas cities.

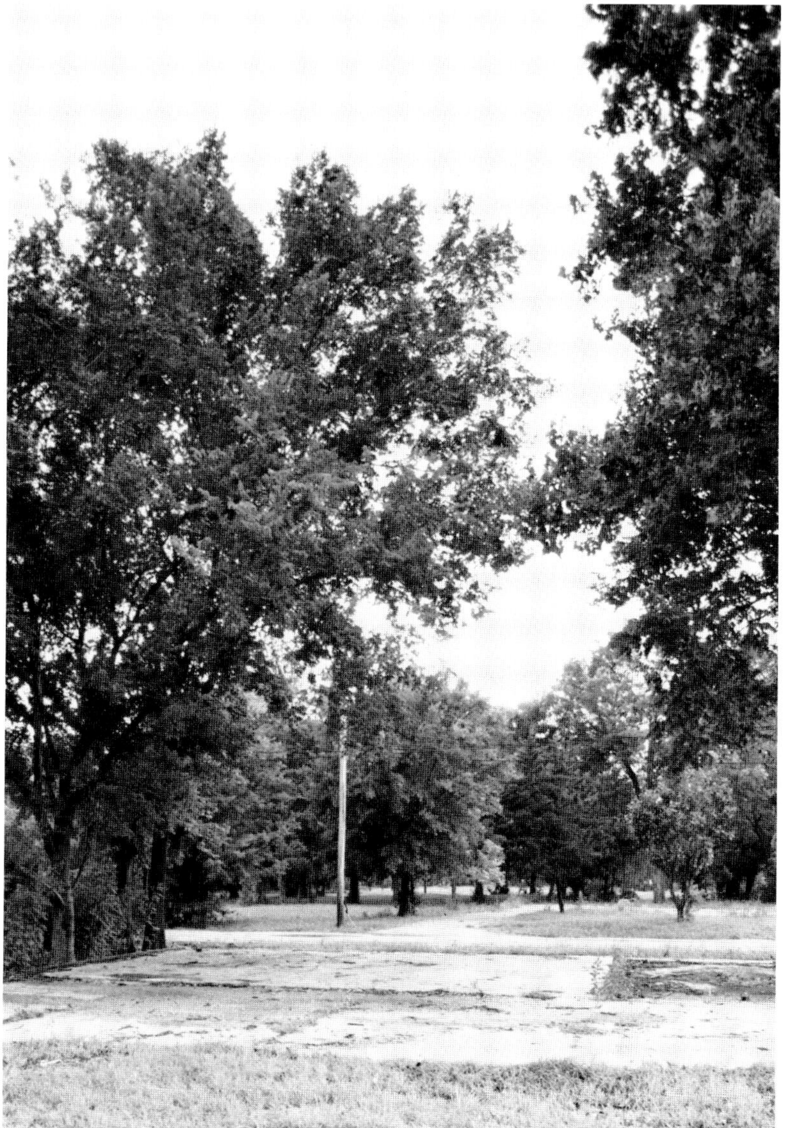

Former neighborhood, Washington at Studemont, Houston

13
Coda

Near the corner of Washington Avenue and Studemont Drive in Houston is a little-noticed landscape, a place of eerie quiet amid the rush of traffic on the neighboring thoroughfares, an arcadian counterpoint to the office towers of downtown Houston a mile to the east. Here, in a space about five blocks from north to south and ten blocks from east to west, one sees at first only widely spaced trees—oaks, pecans, hackberries, elms—and a few shrubs, arranged with an oddly familiar near formality. The streets into the area are blocked off, so it takes a while to notice that the trees are split not just by vacant land, but by driveways, and that, here and there, one can find the remnants of a house foundation. The slight familiarity of the situation becomes clear: This urban grove is made up of the trees of a once-occupied neighborhood. It is as if Christo or Mel Chin or some other environmental artist had been at work, changing what used to be the background into the figurative element, like a Houston version of an eighteenth-century map of Rome by Nolli.

But this is Houston, not Rome, and what lies before us is no intentional work of art. It is a failed real estate development. It was assembled piece by piece over a period of almost ten years by agents acting for the Mischer Corporation (owned by Walter Mischer, who once controlled Allied Bank and a number of Texas S&Ls), then partially cleared, then given back to the lender, First City Bank, when the market fell. The property, which was to have been converted to high-priced residential use or mid-rise office buildings, now belongs to Collecting Bank. This is the suitably unromantic-sounding junk-property arm of First City Bank, created during the latter institution's government-subsidized rescue in the mid-'80s. (The Mischer Corporation, having invented junk for Collecting Bank to own, still manages the property.) The remaining houses in the area were razed when homeless people reportedly started using them to stage muggings of patrons and employees of the nearby ASPCA and YWCA. After the houses were razed, the city had to close the streets because people were dumping trash in the abandoned yards.

The ASPCA, the YWCA, and a few clumps of early twentieth-century commercial buildings, including Rockefeller's nightclub (changed from a small 1925 bank into its present use by Taft Architects in 1978), stand around the edges of the neighborhood, thrown into relief by the emptiness between them. The most poignant of these buildings is the YWCA, more properly the YWCA's Carroll Sterling Masterson Downtown Branch and Metropolitan Offices,[1] designed by Taft Architects and completed in 1980. The Masterson YWCA was one of Taft's earliest relatively large commissions (previous projects had been mostly conversions of nineteenth-century warehouse buildings into offices and apartments on The Strand in Galveston). In it, Taft mixed a lively asymmetrical modernist plan with a strong color palette and a skin-deep exterior wrapping of historical allusions in stucco and colored tile, giving each element of its facade a sense of identity within a unified composition. (The curving parapet-wall shapes around the doors contributed to Nicholas Lemann's slighting reference to Taft in *Texas Monthly* as architects of projects "that look vaguely like the Alamo.")[3] In the process, they produced one of the most influential buildings of the 1980s. Michael Graves, Charles Moore, and Philip Johnson had clearly taken the lead in establishing postmodernism in the architectural mainstream, but when Taft Architects was given a P/A award from *Progressive Architecture* in 1980 and a national honor award for the Masterson YWCA in 1982 by the American Institute of Architects,[4] it showed that even rela-

YWCA Carroll Sterling Masterson Downtown Branch and Metropolitan Offices, Houston (1980), by Taft Architects

tive youngsters way out in the relative sticks could succeed by breaking free of modernism.[5] Within a few cycles of the national design magazines, the means that Taft explored in the Masterson YWCA (and that the other leading postmodernists had ratified) were reduced to a formula that would be repeated by dozens of other architects in hundreds of condos and commercial strips across the country.

With its colors and its billboard-like flat decoration, the Masterson YWCA was always intended to be a foreground building, one that would attract the residents of its mostly Hispanic working-class neighborhood to a place where they could have some wholesome fun in cheerful surroundings. The architectural statement worked. Times have changed, and postmodernism has long since been the mainstream that young architects react against, and Taft Architects has become one of the country's most disparaged firms, if one is to judge by the star architects who come to Texas annually to judge the Texas Society of Architects' design awards competition. That's the way architectural fashions run. The Everest of one year is the Marianas Trench of the next. Such changes also come to developers—Gerald Hines may one day be derided the way that William Zeckendorf and the developers who dominated the 1960s were in the 1980s. Taft's fame came at the expense of earlier modernists, many of whom are now being rehabilitated. In fifteen or twenty years, Taft's work will be rediscovered, and architects will have a new spin on their ongoing controversies. It's a shame that, for now, Taft sometimes gets blamed for the formulaic imitations other people have done of the firm's work, particularly the YWCA, which meshed with its surroundings better than almost any other 1980s building.

What matters most, however, is not architectural style but the fact that the Mischer Corporation took the closest layer of the neighborhood that the YWCA was intended to serve and turned it into a haven for crime and then a multi-block dump. This is a frightening situation to contemplate, but hardly unique.

Take the Lamar Terrace area of Houston, for example. It's easy to find. Just drive west on Hidalgo, a four-lane one-way street through the Galleria area, until it turns into a two-lane, two-way street with potholes big enough to swallow a Cadillac. Speculators led by the Triad Company, owned by international arms merchant Adnan Khashoggi, had reportedly hoped to cash in on the inevitable expansion of the Galleria-Post Oak business center, which is hemmed in to the south and east by freeway overpasses. They had bought up many of the small postwar ranch houses in the neighborhood during the early 1980s. Some householders held out, however; they would later charge that Khashoggi and the other speculators stopped maintaining the properties the speculators held and deliberately rented them to motorcycle gangs and drug dealers, in apparent hopes of breaking the area's deed restrictions and of forcing the hold-outs to accept lower prices. As the condition of the streets also makes clear, city officials began at the same time to neglect the area. A number of houses burned or were cleared away, and commercial uses were established at the neighborhood's edges.[6] Then Khashoggi's Triad Company backed out, leaving the deal's lender, Mainland Savings of Texas City, with a portfolio of very distressed property. Mainland Savings went under soon after.[7] By the early 1990s, another developer had surfaced with a plan for Lamar Terrace; all he wanted was several million dollars in tax abatements, with which he could get some houses and commercial development back in the area.[8] But without a municipal tax subsidy, all agree,

A street in the Lamar Terrace neighborhood, Houston

Lamar Terrace will remain a sinkhole of decay at the edge of the city's most prosperous business center.

There are other examples. In Dallas, preservationists charged that the (now-bankrupt) Campeau Corporation of Canada allowed arson to clear property it had bought in the Vineyard area, just to the north of downtown. And, before the Southland Corporation was driven to the brink of bankruptcy by debt taken on to avoid a hostile takeover, its officials cleared acres of single-family homes and small apartment buildings around North Central Expressway in Dallas in preparation for a never-built cluster of high-priced condos and office projects, marked now only by blocks of broken concrete and weeds surrounding a mostly empty office tower called CityPlace.[9] These neighborhoods are the places where the values of the 1980s were pushed too far and ended up turning themselves inside out. The figure—value—disappeared. The ground—valuelessness—became all that was left.

So here we are. It's probably not fair to say that CityPlace is a fitting example of the '80s vision of the city. That vision, constructed by develop-

CityPlace, Dallas (1989), by Araldo Cossuta

ers and financiers and eagerly embraced by both the architectural profession and the public, is at CityPlace fulfilled by a see-through office building where a for-rent sign marks the penthouse from which the prince was supposed to be taking care of us all. It is wrapped in a neighborhood destroyed by grandiose miscalculation, and it is part of a speculative bubble floated by governmental subsidies at a scale the out-of-work commissars of Moscow might envy.

But that's only a partial view of the 1980s. The decade produced plenty of good things, things we want our children and grandchildren to see, nice office buildings, parks, schools, hospitals, museums, stores, houses, bridges, concert halls, monuments. And surely it can be said that more Americans are better housed and fed than ever before in history; that the distribution of wealth, educational resources, health care, political power, and social justice advanced during the decade, if unevenly. If the decade was not a return to a golden age of American architecture and urbanism, that should be no surprise: As Sam Bass Warner, Jr., has pointed out in *The Urban Wilderness*, there never was such a golden age.

But looking around at what was built in the 1980s, one wonders if this motley collection justifies the hundreds of billions risked and lost in real estate in the decade. It might be if there weren't a sinkhole yawning at the edge of the property, a fault line of hungry valuelessness that threatens to pull us down, a zone of subduction that we helped create by our assent to the myths of the 1980s. Surely it is fair to say that CityPlace, Lamar Terrace, and the neighborhood around the Masterson YWCA, along with dozens of other neighborhoods like them around the state, are markers for the decade's unfinished business, monuments

Blocks cleared for unfinished CityPlace residential development

that rival the bank towers and suburban nodes. The '80s gave some, but the decade took away much more.

Architecture and building, money and meaning, see-through buildings and see-through social institutions, the drawing of lines and the fabrication of structures in the physical world and the collective mind—these are the coordinates of a self-portrait of our society. Architecture may or may not be frozen music; it is certainly frozen social process, a window on a time and a world that has already slipped away, leaving its buildings behind for us to read as best we can.

Reading the architecture of the 1980s for lessons is a lost cause, however. The buildings of the decade have nothing to teach us, because the decade's rituals and myths, the fears fled and dreams embraced, all mixed up as they were, are not things we can separate ourselves from. They are *us*. The decade's creations merely represented the local hypertrophy of ongoing social and economic forces that originated elsewhere and earlier and that continue today unchanged.

Notes

Foreword

1. Douglas Milburn and Thomas Stanley Richmond, *The Last American City, An Intrepid Walker's Guide to Houston* (Houston: Chapbook Press, 1979).
2. Stephen Fox, *Houston Architectural Guide* (Houston: American Institute of Architects, 1990).

Chapter One: J.R. McConnell Died for Our Sins

1. David Dillon, "Constantly Changing Minimalist Tower," *Architecture* (December 1986), pp. 45-49.
2. Stephen Fox, *Houston Architectural Guide* (Houston: American Institute of Architects, 1990).

   Carleton Knight III, "Significant Clients: Gerald Hines," *Architecture* (April 1984), pp. 48-56.

   John Pastier, "Evaluation: Pennzoil as Sculpture and Symbol," *AIA Journal* (June 1982), pp. 38-43.

3. Charles Jencks, *Architecture Today* (New York: Harry N. Abrams, 1988) pp. 10-141.
4. Stephen Fox, *Houston Architectural Guide.*
   Knight, pp. 48-56.
   John Pastier, "A Tale of Two Houston Towers," *Architecture* (April 1984), pp. 39-47.
   Pilar Viladas, "Gothic Romance," *Progressive Architecture* (February 1984), pp. 86-93.
5. Susan Doubilet, "Not Enough Said," *Progressive Architecture* (February 1984), pp. 70-75.
6. John Jacobus, "Philip Johnson: His Work, His Times," *Progressive Architecture* (February 1984), pp. 98-100. This remark, which was first quoted by Jacobus, is usually rendered, "One cannot not know history."
7. James O'Shea, *The Daisy Chain: How Borrowed Billions Sank a Texas S&L* (New York: Simon & Schuster, 1991).
   Stephen Pizzo, Mary Fricker, and Paul Muolo, *Inside Job: The Looting of America's Savings & Loans* (New York: Harper Perennial, 1991).
   Thomas C. Hayes, "Texan Gets Five Years in Big S.&L. Collapse (Don Dixon)," *The New York Times* (April 3, 1991), pp. 1, 3 C.
   Nathaniel C. Nash, "Why they're going to you to rescue S&Ls," *Austin American-Statesman* (July 10, 1989), p. 4 M.
8. Leonard M. Apcar, "First RepublicBank expects record loss for 4th quarter of at least $326 million," *Wall Street Journal* (December 3, 1987), p. 2.
   Jeff Gerth, "Report Faults F.D.I.C. in 2 Bank Bailouts," *The New York Times* (January 31, 1991), p. 1 C.
   Robert Rankin, "NCNB's sweet deal will cost taxpayers billions, study says," *Austin American-Statesman* (January 31, 1991), p. 9 A.
9. Thomas C. Hayes, "Ticor suit charges fraud by developer," *The New York Times* (July 24, 1987), p. 25.
   "Hard Times for a Real J.R." *Time* (September 16, 1987), p. 65.
   Caleb Solomon, "Indictments awaited in real-estate case related to McConnell's collapsed empire," *Wall Street Journal* (October 29, 1987), p. 35.
   Patricia Manson, "Developer indicted in massive title scam," *Houston Post* (October 30, 1987), p. 1A.
   Carl Hooper, "Developer's rags to riches story," *Houston Post* (October 30, 1987), p. 24 A.

Leslie Loddeke, "Dissatisfied homeowners ponder title problems," *Houston Post* (October 30, 1987), p. 24 A.

Caleb Solomon, "McConnell, five others indicted in Houston on bank-fraud allegations," *Wall Street Journal* (October 30, 1987), p. 20.

"Six indictments in title case (largest insurance-fraud case in U.S. history)," *The New York Times* (October 31, 1987), p. 28.

Todd Vogel, "J.R. McConnell: the ballad of a Texas tornado," *Business Week* (November 9, 1987), p. 80.

Jim McTague, "Fugitive turns himself in as fraud hearing begins," *American Banker* (November 19, 1987), p. 3.

Robert Stanton, "McConnell apparently electrocutes himself," *Houston Post* (July 5, 1988), p. 1A.

Mary Flood and Patricia Manson, "'This isn't justice,' creditors say," *Houston Post* (July 5, 1988), p. 1A.

Carl Hooper, "McConnell's death left pledge unfulfilled," *Houston Post* (July 5, 1988), p. 1 B.

Peter Applebome, "Texas real estate tycoon takes his own life in jail," *The New York Times* (July 6, 1988), p. 10.

Eric Gerber, "Driven to die," *Houston Post* (July 8, 1988), p. 2 E.

Jane A. Grandolfo, "McConnell's family blames system, not indicted inmate, for his death," *Houston Post* (July 8, 1988), p. 10 A.

Jeff Awalt, "Tycoon leaves conflicting legacy," *Dallas Morning News* (December 7, 1988), p. 37 A.

"Speculator's bankruptcy case may take 3 years to resolve," *Dallas Morning News* (June 19, 1989), p. 10 B.

Patricia Manson, "Jury returns guilty verdict in McConnell-linked case," *Houston Post* (January 30, 1990), p. 2 A.

10. Michael Graves, *Michael Graves, Buildings and Projects 1982-1989* (New York: Rizzoli Press, 1990).

11. Spiro Kostof, *A History of Architecture: Settings and Rituals* (New York: Oxford University Press, 1985).

12. Ian Angus and Sut Jhally, eds., *Cultural Politics in Contemporary America* (New York: Routledge, 1989).

John Berger, *About Looking* (New York: Pantheon Books, 1980).

———, *Ways of Seeing* (London: British Broadcasting Company and Penguin Books, 1972).

Peter L. Berger and Thomas Luckmann, *The Social Construction of Reality* (New York: Doubleday, 1967).

Neville Brody and Stuart Ewen, "Design Insurgency," *Print* (January/February 1990), pp. 118-125.

Bruce Lincoln, *Discourse and the Construction of Society: Comparative Studies of Myth, Ritual, and Classification* (New York: Oxford University Press, 1989).

Roger Scruton, *The Aesthetics of Architecture* (Princeton: Princeton University Press, 1979).

Bruce Webb and Peter J. Zweig, "Gone to Texas: The Search for a Symbolic Landscape," *Texas Architect* (November/December 1982), pp. 56-61.

13. Constance Perin, *Everything in Its Place: Social Order and Land Use in America* (Princeton: Princeton University Press, 1977).

Carol F. Steinbach, "Shelter Skelter," *National Journal* (April 8, 1989), pp. 851-855.

Katherine S. Newman, *Falling From Grace: The Experience of Downward Mobility in the American Middle Class* (New York: Vintage Books, 1989).

14. Barbara Ehrenreich, *Fear of Falling: The Inner Life of the Middle Class* (New York: Pantheon Books, 1989).

15. Michelle Kay, "Boom or Bust: The '80s in Texas," *Austin American-Statesman* (December 25, 1989), pp. 1, 8 C.

16. Robert D. Bullard, *Invisible Houston: The Black Experience in Boom and Bust* (College Station: Texas A&M University Press, 1987).

Chandler Davidson, *Race and Class in Texas Politics* (Princeton: Princeton University Press, 1990).

Nicholas Lemann, "Healing the Ghettos," *Atlantic Monthly* (March 1991), pp. 20-24.

Sam Bass Warner, Jr., *The Urban Wilderness: A History of the American City* (New York: Harper & Row, 1972).

17. Al Cox, "Map Aimed at Saving Landmarks," *Texas Architect* (November/December 1988), p. 11.

18. David Kaplan, "Suburbia Deserta," *Cite* (Winter 1986), p. 18.

19. Foreclosure figures compiled by Texas Comptroller's Office, Research Division, Austin.

20. Steve Lohr, "Banking's Real Estate Miseries," *The New York Times* (January 13, 1991), pp. C1, C6.

21. Michael Benedikt, "Realness and Realism," *Center* (Vol. 4, 1988), pp. 78-89.

22. Arjun Appurdai, ed., *The Social Life of Things: Commodities in Social Perspective* (Cambridge, U.K.: Cambridge University Press, 1986), pp. 3-63.

Pierre Bourdieu, *Distinction: A Social Critique of the Judgement of Taste*, trans. Richard Nice (Cambridge, Mass.: Harvard University Press, 1984).

23. "Growth in Architects' Income Lags Behind Other Professionals'," *Architecture* (June 1982), p. 22.

24. Robert Sobel, *Trammell Crow, Master Builder* (New York: John Wiley and Sons, 1989).

Jim Powell, *Risk, Ruin and Riches: Inside the World of Big Time Real Estate* (New York: Macmillan, 1986).

25. Stephen Harrigan, "The Governor's New Clothes," *Texas Monthly* (May 1981), pp. 128-132, 212-221.

26. Gary Cartwright, "Paradise Lost," *Texas Monthly* (October 1987), pp. 116-121, 180-187.

Richard Ingersoll, "Las Colinas: The Ultimate Bourgeois Utopia," *Texas Architect* (January/February 1989), pp. 22-30.

27. Lila Stillson, "Robert H.H. Hugman," *Texas Architect* (November/December 1989), p. 59.

28. David Dillon, *Dallas Architecture 1936-1986* (Austin: Texas Monthly Press, 1986).

29. Berger and Luckmann, *The Social Construction of Reality*.

30. Sobel, *Trammell Crow, Master Builder*.

Richard D. Hylton, "Trammell Crow Plans Revamping," *The New York Times* (January 11, 1991), p. 1 D.

31. Joel Warren Barna, "UT conference on the new regionalism," *Texas Architect* (July/August 1986), pp. 28-32, 64.

32. Pamela Lewis, "Excellence in Architecture: AIA honors outstanding home designs," *Houston Post* (March 11, 1990), p. 4 F.

33. Nicholas Lemann, "The Architects," *Texas Monthly* (April 1982), pp. 142-151, 219-232.

Carleton Knight III, "Significant Clients: Gerald Hines," *Architecture* (April 1984), pp. 48-56.

John Pastier, "A Tale of Two Houston Towers," *Architecture* (April 1984), pp. 39-47.

Pilar Viladas, "Gothic Romance," *Progressive Architecture* (February 1984), pp. 86-93.

David Dillon, "A Sibling But Far From a Twin," *Architecture* (January 1988), pp. 50-55.

John Pastier, "Evaluation: Pennzoil as Sculpture and Symbol," *AIA Journal* (June 1982), pp. 38-43

34. "Harold Farb," *Texas Monthly* (September 1990), p. 126.
"This Is Farb," *Cite* (Spring 1983), p. 14.
Sandy Sheehy, *Texas Big Rich* (New York: St. Martin's Paperbacks, 1990), pp. 51-54.

35. David Dillon, "Why is Dallas Architecture So Bad?" *D* (May 1980), pp. 102-109.

36. Mary McLeod, "Architecture and Politics in the Reagan Era: From Post-modernism to Deconstructivism," *Assemblage* (February 1989), pp. 22-59.

37. Peter Dormer, *The Meanings of Modern Design: Towards the Twenty-First Century* (London: Thames and Hudson, 1990).
Patricia Leigh Brown, "When Big Name Talents Tackle Trifles," *The New York Times (*August 21, 1988), pp. 28, 30.

38. Roger Scruton, *The Aesthetics of Architecture (*Princeton: Princeton University Press, 1979), pp. 108-109.

39. Charles Jencks, *Architecture Today.*
Leon Whiteson, "Kentucky Home," *Architecture* (October 1990), pp. 52-53.

40. Knight, "Significant Clients: Gerald Hines."
Brody and Ewen, "Design Insurgency."

41. Thorstein Veblen, *The Theory of the Leisure Class* (New York: Penguin Books, 1967).
John Ruskin, *The Seven Lamps of Architecture* (New York: Dover Publications, 1989).

42. Diane Ghirardo, "Architecture and Taste," *Architecture California* (August 1990), p. 51.

43. Roberta Brandes Gratz, *The Living City* (New York: Touchstone/Simon & Schuster, 1989).
Peter G. Rowe, *Making a Middle Landscape* (Cambridge, Mass.: MIT Press, 1991).

44. Alton Parrish, "Money Down the Drain," *Houston Press* (February 28, 1991), pp. 10-12.
Douglas Pegues Harvey, "Escape from the Planet of the Modernists: Beyond the Growth Syndrome," *Texas Architect* (September/October 1988), pp. 40-43.

45. David Dillon, "Magnets at the city's edge," *Dallas Morning News* (March 11, 1991), pp. 5-6 C.
Joel Warren Barna, "Technology and the Future of Texas Cities," *Texas Architect* (May/June 1991), p. 3.

Chapter Two: Middle-Class Houses of the 1980s

1. Sam Bass Warner, Jr., *The Urban Wilderness: A History of the American City* (New York: Harper & Row, 1972).

   James Marston Fitch, Jr., *American Building: The Historical Forces That Shaped It* (New York: Schocken Books, 1973).

   Kenneth Jackson, *Crabgrass Frontier: The Suburbanization of the United States* (New York: Oxford University Press, 1985).

   Charles Moore, Gerald Allen, and Donlyn Lyndon, *The Place of Houses* (New York: Holt, Rinehart and Winston, 1974).

2. Clifford Edward Clark, Jr., *The American Family Home 1800-1960* (Chapel Hill: University of North Carolina Press, 1986).

   Gwendolyn Wright, *Building the Dream: A Social History of Housing in America* (New York: Pantheon, 1981).

3. Virginia and Lee McAlester, *A Field Guide to American Houses* (New York: Alfred A. Knopf, 1984).
4. Clark, *The American Family Home 1800-1960.*
5. Folke T. Kihlstedt, "The Automobile and the Transformation of the American House, 1910-1935," in David L. Lewis and Lawrence Goldstein, eds., *The Automobile and American Culture* (Ann Arbor: University of Michigan Press, 1983).
6. James J. Flink, *The Automobile Age* (Cambridge, Mass.: MIT Press, 1990).
7. Michael Benedikt, *For an Architecture of Reality* (New York: Lumen Books, 1988).
8. Michael J. Weiss, *The Clustering of America* (New York: Harper & Row, 1988).
9. "2535 Congress Apartments, Dallas," *Texas Architect* (July 1967), pp. 14-17.
10. "Inwood Manor Apartments, Houston," *Texas Architect* (May 1967), pp. 8-12.
11. "Design Excellence: Mark Kaufman and Donald Meeks," *Professional Builder* (January 1983).
12. Marianne Lagerquist Cooley and Leslie Stockman, "Park Place," *Builder* (January 1983), pp. 120-121.

    Tracy Everbach, "Ex-thrift owner Dixon convicted of fraud, jailed," *Dallas Morning News* (December 21, 1990), p. 1 A.

13. Michael Berryhill, "Riding High in Texas," *Builder* (January 1983), pp. 106-109.

    Marianne Lagerquist Cooley and Leslie Stockman, "Richland Trace," *Builder* (January 1983), pp. 110-111.

———, "Emily Lane," *Builder* (January 1983), p. 112.
———, "Country Grove," *Builder* (January 1983), p. 113.
———, "Christiana," *Builder* (January 1983), pp. 122-123.

14. Ray Don Tilley, "Long and Light in a Tight Spot," *Texas Architect* (November/December 1988), pp. 38-39.
15. "Grove Court, Houston, Texas, by Taft Architects," *Architectural Record* (July 1981), pp. 80-83.
16. Lois Smith Brady, "The New Family House," *Esquire* (July 1985), pp. 56-57.
17. Douglas Milburn, "Eight Projects in Houston," *Architectural Record* (June 1985), pp. 117-133.
18. Philip Langdon, *American Houses* (New York: Stewart, Tabori & Chang, 1987).
19. Joel Warren Barna, "Architecture as Understatement (Keating house)," *Texas Architect* (March/April 1986), pp. 38-39.
20. Peter G. Rowe, *Making a Middle Landscape* (Cambridge, Mass.: MIT Press, 1991).
21. Joel Warren Barna, "Texas Houses: Context Versus Subtext," *Texas Architect* (May/June 1989), pp. 24-27.
22. Joseph Rykwert, *On Adam's House in Paradise: The Idea of the Primitive Hut in Architectural History*, second ed. (Cambridge, Mass.: MIT Press, 1981).
23. Frank D. Welch, "On the House," *Texas Architect* (May/June 1983), pp. 58-63.
24. Stephen Fox, *Houston Architectural Guide*, p. 114.
25. Joel Warren Barna, "Power House," *Progressive Architecture* (December 1988), pp. 88-95.
26. ———, "Carraro House," *Texas Architect* (January/February 1992), pp. 30-31.
27. R. Lawrence Good, "Modern Texas Architecture: In the Details," *Texas Architect* (November/December 1991), pp. 34-43.
28. Joel Warren Barna, "Texas Houses: Context Versus Subtext," *Texas Architect* (May/June 1989), pp. 24-27.
29. ———, "House on Sunny Slope," *Texas Architect* (January/February 1990), p. 27.
30. Douglas Brenner, "Mixon House, Houston, Texas, by Taft Architects," *Architectural Record* (Mid-April 1985), pp. 134-139.

Chapter Three: '80s Middle-Class Workplaces

1. Nora Richter Greer, "Deco Lines on a Houston High Rise," *Architecture* (December 1983), pp. 62-65.
2. Stephen Fox, "Transformation: Corporate Imagery in Tall Buildings," *Texas Architect* (May/June 1986), pp. 120-129.
3. Joel Warren Barna, "Company Headquarters in the Second Age," *Texas Architect* (May/June 1987), pp. 28-34.
4. Barbara Lippert, "For AT&T, it's slice of dull after slice of death," *Advertising Week's Marketing Week* (July 11, 1988), p. 11.

   Joel Warren Barna, "Palazzo to Plug-In: Offices are Evolving," *Texas Architect* (July/August 1988), pp. 38-41.
5. Figures on service sector as share of the economy provided by the Texas Comptroller's Office.
6. Adrian Forty, *Objects of Desire: Design and Society from Wedgewood to IBM* (New York: Pantheon Books, 1986).
7. Robert Probst, *The Office–A facility based on change*, fourth impression (Zeeland, Mich.: Herman Miller, 1981).

   George Rand, "Whatever Happened to the Office of the Future," *Architecture* (December 1986), pp. 106-108.
8. Peter F. Drucker, *The Frontiers of Management* (New York: Harper & Row, 1986).
9. Mary S. Gluckman, "The Constant Office: The Dark Side of the Boom," *Omni* (April 1991), pp. 36-94.
10. Tom Peters, *In Search of Excellence: The Leadership Difference* (New York: Random House, 1985).

    Kenneth Blanchard and Spencer Johnson, *The One-Minute Manager* (New York: Morrow, 1982).

    Mary Walton, *The Deming Management Method* (New York: Perigee Books, 1986).
11. Leonard Lane, "Checking Out HEB's Arsenal," *Texas Architect* (November/December 1986), pp. 104-109.
12. Jeffrey Karl Ochsner, "The Past in Our Future," *Texas Architect* (July/August 1986), pp. 38-47.
13. Richard Ingersoll, "Pianissimo: The Very Quiet Menil Collection," *Texas Architect* (May/June 1987), pp. 40-47.

"The Menil Collection: Art Amid the Bungalows," *Wall Street Journal* (June 16, 1987).

John Russell, "At Last, a 'Museum Without Walls'. . . ," *The New York Times* (June 14, 1987), pp. 33-35.

14. Joel Warren Barna, "Houston Builds Civic Projects," *Texas Architect* (May/June 1985), pp. 28-30.
15. ———, "Company Headquarters in the Second Age."
16. Carleton Knight III, "Serene Pavilions Traversing a Lake (Conoco Headquarters, Houston)," *Architecture* (December 1986), pp. 56-61.
17. Scott Burns, "Index Shows devastating erosion of family's buying power in '80s," *Houston Post* (March 11, 1991), p. 3 C.
18. Walter Russell Mead, "The New Old Capitalism: Long Hours, Low Wages," *Rolling Stone* (May 30, 1991), p. 27.

    Don Stowers, "Downward Mobility: employee leasing may be your ticket to the poverty line," *Houston Press* (June 13, 1991), pp. 10-12.

Chapter Four: Schools from the Bottom Up

1. Yolita Schmidt, "Donald Barthelme," *Texas Architect* (November/December 1989), p. 44.
2. R. Lawrence Good, "William Wayne Caudill," *Texas Architect* (November/December 1989), pp. 46-47.
3. William W. Caudill, *Space for Teaching* (College Station: Bulletin of the Agricultural and Mechanical College of Texas), Vol. 12, no. 9, August 1, 1941.

   "West Columbia School," *Architectural Forum* (October 1952), pp. 102-109.

   "New Schools," *Architectural Record* (November 1951), pp. 144-176.
4. Olga Garza, *Interim News #70-6: Edgewood v. Kirby* (Austin: House Research Organization), April 1988, pp. 1-10.
5. Joel Warren Barna, "A New Start at Edgewood ISD," *Texas Architect* (September/October 1988), pp. 30-35.
6. Robert Suro, "Texas to shift money to poor districts," *The New York Times* (April 12, 1991), p. A 10.
7. Garza, *Interim News #70-6: Edgewood v. Kirby*.

   Mike Greenberg, "Plaza Guadalupe, San Antonio," *Architecture* (March 1986), pp. 57-59.

9. Barna, "A New Start at Edgewood ISD."
———, "Edgewood Schools," *Texas Architect* (March/April 1991), p. 37.
10. R. Lawrence Good, "The State of Texas Architecture 1987," *Texas Architect* (November/December 1987), pp. 46-49.
11. James S. Russell, "Back to Bells and Cells?" *Architectural Record* (September 1988), pp. 100-105.
12. Terrence Stutz, "Many fail state's new skills test," *Dallas Morning News* (December 21, 1991), pp. 1 A, 23 A.

Chapter Five: Feeling Better about Medical Buildings

1. Kirk Hamilton and Ray Pentecost, "Health Care: Architecture in an Evolving Market," *Texas Architect* (January/February 1986), pp. 34-37.
2. Joel Warren Barna, "In Health Care, Form Follows Funding," *Texas Architect* (January/February 1986), pp. 38-41.
3. Barna, "In Health Care, Form Follows Funding."
4. Representatives David Stockman and Phil Gramm, *The Administration's Case for Hospital Cost Containment: A Critical Analysis* (Austin: Texas Hospital Association, 1979).
5. Robert Douglass, "Unbundling New Medical Services," *Texas Architect* (January/February 1986), pp. 42-47.
6. Carol J. Loomis, "Killer Cost Stalking Business," in Robert Emmett Long, ed., *The Crisis in Health Care* (New York: H.W. Wilson, 1991).
7. Charles J. Dougherty, *American Health Care: Rights, Realities, and Reforms* (New York: Oxford University Press, 1988).
8. Joel Warren Barna, "A Well-Healed Building Boom," *Texas Architect* (May/June 1990), pp. 34-39.

Chapter Six: Plans and Curses in Downtown Austin

1. Kim Tyson, "Plans begin to gel for building on Alamo Hotel site," *Austin American-Statesman* (July 17, 1986), p. 1 D.
2. Dick Stanley, "Old hotel is 'hexed' on behalf of the needy," *Austin American-Statesman* (August 17, 1984), p. 1 B.
3. Kirk Ladendorf, "Japanese firm to help build Lamar project," *Austin American-Statesman* (February 17, 1986), p. 1 B.

4. ———, "Lamar Savings Sues former executive Stanley Adams," *Austin American-Statesman* (March 2, 1988), p. 1 A.

———, "An American Excess Story: Former head of Lamar did everything in a big way," *Austin American-Statesman* (September 17, 1989), p. 1 J.

———, "Court papers describe Lamar's 'spending orgy,'" *Austin American-Statesman* (September 17, 1989), p. 1 J.

———, "Former Lamar official indicted on 10 bank fraud charges," *Austin American-Statesman* (November 9, 1989), p. 1 F.

5. ———, "Thrift boss files for governor," *Austin American-Statesman* (January 3, 1990), p. 11 A.

———, "Fraud trial of former Lamar Savings executive set to begin," *Austin American-Statesman* (February 25, 1990), p. 1 J.

6. Al L. Ears, "True Stories," *Austin Chronicle* (October 11, 1991), p. 13.

7. Kirk Ladendorf, "Adams pleads guilty to two federal charges," Austin *American-Statesman* (November 16, 1991), p. 1 D.

8. Michael McCullar, "Austin's Heart: Congress Avenue Transformed," *Texas Architect* (May/June 1985), pp. 40-49.

Hank Todd Smith, ed., *Austin: Its Architects and Architecture, 1836-1986* (Austin: Austin Chapter, American Institute of Architects, 1986).

9. *Office Vacancy Index of the United States, December 31, 1987* (Boston: Coldwell Banker/Torto Wheaton Services, February 1988).

10. Sim van der Ryn and Peter Calthorpe, *Sustainable Communities: A New Design Synthesis for Cities, Suburbs and Towns* (San Francisco: Sierra Club Books, 1991).

11. Sinclair Black, "Prospects for Downtown Austin," *Texas Architect* (May/June 1981), pp. 36-45.

12. Ray Ydoyaga, "Civic Identity in the Land of the Laid Back," *Texas Architect* (May/June 1985), pp. 50-59.

13. Michael McCullar, "Proposals for New Austin Downtown Municipal Complex Winnowed Down to Two," *Texas Architect* (January/February 1983), p. 78.

14. ———, "Austin Launches Municipal Hall Competition," *Texas Architect* (September/October, 1983), pp. 21-22, 24.

———, "Austin Announces City Hall Design Competition," *Texas Architect* (January/February 1984), pp. 89-90.

15. Ray Ydoyaga, "Winners Announced in Austin City Hall Competition," *Texas Architect* (May/June 1984), pp. 24-26.

16. Michael McCullar, "Scraping the Sky in Austin: A Problem of Conflicting Views in Texas' Capital City," *Texas Architect* (May/June 1982), pp. 49-51, 81.
 ———, "Austin's Heart: Congress Avenue Transformed," *Texas Architect* (May/June 1985), pp. 40-49.
17. Charles Gallatin, "Austin City Council Rejects Watson-Casey," *Texas Architect* (May/June 1986), pp. 136, 138.
18. Michael McCullar, "Venturi Rauch Scott Brown Announced as Designers of New Laguna Gloria in Austin," *Texas Architect* (May/June 1983), pp. 18-19.
 Blair Fitzsimons, "Venturi Museum Approved by Austin Voters," *Texas Architect* (March/April 1985), pp. 28, 31-32.
 Ray Ydoyaga, "Venturi Talks about Final Plans for Austin Museum," *Texas Architect* (March/April 1986), pp. 20-22.
 James S. Russell, "Living on Borrowed Light," *Architectural Record* (May 1989), pp. 150-155.
19. Ydoyaga, "Civic Identity in the Land of the Laid Back."
20. Jeffrey Karl Ochsner, "The Past in Our Future: New Urban Design in Texas," *Texas Architect* (July/August 1986), pp. 38-47.
21. David Dillon, "The Sinking of Laguna Gloria," *Dallas Morning News* (January 28, 1990), p. 1 C.
22. McCullar, Michael "Austin Convention Center Project Gains Momentum," *Texas Architect* (July/August 1988), pp. 7, 11, 24.
23. ———, "With Allusions to Tuscany Along a Downtown Lake," *Texas Architect* (March/April 1985), pp. 50-51.
24. ———, "Austin's Heart: Congress Avenue Transformed."
25. ———, "Salvation Army's home fits the urban bill," *Austin American-Statesman* (March 12, 1988), pp. 1 B, 11 B.

Chapter Seven: Tower Tops in Dallas

1. Stephen Fox, "Transformation: Corporate Imagery in Tall Buildings," *Texas Architect* (May/June 1986), pp. 120-129.
2. Robert Hughes, "Philip Johnson, Maverick Designer," *Time* (January 8, 1979).
3. Charles Jencks, *Skyscrapers-Skycities* (New York: Rizzoli, 1980).
4. Stephen Fox, *Houston Architectural Guide* (Houston: American Institute of Architects, 1990).

5. Virginia and Lee McAlester, *Discover Dallas Fort Worth* (New York: Alfred A. Knopf, 1988).
6. David Dillon, *Dallas Architecture 1936-1986* (Austin: Texas Monthly Press, 1986).
7. James Baker, "Bank One Center and Interiors of the 1990s," *Texas Architect* (August 1991), pp. 17-19.
8. Jim Murphy, "Trammell Crow Company, Two Generations," *Progressive Architecture* (July 1985), pp. 95-104.

   David Dillon, *Dallas Architecture 1936-1986* (Austin: Texas Monthly Press, 1986).

   ———, "A Sibling But Far From a Twin," *Architecture* (January 1988), pp. 50-55.
9. McAlester, *Discover Dallas Fort Worth.*
10. Ray Ydoyaga, "2200 Ross Place, Dallas, by SOM Houston," *Texas Architect* (January/February 1985), p. 67.

    Paul Goldberger, "Dallas Punches a Hole in the Heart of Its Skyline," *The New York Times* (February 14, 1988), p. 31 H.

    Joel Warren Barna, "Hole in One," *Texas Architect* (November/December 1988), p. 24.
11. ———, "Downtown Blueprint Now Includes People," *Dallas Times Herald* (May 10, 1987), p. 2 D.
12. ———, "Two Dallas Towers," *Texas Architect* (July/August 1987), pp. 42-44.

    ———, "The Texas Commerce Tower," *Cite* (Winter 1987), p. 9.
13. Peter Arnell and Ted Bickford, eds., *Southwest Center: The Houston Competition* (New York: Rizzoli, 1983).
14. "The Hole Truth," *Wall Street Journal* (March 6, 1987), p. 33.

Chapter Eight: Public Housing and Welfare

1. George Rodrigue and Craig Flournoy, "Housing on the Hit List," *Dallas Morning News* (February 17, 1985), pp. 1, 26 A.
2. Rachel G. Bratt, *Rebuilding a Low-Income Housing Policy* (Philadelphia: Temple University Press, 1989).
3. George Rodrigue and Craig Flournoy, "Housing on the Hit List: Reagan proposes deep cuts in HUD funding," *Dallas Morning News* (February 17, 1985), pp. 2, 26 A.

   Carol F. Steinbach, "Shelter-Skelter," *National Journal* (April 8, 1989), pp. 851-855.
4. "It's who you knew at HUD," *Time* (May 22, 1989), p. 39.

5. Jane Baird, "Housing Authority Director Resigns," *Houston Post* (March 16, 1990), p. 1 A.
6. Joel Warren Barna, "Public Housing Master Plan Dropped in Dallas," *Texas Architect* (November/December 1986), pp. 22-24.
   Diane R. Suchman and Marcia I. Lamb, "West Dallas Poised for Change," *Urban Land* (January 1991), pp. 10-16.
7. Rives Taylor, "Fourth Ward and the Siege of Allen Parkway Village," *Cite* (Spring 1991), pp. 21-24.
8. Joel Warren Barna, "Founders Park plan proposed," *Texas Architect* (May/June 1990), p. 8.
   Jane Baird, "Founders Park master plan put on table," *Houston Post* (December 4, 1990), pp. 1, 10 C.
9. Kate Thomas, "Developers eye back-door attack on taxpayers' pocketbooks," *Houston Post* (July 25, 1990), p. 1 C.
10. John Focke, "Founders Park hears citizen needs," *Texas Architect* (November/December 1991), pp. 13, 16.
11. Jane Baird, "Craig Washington Unveils Redevelopment Plan for Allen Parkway Village and Fourth Ward," *Houston Post* (March 16, 1990), p. 1 A.
12. Joel Warren Barna, "A Home of One's Own," *Cite* (Spring/Summer 1989), pp. 12-13.
    ———, "Housing for the Other Houston," *Texas Architect* (May/June 1988), pp. 30-35.
    John Rogers, "Series sounds alarm for public housing," *Texas Architect* (May/June 1990), p. 12.
13 Mitchell Sviridoff, *Community Development Corporations: A strategy for depressed urban and rural areas* (New York: Ford Foundation, 1973).
    Neal Pierce and Carol F. Steinbach, *Corrective Capitalism* (New York: Ford Foundation, 1987).
14. John Rogers, "The Rise of the Community Development Corporations," *Cite* (Spring 1991), p. 11.
15. Luis Alberto Bodmer, "El Mercado del Sol: Pioneering Redevelopment Solutions in Houston" (unpublished manuscript).
    Jane Baird, "Urban Decay's Taxing Problems," *Houston Post* (November 19, 1990), pp. 1-9 F.
16. Joel Warren Barna, "CDCs, a New Force in Affordable Housing," *Progressive Architecture* (June 1991), pp. 72-73.

Kirk Ladendorf, "The Thin Red Line: Law spurs bank lending in low-income areas," *Austin American-Statesman* (February 5, 1990), Capital Business, pp. 1, 13.

17. Kathleen Teltsch, "Charities to Build Housing in 20 Cities," *The New York Times* (February 27, 1991).
18. Charles Jencks, *The Language of Postmodern Architecture*, third ed. (New York: Rizzoli, 1981), p. 9.
19. Katharine G. Bristol, "The Pruitt-Igoe Myth," *Journal of Architectural Education* (May 1991), pp. 163-171.
20. U.S. Census Bureau, *Federal Grants to the States (1981-91)* (Washington D.C.: U.S. Government Printing Office, 1991).

Chapter Nine: Solana, the Electronic Hacienda

1. Joel Warren Barna, "Solana's Place in the Sun," *Progressive Architecture* (April 1989), pp. 65-74.

   Ellen Posner, "Architecture: Visiting Solana," *Wall Street Journal* (November 8, 1989), p. A 16.

   Paul Goldberger, "I.B.M.'s Urbane New Place in the Sun in Texas," *The New York Times* (October 22, 1989), p. 42.

   "Legorreta Arquitectos: IBM Southlake and Village Center Solana, Westlake/Southlake, Texas, 1986-89," *GA Document #24* (1989).
2. Wayne Attoe, assisted by Sidney H. Brisker, *The Architecture of Ricardo Legorreta* (Austin: University of Texas Press, 1990).
3. David Dillon, "Of the Land," *Architecture* (November 1990), pp. 94-101.
4. Gayle Golden, "The Other Perot," *Dallas Life Magazine, Dallas Morning News* (December 10, 1989), pp. 12-25.

Chapter Ten: The Dallas Arts District

1. David Dillon, "Dallas Arts District," *Progressive Architecture* (June 1983), pp. 35-37.

   ———, "The Dallas Arts District: Can It Deliver?" *Texas Architect* (January/February 1985), pp. 56-59.
2. "Dallas Museum of Art," *Architecture + Urbanism* (September 1984).

   "Edward Larrabee Barnes Associates; Dallas Museum of Art," *GA Document* (May 1984).

Bill Marvel, "Dallas Museum of Art," *Arts and Architecture* (1983), pp. 36-40.

Peter Papademetriou, "Art Oasis," *Progressive Architecture* (April 1984), pp. 14, 17.

———, "Dallas Museum of Art: Extending the Modernist Tradition of E.L. Barnes," *Texas Architect* (January/February 1985), pp. 36-46.

Ray Ydoyaga, "Mending Loose Ends: DMA Users' Report Card," *Texas Architect* (January/February 1985), pp. 52-55.

3. David Dillon, "Art and Architecture in Dallas: New Barnes Museum," *Architecture* (April 1984), pp. 32-33.

4. Joel Warren Barna, "Meyerson Symphony Center: A Preview of I.M. Pei's New Twist," *Texas Architect* (September/October 1989), pp. 40-41.

———, "Debut of Meyerson erases public doubts," *Texas Architect* (November/December 1989), p. 8.

———, "Meyerson Symphony Center, Dallas," Progressive *Architecture* (November 1989), pp. 23, 26.

5. Private communication.

6. Louise Rogers, "Dallas Pride," *Architects Journal* (October 4, 1989), pp. 26-31.

7. Paul Goldberger, "After 9 Years, Dallas Concert Hall is Opening," *The New York Times* (September 8, 1989), p. 8 C.

———, "A Year of Years for the High Priest of Modernism," *The New York Times* (September 17, 1989), p. 8 H.

8. Gayle Gordon, "The Other Perot," *Dallas Life Magazine, Dallas Morning News* (December 10, 1989), pp. 11-16, 22-25.

Chapter Eleven: Creating More Perfect Landscapes

1. Douglas Brenner, "Et in Arcadia Ambasz," *Architectural Record* (September 1984), pp. 120-133.

2. "The Lucile Halsell Conservatory," *Progressive Architecture* (January 1985), pp. 120-121.

Paul Goldberger, "Spacious Sunken Garden Will Bloom in San Antonio," *The New York Times* (June 11, 1987), pp. 1, 10 C.

3. Joel Warren Barna, "Light and Fog in San Antonio," *Texas Architect* (July/August 1987), pp. 28-31.

4. Ellen Posner, "Architecture: A Conservatory Grows in San Antonio," *Wall Street Journal* (June 7, 1988), p. 2 B.

5. Frances F. Chamberlain, "Moody Gardens and the World According to Jellicoe," *Texas Architect* (July/August 1987), pp. 32-37.

   Ellen Posner, "Botanical Gardens," *Landscape Architecture* (January 1989), pp. 54-58.

   Warren T. Byrd, Jr., "Recreation to re-creation," *Landscape Architecture* (January 1989), pp. 43-51.
6. Deborah Dietsch, "A Garden of Hope and Recovery," *Architectural Record* (November 1989), pp. 92-98.
7. Geoffrey and Susan Jellicoe, *The Landscape of Man*, revised ed. (London: Thames & Hudson, 1987).
8. Geoffrey Jellicoe, "Gardens of the Moody Foundation," *Landscape Design* (April 1988), pp. 18-22.

   Michael Spens, "Admirable Jellicoe," *Architectural Review* (September 1989), pp. 85-92.
9. David Dillon, "Galveston's Strand hits its stride with restoration," *Dallas Morning News* (January 25, 1986), p. 1 F.

   Joel Warren Barna, "Projects of the 1980s," *Texas Architect* (March/April 1991), p. 41.
10. Chamberlain, "Moody Gardens and the World According to Jellicoe," *Texas Architect* (July/August 1987), pp. 32-37.
11. Gary Cartwright, "The Sleaziest Man in Texas," *Texas Monthly* (August 1987), pp. 86-93, 160-166.
12. Dianna Hunt, "Second Moody is cited in conspiracy," *Houston Chronicle* (July 10, 1991), p. 1A.
13. Dietsch, "A Garden of Hope and Recovery."
14. Douglas Freelander, "Galveston seeks funds to build new causeway," *Houston Post* (January 9, 1990), p. 12 A.

    Jack Stengler, "Bridge won't affect garden development, official says," *Galveston Daily News* (October 11, 1990), pp. 1, 11 A.

Chapter Twelve: Saving the Kimbell for Philadelphia

1. "And Then There Were None," *Cite* (Fall 1983), p. 11.
   Michael Wilson, "Pillot Building Rescued," *Cite* (Spring 1986), p. 4.
2. Patricia Cummings Loud, *The Art Museums of Louis I. Kahn* (Chapel Hill: Duke University Press, 1989).
3. Lawrence Speck, "Regionalism and Invention," in Lawrence Speck, ed., *Center: A Journal for Architecture in America* (Austin: Center for the Study of American Architecture, 1987), pp. 8-19.
4. Doug Suisman, "The Design of the Kimbell: Variations on a Sublime Archetype," *Design Book Review* (Winter 1987), pp. 36-41.
   Lawrence W. Speck, *Landmarks of Texas Architecture* (Austin: University of Texas Press, 1986), pp. 90-93.
5. Charles L. Mee, Jr., "Louis Kahn," in Joseph J. Thorndike, Jr., ed., *Three Centuries of Notable American Architects* (New York: American Heritage Publishing, 1981).
6. Bruno J. Hubert, "Kahn's Epilogue," *Progressive Architecture* (December 1984), pp. 56-67.
7. Loud, *The Art Museums of Louis I. Kahn*.
8. Joel Warren Barna, "Acclaimed museums to see additions," *Texas Architect* (July/August 1989), pp. 7, 13.
9. Romaldo Giurgola and Jaimini Mehta, *Louis I. Kahn* (Boulder, Colo.: Westview Press, 1975).
10. Paul Goldberger, "Romaldo Giurgola," in Thorndike, Jr., ed., *Three Centuries of Notable American Architects*, p. 338.
11. Jim Murphy, "Parliament House, Canberra," *Progressive Architecture* (August 1988), pp. 65-127.
12. Joel Warren Barna, "Giurgola defers to Kahn at Kimbell," *Texas Architect* (September/October 1989), p. 8.
13. Paul Goldberger, "Sincerest Flattery or the Subtlest Form of Dishonor," *The New York Times Magazine* (September 14, 1989).
14. Esther Kahn, "The Kimbell Museum: A Kahn Favorite," *The New York Times* (November 26, 1989), p. 3.
15. Suzanne Stephens, "Controversy: The Kimbell Art Museum," *NYC/AIA Oculus* (November 1989).

16. David Dillon, "Remaking a Masterpiece: The Kimbell should rethink its expansion plans," *Dallas Morning News* (October 29, 1989), p. 1 C.
17. Barbara Koerble, "Kimbell plan draws prominent criticism," *Texas Architect* (January/February 1990), p. 10.
18. Doug J. Swanson, "Expansion proposal for Kimbell museum coolly received in NY," *Dallas Morning News* (January 24, 1990). p. 1 C.
19. Cathleen McGuigan and Maggie Malone, "What becomes a legend most?" *Newsweek* (January 15, 1990), pp. 20-21.

Chapter Thirteen: Coda

1. Ralph Bivins, "Mischer to develop land near downtown," *Houston Chronicle* (February 2, 1990), p. 6 B.
   ———, "Buyer or partner sought on 35 acres lost by Mischer," *Houston Chronicle* (July 17, 1990), p. 1 B.
2. John Morris Dixon, "Garden Gateways," *Progressive Architecture* (June 1982), pp. 65-70.
3. Nicholas Lemann, "The Architects," *Texas Monthly* (April 1982), p. 231.
4. Jeffrey Karl Ochsner, "Tile-Style Triumph," *Texas Architect* (March/April 1982), pp. 80-83.
   "Highly Articulate 'Y,'" *AIA Journal* (May 1983), pp. 254-256.
5. Michael Sorkin, "YWCA Downtown Branch, Houston," *Arts and Architecture* (Winter 1981), pp. 44-46.
6. Curtis Lang, "Greed: The Rise and Fall of Lamar Terrace," *Houston City Magazine* (July 1983), pp. 50-55, 97-99.
7. ———, "One Billion Dollars: The Collapse of Mainland Savings," *Houston City Magazine* (March 1987), pp. 46-49, 92-93.
8. Jane Baird, "2nd step taken to rebuild area near Galleria," *Houston Post* (December 13, 1990), pp. D 1, 4.
   Karen Weintraub, "Mr. Silvers' Neighborhood," *Houston Press* (January 31, 1991), pp. 14-18.
9. David Dillon, "A World Apart: Southland's shining new headquarters stands alone in its unfinished setting," *Dallas Morning News* (March 19, 1989), pp. 1, 8 C.

Index

Photographs are indicated by numbers in italics.

B

E

F

G

H

I

J

M

T

U

V

W

Y